Protestant missionary children's lives, c.1870–1950

Manchester University Press

STUDIES IN IMPERIALISM

When the 'Studies in Imperialism' series was founded by Professor John M. MacKenzie more than thirty years ago, emphasis was laid upon the conviction that 'imperialism as a cultural phenomenon had as significant an effect on the dominant as on the subordinate societies'. With well over a hundred titles now published, this remains the prime concern of the series. Cross-disciplinary work has indeed appeared covering the full spectrum of cultural phenomena, as well as examining aspects of gender and sex, frontiers and law, science and the environment, language and literature, migration and patriotic societies, and much else. Moreover, the series has always wished to present comparative work on European and American imperialism, and particularly welcomes the submission of books in these areas. The fascination with imperialism, in all its aspects, shows no sign of abating, and this series will continue to lead the way in encouraging the widest possible range of studies in the field. 'Studies in Imperialism' is fully organic in its development, always seeking to be at the cutting edge, responding to the latest interests of scholars and the needs of this ever-expanding area of scholarship.

General editors:
Andrew Thompson, Professor of Global and Imperial History at Nuffield College, Oxford
Alan Lester, Professor of Historical Geography at University of Sussex and LaTrobe University

Founding editor:
Emeritus Professor John MacKenzie

Robert Bickers, University of Bristol
Christopher L. Brown, Columbia University
Pratik Chakrabarti, University of Houston
Elizabeth Elbourne, McGill University
Bronwen Everill, University of Cambridge
Kate Fullagar, Australian Catholic University
Chandrika Kaul, University of St Andrews
Dane Kennedy, George Washington University

Shino Konishi, Australian Catholic University
Philippa Levine, University of Texas at Austin
Kirsten McKenzie, University of Sydney
Tinashe Nyamunda, University of Pretoria
Dexnell Peters, University of the West Indies
Sujit Sivasundaram, University of Cambridge
Angela Wanhalla, University of Otago
Stuart Ward, University of Copenhagen

To buy or to find out more about the books currently available in this series, please go to: https://manchesteruniversitypress.co.uk/series/studies-in-imperialism/

Protestant missionary children's lives, c.1870–1950

Empire, religion and emotion

Hugh Morrison

MANCHESTER UNIVERSITY PRESS

The right of Hugh Morrison to be identified as the author of this work has been asserted in accordance with the Copyright, Designs and Patents Act 1988.

Published by Manchester University Press
Oxford Road, Manchester M13 9PL

www.manchesteruniversitypress.co.uk

British Library Cataloguing-in-Publication Data
A catalogue record for this book is available from the British Library

ISBN 978 1 5261 5678 5 hardback
ISBN 978 1 5261 9484 8 paperback

First published 2024
Paperback published 2026

The publisher has no responsibility for the persistence or accuracy of URLs for any external or third-party internet websites referred to in this book, and does not guarantee that any content on such websites is, or will remain, accurate or appropriate.

EU authorised representative for GPSR:
Easy Access System Europe – Mustamäe tee 50, 10621 Tallinn, Estonia
gpsr.requests@easproject.com

Typeset
by Deanta Global Publishing Services, Chennai, India

For my nieces, nephews and god-daughter – Campbell, Emily, Gabe, Harry, Hayley, Katie, Kurt, Lena, Nadia, Rachel and Sam – who both as children and adults have each enriched our lives beyond measure.

Contents

Figures and tables

Acknowledgements

I have long pondered the caution from New Zealand-born historian J.G.A. Pocock that a historian's responsibility is not 'to show that belief systems are ridiculous, but to discover why they were not ridiculous once'.[1] That aphorism has kept me company over the last two decades, as I have worked with the modern Protestant missionary movement as a key historical focus. It is a movement that does not mesh easily with current sensibilities. It is anathema to some, irrelevant to others and for many a historical black hole. And yet recent historians have grappled extensively with the important nexus of empire, nation, society, culture and religion, within which the missionary movement emerges as a significant category of historical analysis. This book reflects some of the breadth and depth of that scholarship, while focusing on the children and young people of missionary families. For the last decade these children – along with other children in metropole locations who supported and learnt about missionary work – have been a more specific focus for me, across a spectrum of imperial, British and Anglo-world settings. At the same time, I have taught undergraduate students about 'children and young people in history', in the context of education studies, and participated widely within scholarly networks interested, respectively, in the history of religion in Aotearoa New Zealand, in World Christianity (and mission history as a cognate field) and in histories of childhood and youth.

This book is one product of that journey and I hope that it contributes further to a nuanced historical understanding of children, young people, missions and empire among other things. I will admit, however, that there have been times when I have questioned the significance of the project and doubted my capacity to bring it to completion. A brief encounter on a train returning from Manchester to Oxford in 2017 helped me to perceive its importance and relevance for a wider audience. I sat with my laptop on my knees, finishing off a presentation for a paper on missionary children that I was to deliver the next day. An older woman sitting beside me glanced from time to time at my screen, in that surreptitious way that people take notice of each other on public transport. We had exchanged brief pleasantries earlier on. As I shut my laptop, I was pleasantly surprised when she commented on my work and asked me some questions about the topic. Shen then made a more personal connection to the subject matter, when she revealed that she had been a vicar's wife and mother, moving often from one parochial charge to another. She mused further that her children were very similar to the children I was writing about. They had forever struggled with a sense of belonging or identity, as a result of constant movement and social re-adjustments. This was a point of regret for her, and a touchstone for further conversation before I alighted at Oxford.

That conversation, the book writing process itself and consequent reflection on the lives encompassed thus prompt me to ask, who really writes a book? Is it the so-called author(s), is it those who contribute ideas and materials (both formally and informally), or is it the historical participants encountered in the archives, the memoirs or at the end of a microphone? Surely all of these and more. While I take responsibility for the choice of content, trajectories of analysis and ultimate conclusions, none of these are possible without the influence of a great multitude of others. Indeed, there have been so many 'others' over the last decade or so, that I would do them a disservice and embarrass myself if I attempted an exhaustive list of 'who is who'. The following acknowledgements, however, aim to cast a wide net of appreciation over the many different people, institutions and groups that have made this publication possible.

Institutional support and associational networks have been pivotal in the execution and completion of this project. The University of Otago funded generous periods of research and study leave (2012 and 2017), along with a University Research Grant (2014–2015) which enabled me to do the interviews in both New Zealand and Scotland. To this I add: the whakawhanaungatanga (warm sense of family) provided by colleagues in the College of Education, which has given me the incentive and courage to persevere; and the chance to share ideas through seminars for the university's History and Theology programmes. Other institutions have also been important. I am grateful for two generous international visiting fellowships, during which I completed the archival research for the book: in the University of Edinburgh's School of Divinity (2012), hosted by Elizabeth Koepping and Brian Stanley in connection with the Centre for the Study of World Christianity; and at Magdalen College, Oxford University (2017), hosted by Laurence Brockliss and Siân Pooley in connection with Oxford's Centre for the History of Childhood. Two societies have also acted as critically important crucibles within which my thinking has developed. One is the Yale-Edinburgh History of Christian Missions and World Christianity Group, especially through its annual conferences. The other is the Society for the History of Children and Youth, through its various networks and conferences, publication in the Society's journal and the key relationships that have developed therein. Other venues in which ideas have been tested include conferences and seminars of the Religious History Association of Aotearoa New Zealand, the New Zealand Presbyterian Research Network, the Scottish Church History Society and the University of Hong Kong's Department of History.

Serendipity, perhaps, has also played its part. My thinking around the application of the history of emotions to children and missions history issues from attendance and presenting at the 'Childhood, Youth and Emotions in Modern History' conference hosted by the Max Planck Institute for Human Development in Berlin (2012), and the publication opportunities that came from that thanks to Karen Vallgårda (with Claire McLisky and Daniel Midena) and Stephanie Olsen. I am forever grateful for chance meetings with Mary Clare Martin (University of Greenwich, UK) at seminars and conferences in 2010–2011, which has translated into a longer-term friendship cemented by similar scholarly interests, involvement with the UK-based Children's History Society and the shared project of editing a book together on children's religious history. And in no small part, my own work on children's history is due to the chance connections as a contract history lecturer at the University of Waikato, in 2005–2006, with Jeanine Graham, who is the pioneer in developing this field of study in Aotearoa New Zealand.

All of this rests on the shoulders of giants – the archivists, librarians and their institutions – who are often unseen or unbidden but who are utterly indispensable. I have been helped by too many people to name, but want to thank especially the staff of the following institutions for generous access and support: in China – the Au Shue Hung Memorial Library (Special Collections and Archives), Hong Kong Baptist University; in England – the Angus Library and Archives, Regent's Park College, Oxford, the Bodleian Library, Oxford, the Special Collections, School of Oriental and African Studies, London, and the Cadbury Research Library, University of Birmingham; in New Zealand – the Presbyterian Research Centre, Dunedin, Uare Taoka o Hākena/Hocken Collections, Dunedin, and the Alexander Turnbull Library, Wellington; and in Scotland – the Centre for the Study of World Christianity, the Centre for Research Collections and the New College Library (all in the University of Edinburgh), the National Library of Scotland and National Records of Scotland, Edinburgh. I also acknowledge gratefully the access kindly given to privately held Scottish materials, by Ian Waldram and Michael Orr (and family) respectively. Kind permission has been given to quote more extensively from: Pat Booth, *Pat's India: Memories of Childhood* (Wellington: Philip Garside Publishing Ltd., 2017), at https://philipgarsidebooks.com/products/pat-s-india-print; Ian Gray, *We Travel Together: Lesley's and Ian's Journey* (Nelson: The Copy Press, 2014); Catherine Hepburn, 'The Burning Rosebush', the Handsel Press www.handselpress.co.uk; Stephanie Vandrick, *Growing Up with God and Empire: A Postcolonial Analysis of 'Missionary Kid' Memoirs* (Bristol and Blue Ridge Summit, PA: Multilingual Matters, 2019); and Faith Cook, *Troubled Journey: A Missionary Childhood in War-Torn China* (Edinburgh: The Banner of Truth Trust, 2004) http://www.banneroftruth.org.

Three important sets of people require further acknowledgement. First, words are simply not enough to say thank you to the twenty-two people who took part in this study through 2014–2015, as interview participants – sixteen in Scotland and six in New Zealand. There were also others who were willing to be interviewed, but for whom time or circumstances ultimately prevented this from happening. This remains one of the most special 'moments' of my research career. I was generously hosted in their homes, spending time conversing and listening around meal tables alongside the formal interviews completed. Their stories are rich and detailed, and I am keenly aware that I have represented in this book but a fraction of what they said. These stories deserve a fuller telling, a project ahead perhaps. While I have attempted to interpret their stories against a wider historical and historiographical canvas, I hope that I have done some justice to the words and memories entrusted to me through the interviews. Second, I acknowledge with gratitude the support of both Manchester University Press and Deanta Global Publishing Services in bringing this book to final publication. In particular I thank the series editors and peer reviewers, Emma Brennan, Meredith Carroll, Paul Clarke, Humairaa Dudhwala, Jen Mellor and Lillian Woodall. Finally, I am deeply grateful to my own wider family, who have a sense of their own stories and who continue to support me in my mad adventures in scholarship. In particular, I dedicate the book to my nieces, nephews and god-daughter, mindful of the many ways in which my life and journey would be much impoverished without them. And as always, I am grateful to you, Anne, for your solid and unvarying belief in me and your sense of empathy with the writing projects that have occupied me over the years. Thank you.

Note

1 Pocock, 'Tangata whenua', 29.

Abbreviations

ABCFM	American Board of Commissioners for Foreign Missions
ATL	Alexander Turnbull Library
BIM	Bolivian Indian Mission
BM	Basel Mission
BMS	Baptist Missionary Society [England]
CIM	China Inland Mission
CMS	Church Missionary Society
COS	Church of Scotland
FCS	Free Church of Scotland
LMS	London Missionary Society
NLS	National Library of Scotland
NMS	Norwegian Missionary Society (Det Norske Misjonsselskap)
NRS	National Records of Scotland
NZP	New Zealand Presbyterian (mission)
NZPC	New Zealand Presbyterian Church
PIVM	Poona and Indian Village Mission
PRC	Presbyterian Research Centre (New Zealand)
SIM	Sudan Interior Mission
SIM	SIM International Archives
SOAS	School of Oriental and African Studies
SPG	Society for the Propagation of the Gospel
UFC	United Free Church of Scotland
UPC	United Presbyterian Church of Scotland
WMMS	Wesleyan Methodist Missionary Society

Introduction

Children, missions, empire and emotions

By way of introduction, this chapter outlines a rationale for writing a history of Protestant missionary children, in the process traversing key trends in the scholarship to date, outlining the main conceptual emphases and fleshing out the lines of argument for each chapter. It begins with a story whose emphases have been somewhat paradigmatic in shaping the historiography of missionary children, not always helpfully. In 1992 English educationalist Joyce Wilkins wrote and published an account of her childhood, teenage and early adult life written from a 'child's eye view'.[1] Born in England in 1902, Joyce spent her early years in India with Baptist Missionary Society (BMS) parents Nellie and Gordon Wilkins, before returning to England with her family in 1908 at the age of six. Her story will be expanded on at various points and her transition from India to England as a child is an appropriate starting point for this book. For Joyce this was a definitive return, following in older sister Dorothy's footsteps into the Walthamstow School for Girls at Sevenoaks, London in 1909.[2] At that point, her parents, with two younger children, returned to India. Eighty years later she leafed through her father's diary of that period, noting his habit of systematically writing points 'for which he could give PRAISE TO GOD'. At the point of the parents' departure from the two older girls, she found that he had given thanks, among other things, for 'the splendid attendance and kindly spirit manifested at the farewell meeting', 'Joyce's birthday', 'that Miss Hare was so pleasant and thoughtful when we took the children to the school for the last time' and 'for the contingent of Christian Endeavourers who saw us off at Sevenoaks station'. There was no indication of what he felt upon leaving Dorothy and Joyce behind nor any rumination on how they might be coping. Thinking about her own very different feelings and memories engendered by that departure and pondering the adult-centric tone of these observations, Joyce 'decided to write "A Child's Eye View" of these same days, and of my childhood from my earliest memories up until the time I left school and "put away childish things"'.[3] While repeating this intention further on in her account, Joyce then conceded that 'now re-reading' her father's diary, 'I have more sympathy for the writer'.[4] In her postscript, pondering her own experiences alongside those of others, she empathised further:

> I think that many of us felt the deep sense of deprivation because of our separation from our parents. The children had to be sacrificed because the parents had answered the 'call'. (How deeply disturbing I found the story of Abraham, willingly preparing to sacrifice his son Isaac to the Lord.) Now, as an adult I can feel more sympathy for the parents – and Abraham. I realise too that many of our teachers … were well aware of our problems and tried their best to give us a 'home' as well as school.[5]

Joyce's experience and response as a child was not unique. Leila Brown (from India) made her way back to England with her mother and brother Charles in 1916, also to enter the Walthamstow school. En route, their ship was nearly torpedoed, but in her memory, this peril was overridden by a more painful memory: 'of her mother's walk away from Walthamstow Hall towards Sevenoaks Station at the start of her journey back to India in 1918'. Leila said that she 'never really got over that' and was still upset in her nineties when this memory was recalled.[6] Leila and Joyce, in turn, were two among a large body of Western children routinely separated from parents from the 1840s well into the twentieth century, mostly for education, in the name of empire and/or religion.[7] One was Rikard Jacobsen, from a Norwegian Missionary Society (NMS) family in Madagascar who, in 1881, remained with sister Elisabeth and brother Jakob in the mission's home and school in Stavanger, southern Norway, while his recently widowed father returned to mission work. He did not see him for another ten years. Rikard's letters bear witness to the details of daily life mixed in with stories of bad behaviour and low school grades reflecting confusion and anger.[8] A later child was Faith Cook, daughter of English China Inland Mission (CIM) parents in the 1940s, whose story of wartime separation makes for painful reading (her story also appears further on). In her published memoir she stated that

> at the repeated request of my family and friends, I have at last agreed to write an account of my childhood years – years of high adventure, unusual circumstances, deprivations and deep sorrows. It has not been an easy account to write as it touches on a number of hurtful memories. It also involves issues that have been a problem, not only to me, but to many other children of missionary parents.[9]

In this, she also recognised that her own story of childhood hardships might resonate with adult readers who had experienced difficult lives in various other contexts.

This book zeroes in on the children of British and Anglo-world Protestant missionary families, seeking to engage with the details and contexts of their lives. For them and their families, separation was a defining experience. As Emily Manktelow observes for the London Missionary Society (LMS), it 'formed a painful commonality among mission communities. It was the most difficult aspect of missionary parenting, and yet remained the most basic shared experience of missionaries in different corners of the globe.'[10] While made for one British mission operating in specific geographical spheres (the South Pacific and southern Africa) during the early to middle decades of the nineteenth century, this observation also applied to a host of families from different missions, nationalities and periods. Stereotypes of historical missionary children (as endangered, deprived, pitiable, traumatised etc.) potentially muddy or simplify understanding and can act to disenfranchise children within the historical record in terms of how they might narrate their own childhood stories (both as children and adults). The fact that separation became normative over many decades, to the extent that it was institutionalised for so many children, reflected the powerful influence of a sustained parental and organisational discourse concerning childhood more generally. Its controversial nature – now perceived more clearly through published memoirs, the more recent conceptualisation of such children as 'third culture kids' and a much-needed current focus on children's welfare combined with redress of historic and contemporary institutional abuses – explains its dominance within both popular, professional and academic discourse. While legitimate, if this is the only focus then it tends towards a reductionist view of such children, with little regard for time, place, culture or juvenile agency.

At the same time, separation was not the only defining characteristic of missionary children's lives – especially from their own perspectives – and if it was, then it was not always felt negatively or represented as overly problematic. Two examples illustrate this by way of introduction. Murray Crozier and younger sister Judith were born and grew up in western India, in the 1930s and 1940s, children of New Zealand missionaries working for the Poona and Indian Village Mission (PIVM). They went through two different periods of separation from their parents for their schooling – in southern India and later in Western Australia. They each acknowledged the hardships that this created both for them and their parents. Yet these do not dominate their later estimation of those years. They appreciated the 'special dimension' and 'privilege' given to their lives by the relationships formed with people in their village, expressing gratitude to their parents for their 'early life in India'.[11]

Pat Booth writes in a similarly reflective mode, introducing her memoir of life in northeast India during the 1940s and 1950s:

As I pondered on my children's New Zealand childhoods during the 1970s and 1980s – living in the same house in the middle class, monocultural Wellington suburb of Karori, walking to and from school each day, seeing both parents every day, being monolingual – I began to realise how different my childhood had been.[12]

Pat's story, like that of Joyce Wilkins, will be encountered at a number of points throughout this book. Separation was also a big part of her childhood journey but one that was not necessarily negatively construed. In her postscript, Pat drew out both the richness and the messiness of being a child who grew up with and still identifies with two cultures (India and New Zealand), which is further mingled with a mix of Māori culture and Christian spirituality to create a sense of meaningful adult identity.[13]

This book engages with these complexities by expanding the historical and conceptual parameters, to advance scholarship in what is still arguably an underdeveloped category of historical research. We now know quite a lot about discrete groups of missionary children in particular periods and places but still lack a more 'global' view. Here a broad and deliberately comparative approach considers Protestant missionary children[14] across selected nations, missions and non-Western locations, within the period from the late nineteenth to the mid-twentieth centuries. To date, this later period is underrepresented in the literature. As such, the book makes a case for the importance of historicising these children's lives and in the process raises questions as to what might be meant or understood by the phrase 'missionary child' at particular historical moments. It argues that missionary children in these imperial decades represent a distinct subset of the British Empire's children. Their lives were differentiated and defined by the religious identities, motivations and functions of their parents as well as by a combination of other geographical, cultural, political and social influences. Furthermore, it argues that from just after World War I onwards, they increasingly emerged in literature, academia, mission policy and practice as a definable juvenile category that increasingly required specialist thought and care. In the process, they emerged on their own terms as authors of their own lives as much as they were the product of other factors.

Both conceptually and methodologically, therefore, this book argues for a holistic history of missionary children, one that considers equally the separate yet interwoven perspectives of children, parents and religious institutions. By using the concept of three overlapping narrative lenses (parents, organisations, children), it offers a 'triangulated approach' that 'deals "more holistically" with the data, discerning both the story lines that different groups used and the narrative "artifacts" that emerge'.[15] It takes seriously the recognition that '[c]hildren and adults have different positionings in becoming human, there are adult-becomings and child-becomings that are folded together in any search for understanding children and childhood'.[16] Here, then, missionary children appear, in part, on their own terms but in a way that is both historically differentiated and contextually specific.[17] To this end, the book excavates a diversity of archival, published and oral history sources that are then placed in conversation with wider scholarship in the histories of childhood, missions, empire and emotions. It hopes to bring a degree of conceptual and methodological cohesion to what is, at present, a rich but relatively inchoate and piecemeal body of literature.

Historical and historiographical perspectives

Missionary children were integral to the changing demography of imperial white populations in British colonial settings. By the end of the 1800s, Western children and young people in general were a growing and important component of imperial populations, becoming much more visible and contentious across a multiplicity of colonial or colonised locations. They came with or were born into families whose parents (often fathers) were engaged either in imperial institutions like the military, administration and education or employed in colonial commerce, agriculture and industry: youngsters like Eric Blair (George Orwell) born in 1903 to an English imperial civil servant in India, with grandparents who had also worked or served in India and Burma.[18] By the 1890s in Asian settings, European children made up a disproportionately large part of white populations, and this persisted up to World War II.[19] As a broad social and demographic group, they have received increasing attention from scholars interested in imperialism and colonialism, with a particular focus on empire families, imperial domesticities and trans-colonialism.[20] In this same period, they were also the children of countless migrant families, moving from so-called old to new world locations with their families or often unwittingly as the subjects of now contentious political and religious schemes to relocate working-class children from industrialised Britain to the open, agrarian spaces of Australia, Canada and New Zealand.[21]

From the inception of the modern Protestant missionary movement in the late eighteenth century, children were continually present but often hidden as Western missionaries moved into increasingly diverse non-Western contexts. They existed in considerable numbers, and by the late nineteenth century, missionary policy makers could not ignore the implications (particularly how to support families to educate their children). Comprehensive statistics are lacking, but some examples indicate the potential scope of that population. For the British context, from about 1796 'around 10,000 missionaries were dispatched from Britain in those first hundred years; over 1,300 by the LMS [London Missionary Society] alone – all this, "not including the wives", yes, but also not including the children, the grandchildren, the sisters and aunts'. In India and the South Pacific alone there were some 650 LMS children between 1860 and 1940.[22] More generally, in China there may have been at least 3,800 children born to a wide range of Protestant missionaries between 1868 and 1949.[23] Further afield, among Scottish Presbyterians, there were at least 796 missionary children between 1870 and 1940 living in such diverse regions as southern Africa, China, India and the Caribbean. Again, over the same period, some ninety-three New Zealand Presbyterian children almost doubled the number of missionary adults in India, south China and the New Hebrides (Vanuatu).[24] These indicative statistics are likely the tip of the iceberg and suggest that children comprised a significant proportion of missionary and white imperial populations. Yet their voices were seldom officially heard and, consequently, their stories have remained largely untold – both at the time and, until recently, in the historiography of the modern Protestant missionary movement.

In the contemporary literature of missions – aimed especially at home-base constituencies – such children were often taken for granted or were obliquely referred to with respect to missionary families or education, their presence assumed and rarely acknowledged. More typically they were hidden behind exotic stories of heroic men and women or were glossed over in favour of published writing on theology, grand policies, strategies and movements. Alternatively, they were discussed with reference to women's groups and missionary involvement and therefore subsumed within those narratives. Some details did appear in published form, but within certain parameters; for example, in magazines aimed at home-base children or in the births and deaths lists published in some missionary literature (Chapter 1). Look hard and they are also found in many of the ubiquitous missionary biographies of the period, albeit again briefly. It was only in the 1920s and early 1930s that missionary children began to be considered a distinct group and to gain a more public profile in professional and academic literature (Chapter 3).

Over recent decades a growing body of published memoirs by ex-missionary children more visibly profile their experiences. These remain important but relatively untapped historical and sociological sources.[25] Memoirs often highlight missionary children's hardships and seek to address these from a range of theological, psychological, therapeutic and sociological angles.[26] For the purposes of this study, they are also helpful in that when taken together, they 'provide a fascinating glimpse into the world of missionary children, one that often turns out to be far different from what their parents might have imagined beforehand'.[27]

The history of Christian missions and its cognate World Christianity are significant scholarly fields with a now voluminous and nuanced body of literature.[28] Within this, the connections between missionaries and empire are also well drawn in historical scholarship.[29] However, as noted trenchantly by the South African scholar John W. de Gruchy in a wide-ranging theological reflection, 'what of their children? That is surely an interesting subject for consideration and research, not least because of everything children had to endure for the sake of the missionary cause.'[30] Within mission history scholarship to date, most energy has been expended on Indigenous or colonised children as missionary subjects and, within that, a focus on the relationship between Christian missions and education.[31] To a lesser extent, Western children's pedagogical and practical imbrication in the missionary movement in British or settler metropoles is now receiving increased attention.[32]

Fewer historians to date have picked up this challenge to focus on missionaries' children, and arguably those who have would not strictly define themselves as historians of Christian missions. Emergent understandings in English-language literature are very much in debt to scholars more specifically aligned with histories of empire, childhood, gender, American identity or internationalisation and emotions, or with postcolonial literary studies (these are encountered throughout the book). Yet the same issue pertained, until recently, to wider historical scholarship. For instance, writing about the Hawaiian missionary context, Jennifer Kashay observed in the 1990s that American historians have 'failed to incorporate children in the histories they study' and that by 'limiting the scope of their analysis' they have only told part of a much larger story.[33] In turn, Kashay echoed an earlier observation by Sarah Mason in 1978 that 'very little has been written about the sons and daughters of China missionaries' hailing from America in the early twentieth century.[34] By the 1990s children and young people were clearly on the agenda of historians of society and culture, but missionary children as a particular subset were still largely a missing historical and historiographical link. That has begun to change as the following discussion outlines.

In some respects, emergent scholarship is a product of a more interdisciplinary approach to mission history and of the new imperial history's integration of religious factors.[35] It also builds on the important pioneering works of historians like Catherine Hall and Patricia Grimshaw, with their focus on empire, culture contact, Protestant missionary families (among other empire families) and women's history.[36] In the case of Hawaii, that lacuna has now been addressed both by Kashay and through the more recent work of another American historian Joy Schulz;[37] the latter reflects broadening intersections between histories of childhood, culture, missions, education, politics, nation and empire. To some extent, this body of emerging English-language scholarship is more concerned with the early to mid-nineteenth century and focuses on such geographical domains as the Pacific, South Asia and Africa. Two recent monographs, on Danish missionary families in South India and on the legacies of American Protestant missionaries, include significant discussions of missionary children across national origins and extend analysis into the twentieth century.[38]

At the same time, there are other emphases. One such is a focus on missionary families, including consideration of the children. The ideology and roles of missionary families and homes is an important topic with an extensive literature outlined further in Chapter 2.[39] Current scholarship is beginning to unravel the extent to which the missionary family co-existed on two planes: that of idealisation and that of reality. Manktelow quotes the LMS centenary historian Richard Lovett who wrote that while 'the idea was that the Christian family would be an educative and helpful influence to the natives, [in which] the European children … would take part in missionary labour, and be all the better qualified [for it]', in reality this 'was a fond imagination'. She notes that over many decades 'the LMS was constantly disappointed with the behaviour and function of missionary families'.[40] Thus, scholarship continues to engage with the complexities of missionary families, paying attention among other things to the interplay of gender, literary representations and both transnational and trans-generational arcs.[41] Beyond the family, there is also a growing body of scholarship that considers missionary children with respect to colonialism, race, play, education and emotions, all of which are considered in the following chapters.[42] Across this scholarship, children are considered in context but can easily be lost as a distinct or unique focus.

British world scholarship also tends to subsume missionary children within the broader category of 'empire children',[43] for whom Britain or British settler societies were thought of either ideologically or actually as 'home'. Here family separation is an important focus, with a consequent emphasis in contemporary comment and scholarship on children as 'victims' or 'casualties of Empire'.[44] Thus in India, for example, separation for the purpose of education took on both positive and negative connotations. These included, argues Elizabeth Buettner, the 'physically and culturally threatening contacts with India's climate and indigenous and mixed-race populations', the benefits 'from exposure to Britain's climate, culture, and schooling provisions' and, especially for boys, an education that provided a 'stepping stone into professions that brought a higher socio-economic (and racial) status both in Britain and overseas in adulthood'.[45] This came at a cost for many, exemplified in the narratives of those who attended or resided in schools and institutions for missionary children, both *in situ* and in metropole locations (see further in Chapters 4 and 5).

A recent scholarly focus on deviance and empire suggests at least one alternative approach to historicising empire and missionary children's lives, one that raises the possibility of also finding instances of children's voices in the historical record. Here the non-exemplary missionary child, resisting or transgressing family or social conventions, is one example among others. Notable examples from the South Pacific include Neil Gunson's genealogy and account of the Henry family (LMS) in early nineteenth-century Tahiti and Ewen Johnston's unpublished description of the long-serving New Zealand Presbyterian Oscar Michelsen and his family in early twentieth-century New Hebrides.[46] More recently Manktelow has argued extensively and sensitively for a degree of children's agency in terms of their quotidian lives. In doing so she extends the motif of the deviant missionary child to broader discussions of family, sexuality, child abuse, the body and colonial politics.[47] This scholarship accentuates the fact that while family separation is one important thread, with its focus on the impact on children, there are other important themes to consider, in order to depict lives that were varied, complex and both historically and culturally specific.

Since 1945 a growing body of literature issuing from anthropological, sociological and educational scholarship – focused on multiple international settings – has tended to redefine and position modern groups like missionary children as 'third culture kids' or as 'global nomads'.[48] In this post-Empire literature, different nationalities of children from military, diplomatic, corporate and missionary families are often conflated in a fashion similar to the category of Empire children.[49] Yet the focus has changed somewhat, with a new emphasis on their liminal status wherein they occupy a third 'interstitial' and cultural space, lying somewhere between the cultures of origin and immediate location. Literature emphasises the need to understand the often negatively framed elements of those spaces – a 'neither/nor world', resulting problems of identity formation and dislocation and the grief attached to movements from the familiar to the unfamiliar – to then help children and young adults make the requisite cultural and social adjustments.[50]

In this respect, mobility emerges as an integral feature and an important motif for considering children and young people of both the imperial and post-World War II eras, especially when set amid the large-scale migrations of the nineteenth and twentieth centuries.[51] Discussion in Chapters 5 and 6 addresses this as a major gap in scholarship on missionary children to date, as it is for children and youth more generally.[52] Juvenile and youthful mobility was arguably central to the narratives and identities of missionary and Empire children.[53] Manktelow, in this respect, further argues that 'children flowing across and between cultural boundaries is potently relevant to the lives and experiences of missionary children'.[54] Across both nineteenth- and twentieth-century settings, missionary children's mobility was therefore as much cultural as it was geographic. Yet the spatial element was important, especially for missionary children of the early to mid-twentieth century. For these children, as for others more broadly, the new century increasingly provided more frequent and faster opportunities to move 'across borders and over much larger distances' and emerging local and national identities were transnationally configured in the process.[55] Thus it seems important to consider the ways in which missionary children experienced their lives dynamically within and between spaces (Chapter 6). Furthermore, a focus on mobility again accentuates the notion of complexity with which this book seeks to engage, taking seriously the many and varied experiences through which children, past and present, 'may feel "at home" everywhere and nowhere with lives punctuated by moving, adapting, surviving, coping and constantly feeling different from others'.[56]

Conceptual approach

Where then does this book fit in terms of its focus on missionary children positioned within the broad period from the late nineteenth to the mid-twentieth centuries? Is it primarily mission or religious history, imperial or transnational history, social or cultural history, migration history, family or gender history or childhood and youth history? Mission history is its obvious starting point, in that the book aims to address a gap in the scholarship (by profiling missionary children as named and known participants in the historical record and by nuancing how their lives might be historically interpreted) and, in the process, to integrate mission history more deliberately into other modes of historical research and writing. As such, religious history provides a wider hermeneutical frame within which to advance understandings, more generally, of the many and varied relationships between children and religion, nuanced here by empire as a physical, ideological and discursive space.

However, I would argue that this subject is broader than just one analytical category and that it needs all of the above. I am honour bound to say that. My undergraduate grounding was in a mixture of geography, history and theology going on to high school teaching in the social sciences. Over the last two decades my scholarly trajectory has arced its way from doctoral studies in New Zealand-focused religious and mission history (informed significantly by religious, social and cultural historiographies and my own positioning within postcolonial Aotearoa New Zealand); along a trajectory of an increasingly comparative and transnational/British world research focus on children, missions and religion; to a sustained involvement in teaching and researching within broader histories of childhood, youth, religion and education. This journey has been influenced by an international community of researchers, scholars and teachers. Consistent through it all is my commitment to what Karen Vallgårda, Kristine Alexander and Stephanie Olsen helpfully describe as a 'global-historical approach'. This 'forces us to reckon with a multi-centred world, characterized by ambiguity and contradiction' and through which 'contingency and cultural temporal-specificity' are 'key concepts' in a 'geographically broad approach to the past'.[57] Throughout the book these different types of history are brought into mutual conversation, bringing their respective wisdom, ideas and methodologies to bear on historical missionary children and thus fleshing out a 'global-historical approach'.

Four emphases require introductory comment at this point, while their conceptual and methodological details will be mapped out in the relevant chapters. First, this book continues to engage with the complexities of the relationship between empire, religion and missions already touched upon and which historians of empire and religion take seriously. In particular, it sits within a wider imperial historiography interested in the mundaneness, complexities and decentred nature of empire as experienced or witnessed across and between both metropole and colonial contexts. In broad fashion it supports Manktelow's contention, referencing a significant case of missionary child abuse within the LMS school in 1840s Tahiti, that imperialism 'was a messy and complicated business … uneven and sometimes ambiguous … constituted in the performance as much as the practice of superiority and power'.[58] This observation reflects a turn in imperial history over recent decades that emphasises empire's (and imperial processes') interconnected and mutually constitutive nature – Tony Ballantyne's multilateral 'webs of empire'.[59]

Among other things, this becomes most evident when we consider the contemporary literature in which missionary children commonly appeared. This literature was important in shaping popular public conceptions of such children in a multiplicity of imperial locations (Chapter 1), even though arguments for the reflexive impact of empire have been rightly tempered by scholars who call for a more carefully nuanced analysis of imperial reflexivity.[60] Andrew Thompson argues, for example, that 'the effects of empire on the structure of British society, the development of British institutions and the shaping of British identities were complex and (at times) contradictory'. Therefore, we need to look for 'how different parts of society became caught up in the process of overseas expansion in different ways'.[61] Children and childhood in the imperial metropole comprise one such grouping. In turn, highly mobile missionary children became active agents who conveyed the realities of empire back 'home' while on temporary furloughs or through permanent residency for further education, whether that was in Belfast, Liverpool, Swansea, Dundee, Cape Town, Dunedin, Melbourne or Edmonton. Missionary children in this period lived within and across empire, both experiencing and mediating its ambiguities and idiosyncrasies. This is a focus throughout the book, and especially in Chapter 6. More generally, however, children have tended to appear incidentally in past empire histories or have been subsumed within wider discussions of gender and family.[62] Hence Manktelow's two major monographs are highly welcome. Even though they are historically and geographically specific, they open up a host of questions for empire and religious historians to pursue both discretely and comparatively.[63]

Therefore, this book aims to contribute further to the wider field of 'imperial history' by giving a clearer profile to a significant group of juvenile Empire citizens who were differentiated further by their parents' religious motivations and livelihoods; who experienced empire in a range of modes both *in situ* and dynamically through diasporic lifestyles; and whose lives as Empire citizens were shaped and (mis)represented across a wide diversity of literature and institutional policy. Here we encounter a specific form of juvenile 'lived religion' that was 'experienced ... within a certain time and space, framed by societal and economic structures and affected by cultural categories'.[64]

Second, this book also sits within and is shaped by the currently dynamic field of children's and youth history. This is now a mature and complex international historical discipline, arguably a product of historiographies inspired by the French *Annales* and subaltern 'histories from below' movements of the 1960s and 1970s, and further influenced by a 1990s focus on historical representation and the constructed nature of childhood. It is variously represented by an explosion of published writing over the last three decades, a range of dedicated journals or book series, and both regional and international academic and professional societies – all of which embrace a plethora of interdisciplinary approaches and a diversity of cross-culturally comparative perspectives.[65]

While this book draws on a wide body of literature from that larger pool, it is written with two emphases in mind. On the one hand, it seeks to add to a growing body of scholarship on children and religion. As Mary Clare Martin and I have written previously, '[r]eligion, despite arguments about secularization, is not disappearing but continues to be politically, socially and culturally significant in the twenty-first century', and historically 'religion ... was an abiding influence among children of British or Anglo-world societies'.[66] From a contemporary perspective, Americans Marcia Bunge and Don Browning point to the present as a critically important moment to focus on children and religion – including the influence of the past – because 'religious diversity is now the experience of every society and [therefore] of many children'.[67] If there has been a 'historical lacuna',[68] in scholarship in general, this is now beginning to change, and this book is one deliberate attempt to help fill that gap.

On the other hand, it attempts to further engage with scholarship that grapples with hearing children's voices in the historical record and the relationship of this to juvenile historical agency. Nell Musgrove, Kristine Moruzi and Carla Pascoe Leahy helpfully differentiate children's voices (that is 'the opinions, emotions and behaviours of young people ... what [they] *actually* [emphasis original] thought, felt and did [as opposed to what was] *expected* or *assumed*') from agency (which has 'often been taken to refer to a young person's ability to resist adult-imposed structures').[69] As an alternative, they call attention to Mona Gleason's emphasis on children's voices being heard in different contexts and in conversation with other key people in their lives. She suggests that 'Approaching questions of agency as *relational and contextual* [emphasis original] enables historians to move beyond binaries and undifferentiated approaches towards a more fruitful exploration of *how* the social construction of age and social relations of power propelled change over time.'[70] Here the use of an overlapping narrative lenses approach across the chapters combined with the use of oral history – especially in Chapters 4, 5 and 6 – is a deliberate strategy to discern more clearly the different voices (of children and adults in conversation with one another) both at the time and in hindsight, in order to arrive at what is hopefully a more representative picture of both experience and response.

Therefore, this book aims to contribute further to the wider field of childhood history by a combination of reclamation history (profiling the historical experiences and reactions of missionary children); a refocus on 'religious childhoods' in imperial spaces over the transitional period of the late nineteenth and early to mid-twentieth centuries; and a methodological approach that further exemplifies how to interpret and situate children both contextually and relationally.

Third, this book looks to the relatively recent but equally dynamic history of emotions to further enhance interpretations of missionary children's lives – both in their historical details and how those details might be contextually understood. A useful definition is provided by Rob Boddice, who argues that the central claim is that 'emotions have a history. They are not merely the irrational gloss on an otherwise long narrative of history unfolding according to rational thought and rational decision-making. Nor are emotions merely the effect of history; they also have a significant place, bundled with reason and sensation, in the making of history.' Such 'central claims', he suggests, 'require both a sophisticated understanding of what emotional experience is (or could be) and an openness to new understandings of historical causality and change'.[71] This is now a significant scholarly focus in its own right, with William Reddy arguing that emotions' history is 'a way of doing political, social, and cultural history', more than simply an adjunct field.[72] At the same time, it is inhabited by a somewhat frighteningly diverse array of concepts and approaches. In a recent emotional history of late nineteenth-century Italian nationalism, for example, Mark Seymour employs at least seventeen different emotional phrases or concepts, indicating both the scope and complexities of this field.[73] 'Anyone interested in the history of emotions', suggests Barbara Rosenwein and Riccardo Cristiani, 'will find the terrain difficult without a map'.[74] Thankfully such maps (or perhaps atlases is a better term) now exist as the field reaches a point of helpful self-reflection.[75] Concepts like 'emotional regimes and styles', 'emotional communities' and 'emotional practices' are now well-accepted concepts applied to a wide range of historically and contextually differentiated settings.[76] In the process, such broader fields as imperial or colonial history are also embracing emotional concepts to better understand empire-making and experiences of empire in a range of global settings.[77]

While drawing selectively from the history of emotions, this book sits squarely in the middle of two streams of inquiry that engage further with the history of emotions – mission history and children's/education history. In the first instance, historians have begun to broach both the relationship between Christian missions and emotions and how the concepts and methods of emotions' history might further inform historical understanding. In this respect, Claire McLisky and Vallgårda suggest that missions form an 'interesting and unusual case study' for emotions' history, especially because 'so many of the historical actors involved in the project *at the time* [emphasis original] recognised and discussed this importance' which, in turn, 'has left mission historians with an archive rich in both emotional expression and explicit commentary on the subject of emotional expression'.[78] Aside from their rich edited collection, this is still a work in progress, with a focus on women and children as subjects of missionary projects, but only a little written about missionary children.[79] This book is one attempt to address this more thoroughly.

In the second instance, historians of childhood and education find in the history of emotions a scholarly stream that potentially enriches our historical understanding of children and youth. Education historians, for example, have used concepts such as emotional communities, practices and regimes to emphasise the centrality of children's experiences of schooling, of using literature, of relating differently between home and school, of informal education and as racialised or gendered educational subjects.[80] At the same time, scholars like Olsen have critiqued emotions' history for its 'heterodoxy of approaches', its 'theoretically inchoate' nature and its tendency to be 'adult focused' in its inability to account for 'the formative years of initial emotional development, where the learning curve of emotional expression and belonging is steepest'. Therefore, she suggests, we need to examine 'how emotions themselves are formed in childhood, with their specific historical meanings and qualities'.[81]

To this end, Olsen, Vallgårda and Alexander offer their own conceptual reconfiguration of concepts like communities, styles and practices for the contexts of children, in the shape of 'emotional formations' and 'emotional frontiers'.[82] Elsewhere I have attempted to summarise these as follows.

> An emotional formation is doubly defined as 'a set of emotional structures ordered in a particular pattern' (akin to emotional communities and which at a range of scales display coherence but might also be quite diverse across such things as space, gender or class) and as a 'process that depends on each individual learning the imparted codes of feeling' (which are mutable over time). An emotional frontier is conceptualised as 'the boundary between different emotional formations'. These might be 'encountered in various ways, from a minor understanding to a seemingly insurmountable conflict' and doubtlessly 'difficult to traverse' in 'encounters between people raised in different emotional formations'.[83]

I will return to these as appropriate in the following chapters, noting here that they are now noted, developed or critiqued by a range of historians of childhood.[84] Here I also acknowledge the burgeoning, sometimes related and increasingly theorised field of the 'history of experience'. Rob Boddice helpfully suggests that this history

> assumes that past lives were lived in past contexts, according to past epistemologies and, importantly, through past ontologies and situated affective and sensory biocultural systems. What it means to be human – to experience life as a human being – is historical. It changes over time. The human itself is a biocultural historical artefact.[85]

This book, while not engaging extensively with this field, keeps it in view where appropriate.

Therefore, this book inhabits a dynamic space, seeking to engage further by drawing from and adapting how we might think about emotional labour and happiness in the context of missionary children's lives; arguing that the overlapping narrative lenses used across the chapters can primarily be thought of as emotional narratives doubly constructed *in situ* and in hindsight through memory; and focusing on particular emotionally constructed sites, communities and frontiers inhabited, navigated or negotiated by missionary children in diverse colonial/imperial and metropole locales.

Fourth, this book considers the spatial nature of missionary children's lives. Children and young people inhabited at least two important spaces – figuratively that of literature (Chapter 1) and in a more embodied way that of empire (Chapter 6). But they also inhabited spaces more discretely defined: missionary houses and compounds, local streets and bazaars, churches, schools (of various sizes, types or locations), public transport *in situ*, ocean-going vessels, trans-continental trains or sometimes planes, missionary children's homes in metropole settings and the parlours or kitchens of far-flung relatives. In all of these, they were important actors but, depending on context, their representations were variously either self-defined (albeit often in hindsight through memory) or mediated by adults. Therefore, space (as well as time) was equally important in terms of being a discursive influence on their lives and deserves more careful consideration.[86] One approach to this is to think about missionary children's spaces – geographic, figurative, cultural, gendered – as 'sites', conceived of as both physically defined entities and as places that are 'created by socio-spatial practices', on a sliding scale from small to large, with 'fluid and overlapping boundaries (social and spatial) created and maintained by practices of power and exclusion'.[87]

In historical scholarship, this concept has been applied to 'education' or 'the mission field', rather than to geographically defined places (but with little conceptual development),[88] and is derived more from the social sciences.[89] Outlining its potential for analysing missionary education in early twentieth-century Bolivia, I have previously argued the following, which I contend is also relevant for pondering missionary children's spatiality.[90] In particular, sites have been thought about in terms of place and gender, firstly referring to '"the kinds of places … which were physical entities in socially and culturally mapped space" and which "bear gendered cultural meaning", and secondly referring "to a domain or a cluster of social practices and ideas that are expressed in a variety of physical spaces"'. Here there might be multiple narratives in play for any one site, in turn emphasising their unbounded, porous and interconnected nature at a range of geographic scales. Nina Laurie et al. note that 'places are constituted by, and in turn constitute other places, and connect in various ways to wider processes, being constituted through shifting global/local connections'. Crucially these connections are 'unequal and result in differential access to "power" in its widest sense'. They are also historically constituted, in that 'circumstances cohere and coalesce across time as well as space, and while inequalities remain they do undergo temporal change'.[91]

Therefore, this book integrates spatial complexity into its consideration of the range of sites that were important across the narratives and which were constitutive of missionary children's experiences, identities and responses. Furthermore, it draws connections to the large conceptual pool of emotions' history, by thinking of the places and spaces filled or occupied by children as being emotionally constructed, experienced and managed. Missionary children's sites, in these terms, are thought of as 'spaces for feeling' that were simultaneously or variously 'physical or conceptual' in nature (Chapter 6).[92]

Structure

This book aims therefore to add complexity and breadth to current scholarship on historical missionary children for discrete periods and places. More specifically it does so through a comparative approach across geographic and national settings and through its focus on the transitional decades of the late nineteenth and early to mid-twentieth centuries which, to date, have been less considered. It focuses doubly on geographical similarities or differences and on historical continuities or discontinuities, approached conceptually through the notion of overlapping narrative lenses (of parents, organisations and children) and drawing on a range of interpretive historiographies. At its core is an in-depth focus on children who lived in Scottish and New Zealand Presbyterian missionary families, using a set of selected oral history interviews, further supported by a wide-ranging dossier of published, archival and private sources. These children lived in a mixture of India, Japan, northern China, southern Africa and Vanuatu, in the decades most immediately before and after World War II. The focus on one denomination across two national points of origin is both pragmatic and strategic. It is constrained by the normal exigencies of research time and the potential expanse of archival sources and therefore focuses on a denomination whose missionary endeavours and apparatus were representative both of major religious affiliation (in each of New Zealand and Scotland) and of the wider collective of Anglo-American Protestant missionary activity. This core of material is further augmented by research in a range of selected British missionary archives;[93] selected missions documented in secondary sources;[94] selected published missionary children's memoirs (American, British and New Zealand); and British, British settler and North American newspapers and periodicals.

Oral history interviews represented a second research phase, following initial Presbyterian archival work, which was then followed up by research in other denominational or organisational archives as a third and final phase. Interviews are both a standard qualitative methodology and a well-attested means of historical research[95] deemed, in the context of this project, to be a vital means by which to take a more child-centred approach to the lives of missionary children. In this case, the interviews were clearly done with older adults and thus are not strictly 'interviews with children'; they are hindsight documents and artefacts. However, this does not negate their value in terms of narrating or interpreting the past.[96] Due ethical process was followed with respect to recruitment of interview participants, information and consent, the conduct of the interviews themselves and the follow-up of transcripts with the participants. Through this book, interviewees are identified by first name, nationality and mission location. Full names are given for those also found in published writing and pseudonyms are assigned for others who chose not to be identified. Two are unnamed with their mission locations generalised for reasons of sensitivity.[97] At the same time, limitations are noted in two respects. The number of interviews conducted with Presbyterian participants (sixteen in Scotland and six in New Zealand) was dictated by practicalities of time and finances and are therefore presented here as indicative rather than fully representative. Likewise, those who responded to advertisements or approaches to participate were individuals who, for the most part, had generally positive or benign missionary child experiences and therefore might be considered again as indicative, and not fully representative of those whose experiences were less than positive. Memoir material tended to elicit more negative stories and experiences. Hence these two different sets of autobiographical sources are read together all the way through this book.

The chapters that follow spiral around each other, rather than proceeding in a straight line, building a kaleidoscopic picture through the coalescence and differentiation of the multiple operative narratives. Chapter 1 focuses on missionary children as inhabitants of the vibrant and extensive religious and secular literary spaces ubiquitous throughout the period under study. It argues that this was where the wider reading public often encountered missionary children and that this was a constitutively important encounter. Conceptually it suggests that literature, as a site, formed a mixture of emotional community, culture contact zone and imperial textual commons within which missionary child subjects were encountered and 'known'. Through such representations, certain public perceptions of missionary children were formed, cemented and sustained over many decades, which were often pejorative or negatively framed and from which missionary children emerged as objects of pity. In the longer term, they helped to feed or sustain identifiable adult-centric narratives. Chapters 2 and 3 then pick up on this thread considering, in turn, the parental and institutional narratives that were formed. They argue that parental narratives, focused primarily on the family and domestic issues, should be the starting point. First, family provided the primary parameters for children's lives and was the reference point by which children often interpreted their own experiences and memories. Second, they were often then the catalyst for institutional debates and policy making that underlay consequent institutional narratives. Chapter 2 outlines the nature and demographic shape of the missionary family over this period, its religious and domestic parameters, parental anxieties and the adult emotional labour expended in rationalising or supporting parent–child separations. Chapter 3 then canvasses how institutions shaped a response to parents' anxieties, with a focus on missionary children's residential homes as sites of emotional well-being, and how an emerging academic/professional discourse in the interwar period signified the possibilities of a more child-centred approach to their welfare and education.

Therefore, Chapters 4 and 5 bring children's narratives into the spotlight, both in conversation with and sometimes tangential to the adult-framed narratives. Together they present two interwoven narrative threads whereby children interpreted their lives as variously ordinary and complicated. In each case, discussion is differentiated by a range of contextual factors. Chapter 4, outlining 'life as ordinary', focuses on themes of domesticity, education and recreation. Chapter 5, outlining 'life as complicated', focuses on complex experiences (especially language, mobility, education and separation), consequent emotional navigations and related issues of identity. Both chapters detail and reflect on children's perspectives as forming 'emotional narratives' and on children's emotional labour as a counter-narrative concerning happiness and well-being. Chapter 6 returns to the spaces inhabited by children, namely those constructed through imperial and colonial processes. Drawing again primarily on children's autobiographical material, it argues that children physically, mentally and emotionally navigated their way within and between a range of imperial sites, wittingly or unwittingly mediating empire or militating against it at various points. This is illustrated through examples of children's relationships with Indigenous or local people, their mobility and their responses to how missionary parents re-appropriated traditional architectural spaces for Western or Christian purposes. By way of conclusion, the book outlines both commonalities and differences elicited through the overlapping narrative lenses' approach and across the decades under study; assesses the extent to which these narratives can be more fundamentally considered 'emotional narratives'; evaluates the concepts employed; and ponders the question 'how then can we talk about missionary children in history?'

Notes

1 Wilkins, *A Child's Eye View*. Joyce also recorded elements of her school years in England for an oral history project in Wood and Thompson (eds), *The Nineties*, pp. 134–40. The experiences of separation from parents, for all three

sisters – Joyce, Dorothy and Phyllis – are also narrated in Brendon, *Children*, pp. 189–93.

2 For an introduction see Pike, Curryer and Moore, *The Story of Walthamstow Hall*.

3 Wilkins, *A Child's Eye View*, p. 9.

4 *Ibid.*, p. 43.

5 *Ibid.*, p. 135. A similar theme is taken up in Devereux (also with respect to the English BMS) in 'Narrating', pp. 78–84.

6 Brendon, *Children*, p. 197.

7 For imperial India, see Buettner, *Empire Families*, pp. 110–45; and of an example from non-English speaking countries see: Maß, 'Constructing', 340–61.

8 Ask, *Dear Rikard*.

9 Cook, *Troubled Journey*, pp. ix–x.

10 Manktelow, *Missionary Families*, p. 149.

11 From recollections included in Crozier, *Will the Rajah?*, p. 183.

12 Booth, *Pat's India*, p. 9.

13 *Ibid.*, pp. 129–38.

14 Throughout this book, 'children' is used as shorthand for infants, children and young people up to high school leaving age (which in this period might be anywhere from sixteen to eighteen years of age). Where context demands more age specificity, children are identified appropriately.

15 See Morrison, 'Three Variations', 200, in turn citing Hatavara et al., 'Introduction', pp. 1–10. Also Punch, *Introduction*, pp. 216–17.

16 Millei, Silova and Gannon, 'Thinking through Memories', 328, in turn citing Jones, 'True Geography', 195–212.

17 This also is a response to a dilemma noted by Lindsey Dodd that although 'all historians must accept the epistemological and methodological impossibility of including everyone and everything in the account they construct', disparate voices and perspectives do need to be taken account of. Dodd, 'It's Not What I Saw', 4.

18 Williams, *Orwell*, p. 7.

19 Pomfret, *Youth*, pp. 2–3.

20 Alongside Buettner and Brendon's Indian studies, two important contributions that inform wider scholarship are: Pomfret, *Youth*; and Stoler, *Carnal Knowledge*.

21 Two important monographs are: Boucher, *Empire's Children*; and Lynch, *UK Child Migration*. Children as migrants with their families are included in McCarthy, *Personal Narratives*.

22 Manktelow, *Missionary Families*, p. 2; India and South Pacific figures are calculated from Volumes 1 and 2 of the 'London Missionary Society Register of Missionaries' Children up to 1940', Archives and Special Collections, School of Oriental and African Studies (hereafter SOAS), London.

23 Mason, 'Missionary Conscience', p. 6.

24 See Chapter 2 for detailed notes on the sources used to reconstitute the families to which these Presbyterian Scottish and New Zealand children belonged.

25 A recent review of such literature is the postcolonial literary analysis by Vandrick, *Growing Up*. Vandrick bases her analysis on forty-two North American memoirs published between 1975 and 2014.

26 For example Van Reken, *Letters*; and Ostini et al., *Sent*.

27 Addleton, 'Missionary Kid Memoirs', 30.

28 Representative examples that provide scholarly road markers are: Latourette's seven-volume *A History*; Neill, *A History*; Robert, *Christian Mission*; and Stanley, *Christianity*.

29 Representative examples include: Adogame and Lawrence (eds), *Africa in Scotland*; Breitenbach, *Empire*; Porter (ed.), *The Imperial Horizons*; and Stanley (ed.), *Missions*.

30 de Gruchy, 'Who Did They Think They Were?', p. 217.

31 Useful surveys are: Raftery, 'Religions', 41–56; Raftery, 'Themes and Approaches', pp. 17–25; and Jensz, *Missionaries and Modernity*.

32 The scope of this literature is examined more thoroughly in Morrison, *Protestant Children*.

33 Kashay, 'Problems in Paradise', 81. This neglect of missionary children within Hawaiian historiography has been answered in part by Schulz, *Hawaiian by Birth*.

34 Mason, 'Missionary Conscience', p. 2.

35 See for example: Robert, 'From Missions', 146–62; and Ballantyne, 'Review Essay', 427–55.

36 Hall, *Civilising Subjects*; Grimshaw, *Paths of Duty*.

37 Schulz, *Hawaiian by Birth*.

38 Vallgårda, *Imperial Childhoods*; Hollinger, *Protestants Abroad*. As this book goes to publication a further doctoral dissertation on American missionary children in republican Shanghai has just been completed, which further adds to a better understanding of the early twentieth century – Keon, 'Making Americans'.

39 Exemplified here by scholarship for the earlier nineteenth century and the early to mid-twentieth centuries: Manktelow, *Missionary Families*; and Robert, 'The "Christian Home"', pp. 134–65.

40 Manktelow, *Missionary Families*, p. 1, in turn quoting from Lovett, *London Missionary Society*, vol. 1, pp. 295–96.

41 Recent scholarship includes: Manktelow, 'Forging the Missionary Ideal', 195–216; Maß, 'Constructing'; and Morrison, 'Reimagining the Missionary Family', 465–88.

42 Representative examples include previously cited works by Schulz and Vallgårda, as well as: Martin, 'Play', pp. 61–84; Morrison, 'I Feel That', pp. 218–39; and Semple, 'The Conversion', 29–50.

43 Brendon, *Children*, pp. 185–212; Buettner, *Empire Families*, pp. 154–62; Cleall, *Missionary Discourses*.

44 See further: Buettner, 'Parent-Child Separations', pp. 115–32; Pedersen, 'Anxious Lives', 7–19; and Brendon, *Children*, p. 212.

45 Buettner, *Empire Families*, p. 110.

46 Gunson, 'The Deviations', pp. 31–54; Johnston, 'Cannibals Won for Christ!'.

47 Manktelow, *Gender, Power*. Also see: Jackson and Manktelow (eds), *Subverting Empire*; and Manktelow, "Making Missionary Children', pp. 41–60.

48 Pioneers in this field were American sociologists John and Ruth Hill Useem, coining the phrase 'third culture kids' and initiating a stream of academic and professional literature on this subject. See further: Useem, 'A Third Culture Kid Bibliography'; Pollock and Van Reken, *Third Culture Kids*; Langford, 'Global Nomads', pp. 28–43; and Hopkins, 'Coming "Home"', 812–20.

49 Langford, 'Global Nomads', pp. 29, 30–34.

50 Hopkins, 'Coming "Home"', 813–14.

51 As a sociological theme this is helpfully backgrounded in Kwon, 'Third Culture Kids', 113–22.

52 Jobs and Pomfret, 'The Transnationality of Youth', p. 6.

53 Again see especially: Buettner, *Empire Families*; Brendon, *Children*; and Cleall, 'Far-Flung Families', 170–73.

54 Manktelow, *Missionary Families*, p. 164.

55 Jobs and Pomfret, 'The Transnationality of Youth', p. 6.

56 Devereux, 'Narrating', p. 197; in turn quoting from Walters and Auton-Cuff, 'A Story', 755. Note that the simultaneous living at home 'everywhere' and 'nowhere' imagery may originate from the author Pearl Buck, herself an American missionary child in China between the late nineteenth and early-twentieth centuries. Addleton, 'Missionary Kid Memoirs', 34.

57 Vallgårda, Alexander and Olsen, 'Emotions', p. 14.

58 Manktelow, *Gender, Power*, p. 178.

59 Ballantyne, *Webs*. For wider reference see: Lester, *Imperial Networks*; O'Hara, 'New Histories', 909–25; and Pietsch, *Empire of Scholars*.

60 Hall and Rose (eds), *At Home*; Thompson, *The Empire Strikes Back?*; and Thompson (ed.), *Britain's Experience*.

61 Thompson, *The Empire Strikes Back?*, pp. 5, 239, 241.

62 An example of this in an otherwise important essay on gender and empire is Grimshaw, 'Faith, Missionary Life', pp. 260–80.

63 Manktelow, *Missionary Families*; Manktelow, *Gender, Power*.

64 Katajala-Peltomaa and Toivo, 'Introduction', p. 4.

65 The evolution of childhood and youth history, as a discipline, is traced out in Heidi Morrison, *Global History of Childhood Reader*, pp. 1–5. The breadth and depth of historiography is usefully represented in: Fass (ed.), *Encyclopedia of Children*, 3 vols; Fass (ed.), *The Routledge History*; and Stearns, *Childhood*.

66 Morrison and Martin, 'Introduction', p. 1.

67 Bunge and Browning, 'Introduction', p. 3.

68 This quote is from one such recent contribution exploring more comprehensively and comparatively the child–religion relationship, in Strhan, Parker and Ridgeley, 'Introduction', pp. 1–13. Further examples of significant or benchmark scholarship include: Bunge (ed.), *The Child*; Browning and Bunge, *Children and Childhood*; Clapp-Itnyre, *British Hymn Books*; Morrison and Martin, *Creating Religious Childhoods*; and Parker et al., *Religion and Education*.

69 Musgrove, Pascoe Leahy and Moruzi, 'Hearing Children's Voices', p. 12.
70 *Ibid.*, p. 12; Gleason, 'Avoiding', 457.
71 Boddice, 'The History of Emotions', 11.
72 William Reddy quoted in Plamper, 'The History of Emotions: An Interview', 249.
73 Seymour, 'Emotional Arenas', 177–79.
74 Rosenwein and Cristiani, *What Is?*, p. 2.
75 Alongside Rosenwein and Cristiani's overview, also see: Boddice, *The History of Emotions*; and Plamper, *The History of Emotions: An Introduction*.
76 While particular emotions' history concepts will be elaborated in following chapters, representative scholarship includes: Reddy, *The Navigation of Feeling*; Rosenwein, *Emotional Communities*; and Scheer, 'Are Emotions a Kind of Practice', 193–220.
77 For example, the extensive range of essays in Pernau, Jordheim et al., *Civilizing Emotions*; and Pernau's writing about South Asia exemplified in 'Space and Emotion', 541–49.
78 McLisky and Vallgårda, 'Faith through Feeling', p. 3.
79 For example: Haggis and Allen, 'Imperial Emotions', 691–716; and Cummins and Lee, 'Missionaries'. Vallgårda's *Imperial Childhoods* is an important contribution to discussion on children, families, missions and emotions. Also see an exploratory essay on emotions history for children and missions broadly defined by Morrison, 'I Feel That', pp. 218–39.
80 Barron and Langhamer, 'Feeling', 101–23; Frevert, Eitler et al., *Learning*; Olsen, *Juvenile Nation*; Swartz, 'Educating Emotions'; and Swartz, *Education and Empire*.
81 Olsen, 'The History of Childhood', 1, 2.
82 Vallgårda, Alexander and Olsen, 'Emotions', pp. 20–26.
83 This is a summary of Vallgårda et al., 'Emotions', pp. 20–23, in Morrison, *Protestant Children*, p. 84. For further elaboration see Olsen, 'Children's Emotional Formations', 644–45.
84 Olsen, 'Children's Emotional Formations'; Kaarninen, 'Red Orphans'; Bruce, 'Encountering Emotions'; and Barron and Langhamer, 'Feeling'.
85 Boddice, 'What Is the History of Experience?', www.tuni.fi/alustalehti/2019/04/18/what-is-the-history-of-experience/ (accessed 13 February 2023). Sari Katajala-Peltomaa and Raisa Maria Toivo helpfully elucidate this field further through a model that simultaneously identifies or differentiates 'everyday experience', 'experience as process' and 'experience as structure', in 'Introduction', pp. 11–15.
86 The historiography of the relationship between children, young people and space is touched upon at a number of points through the chapters and is exemplified in Sleight, *Young People*.
87 Brookes, Cooper and Law, 'Situating Gender', p. 10.
88 For example: Chiu, 'A Position of Usefulness', 789, 791; and Prevost, *The Communion of Women*, p. 5.
89 In particular note the influence of Laurie, Dwyer, Holloway and Smith, *Geographies of Femininities*.

90 The following is quoted from Morrison, 'Theorising', 8–9; in turn quoting from Laurie et al., *Geographies of Femininities*, pp. 11–14 and from Brookes et al., 'Situating Gender', pp. 11–12.

91 Laurie et al., *Geographies of Femininities*, pp. 11–14.

92 See Rosenwein and Cristiani, *What Is?*, pp. 90–91; Broomhall, 'Introduction', p. 1.

93 The English Baptist Missionary Society; the English Church Missionary Society; and the London Missionary Society.

94 In particular: the American Board of Commissioners for Foreign Missions in the Hawaiian Islands; the Basel Mission; the China Inland Mission; the London Missionary Society; and the Norwegian Missionary Society.

95 For wider reference see: Punch, *Introduction*, pp. 168–78; Thompson, *Voice of the Past*; Perks and Thomson (eds), *Oral History Reader*; and Green and Hutching (eds), *Remembering*.

96 See both further discussion in Chapter 4 and Maynes, 'Age', 114–24.

97 Under University of Otago ethics and consultation procedures, this project was formally accepted by the Ngāi Tahu Research Consultation Committee in June 2013 and approved by the university's Human Ethics Committee in December 2013 (reference number D14/015). For wider discussion on the ethics of using real names or pseudonyms for interview participants, see Nys, 'I Am F.B.'.

1

Public representations: missionary children inhabiting literary spaces

This chapter begins with missionary children as literary representations, who inhabited a diversity of literary spaces but whose lives, in the process, were not always well understood and at best misconceived. Historically the children of missionary families were mostly either completely invisible or partially visible by implication within formal reporting processes. Children were also noticeably absent from many of the missionary biographies of the late nineteenth- to early twentieth-century period, with readers perhaps taking the presence of children for granted within family narratives. In many cases, their appearance was anonymous and lacking detail. Unelaborated statistical representations, like the reported 800 missionary children with the China Inland Mission (CIM) in the 1920s, were common.[1]

Yet that was not the full story. Both in missionary circles and in the wider reading community, children did appear in varying degrees of detail and individual identity in a range of literary spaces – books, magazines, newspapers and photographs among others. Three brief introductory examples indicate the potential of these. In their monthly missionary magazine, New Zealand Presbyterian children were reminded of their responsibilities through the 1919 'missionary catechism': 'Q. How many young children of the missionaries are there? A. There are five children of missionaries in the New Hebrides, fifteen in China, and eleven in India – altogether thirty-one missionaries' children.'[2] In February 1935, Australian readers picked up their newspapers and read the headlines '70 British Children on Pirated Ship – Safe after three days in locked saloon', which referred to an incident wherein students returning to the CIM school at Chefoo (now Yantai) in eastern China were caught up in a pirate attack, but without coming to any harm.[3] Also appearing in a weekly children's pen pal and hobbies page in 1937 and 1938 were two sisters – Yvonne and Corinne Engwall – writing from the Belgian Congo, of their daily lives as daughters of Swedish Baptist missionaries. They told children in Christchurch, New Zealand, about playing with local girls, pet monkeys, gardening and cooking traditional foods like manioc and bananas.[4]

Missionary children inhabited a great variety of physical, emotional and conceptual spaces. Yet these specifically literary spaces were significant. Here domestic audiences around the Empire – children and adults – had their first, and perhaps only, encounter with missionary children. In this respect, public literary representations mark an important starting point for the present discussion. Therefore, this chapter engages with the question 'in what ways were missionary children visible to the wider public and to what effect?' As such, it conceptualises such literary spaces as a mixture of emotional community, virtual contact zone and imperial textual commons, beyond their obvious function as sites of recreational reading and formal or informal education.

In the first instance, the concept of emotional communities emerges from history of emotions scholarship and is identified especially with the work of Barbara Rosenwein. Countering the grand narrative that 'the history of the West is the history of increasing emotional restraint', she developed the idea of 'emotional communities' as 'a way of thinking about the social foundations of emotion'.[5] This has been elaborated at a number of points,[6] and most recently thus, where emotional communities are conceived of as 'groups – usually but not always social groups – that have their own particular values, modes of feeling, and ways to express those feelings'. Such communities 'may be very close in practice to other emotional communities of their time', but they are not necessarily 'bounded entities' and may be defined 'quite broadly' within historical research. However, '[m]ore narrowly delineated communities allow the researcher to characterize in clearer fashion the emotional style of the group. Larger communities will contain variants and counterstyles.'[7] The concept has been widely applied in historical scholarship and, for children's history, reformulated through the related ideas of 'emotional formations' and 'emotional frontiers' (see Introduction). In both mission and children's religious history, to date, scholarship has focused on gendered emotional communities and on children belonging to theological-emotional communities.[8] Here, the focus is on emotional communities constituted through shared texts.

The other two concepts derive from wider scholarship in imperial history. On the one hand, contact zones, developed by Mary Louise Pratt relating to imperial travel writing, can be thought of as 'social spaces where disparate cultures meet, clash, and grapple with each other, often in highly asymmetrical relations of domination and subordination'. Pratt applies the concept to physical encounters like explorer Peter Kolb's eighteenth-century journeys among the Khoikhoi in the Cape region of South Africa. More recently it has been applied to a study of British Arctic exploration in the mid-1800s and, in passing, to missionary children's play.[9] Here it is reapplied in a more virtual mode, thinking about literature as a space in which domestic readers encountered and formed attitudes about people different from themselves, which I would argue sometimes included missionaries and their children alongside the Indigenous or national peoples among whom missionary children lived.

On the other hand, the idea of an imperial textual commons highlights an international community of readers brought together through a mutually shared and multi-lateral print network. We now have a very good sense of how the British Empire was 'sustained by a fundamental mobility of people, commodities, capital and information, and by novel technologies of global communication'.[10] With respect to imperial literature, South African scholar Isobel Hofmeyr draws attention to the masses of magazines and newspapers that 'poured' out monthly from both so-called metropole centres like London but also from other imperial centres and which constantly moved backwards and forwards along lines of distribution so that all imperial readers potentially consumed materials from all parts of the Empire.[11] In the process, newspapers and magazines liberally copied material from one another, accentuated perhaps by the ubiquity of shared cablegram news stories in both national and provincial papers.[12] Hofmeyr argues that this 'periodicalism in empire' was a form of 'imperial textual commons', constituted by a 'weave of uncopyrighted text that criss-crossed empire' and which became pervasive across a vast reading audience, both religious and secular.[13] In particular, she points to the significance of this for periodical literature, which as the following discussion indicates was very important for children's religious reading and engagement in this period. With Antoinette Burton, she argues that

> this periodical exchange system was especially important in creating a mobile imperial commons ... These interwoven periodicals produce the textual format so familiar to anyone who has worked with imperial newspapers. Any one page will largely be composed of cuttings from elsewhere, each page convening its own miniature empire ... The juxtaposition of these pieces invited readers to construct their own empire without copyright.[14]

Thus, this chapter suggests that the literary spaces in which missionary children appeared served simultaneously as points of imperial contact and commonality, doubly drawing together juvenile readers into the orbit of a shared emotional community with their missionary peers and inscribing missionary children as both an exotic focus and as a cause for collective concern. At the same time, missionary children were drawn into fellow commonality with their peers in countries of origin, sometimes speaking for themselves while often filling the role of 'other'. For adults, these representations acted as powerful drivers of the parental and institutional narratives considered in the following two chapters. In turn, adult perspectives were challenged, to a certain extent, by children's narratives. This chapter therefore sets the scene by outlining in some detail the literary sources and their scope by probing apparently dominant tropes of deprivation, danger and difference and by thinking further about audience and context.

Sources and scope

In the first instance, the literature considered here derives from publications of the period under study. This does not include the many memoirs written in hindsight by adults looking back on their missionary childhoods, nor those missionary biographies also published later in which children might appear. Such publications are important and will be considered in later chapters.[15] Here the focus is primarily on contemporary books, newspapers and periodicals which act as sources in their own right as well as interpretative sites. This broad period was one in which overall literacy in the West increased for all ages, print technologies improved (giving readers access to an increasingly greater mix of print and visual material) and both transport and communication technologies ensured quicker access to news and reading materials. Producers and distributors of religiously focused literature quickly took advantage of these developments, placing voluminous amounts of literature into people's hands and houses. What was published in Britain or North America quickly found its way to places like South Africa, Australia and New Zealand and vice versa.

Newspapers were one way by which missionary children became visible and 'known' to the general public, albeit on a limited and somewhat stereotyped basis, and which most clearly constituted a ubiquitous form of textual commons. Here children were at their most anonymous, often simply referred to as 'missionaries' children' or mentioned in reference to events or wider issues. Across a broad survey of digitised newspapers from Australia, Britain and New Zealand, the Engwall sisters were among the very few to be named, although this does not discount the appearance of others by name and was dependent on context. Children might, for instance, be glimpsed simply as the 'daughters' of a family returning to Australia from Korea in 1931, the 'missionaries' children in China, India or the South Seas' who received correspondence school materials from Melbourne through the 1930s or the 'Michell' and 'Nicholls' children reunited with their parents after internment by the Japanese in China during World War II.[16] Common, too, were travellers' reports of visits to missionary children's schools like that at Chefoo, China, where children were anonymously lumped together as 'boys' or 'girls' or as candidates for 'the Oxford examinations'.[17]

Extensively shared and detailed newspaper coverage enlarged missionary children's profiles on at least three occasions, accentuating perceptions of danger common across provincial and national imperial readership. One was a natural disaster that devastated Darjeeling, in northern India, in late 1899, that engulfed one American missionary family (see further). Other occasions involved missionaries and their children caught up in incidents in China: namely the Kucheng massacres of 1895 and the Boxer War of 1900, but also one-off instances of families being kidnapped during periods of local conflict. Multiple iterations of the same news stories appeared, for example, in Australian and New Zealand papers, broadly citing the numbers of unnamed children killed or injured in those conflicts. One such report in 1900, shared by many papers, highlighted the plight of children forced to escape to Hankow (Hankou) on a fifty-day march, arriving 'emaciated' with 'their little bones all showing, and no flesh on their limbs', having survived on little or no food for an extended period.[18] More commonly, newspapers tended to accentuate perceptions that children occupied hazardous environments and were in need of public philanthropy. In some contexts, newspapers also differentiated missionary children abroad (living in various geographical or cultural settings) and missionary children in the metropole (especially inhabiting missionary children's residential homes for their education). This latter aspect was the dominant representation in Scottish and English newspapers of the period. Very rarely, but echoed across other literary sources, missionary children were sometimes cast in an exemplary role to showcase attitudes, morals or values desirable in the wider population.[19]

For more specifically defined Protestant or religious reading audiences across the British Empire in this period, books and periodicals emerge as important literary sites for encountering missionary children. Throughout the long nineteenth century, Protestant denominations and missionary organisations developed sophisticated literary infrastructure that included long runs of targeted periodicals and vibrant printing houses.[20] These sustained a perpetual flow of missionary literature for the wider reading public, adding greatly to shared perceptions and knowledge of their Empire.[21] Children were a central focus. Mary Ellis Gibson captures the scope of this huge swathe of children's literature when she comments that '[n]o life is long enough for a scholar to read the deluge of print that engulfed the Victorian young'.[22] Periodicals were the most obvious manifestation of this, appearing from the 1840s onwards across Anglo-American Protestantism and were well established as an effective form of educational propaganda by the late nineteenth century.[23] A perusal of library catalogues for the period also indicates the ubiquity of missionary biographies aimed at both child and adult readers. Across English and North American Sunday school libraries, for example, these books were religiously didactic while promoting 'more secular ideals incorporating the style and format of contemporary books and magazines' and which 'importantly included ideas linked to self-improvement, character building and imperialism, which were all deemed important by the Sunday school network'.[24]

Jeffrey Cox suggests that 'for most British children in the nineteenth century, the single largest source of information about what foreign people were like came from the foreign missionary societies of their respective denominations'.[25] While true, this observation needs to be tempered by noting the ubiquity of children's periodicals in Britain and the Empire – like the *Boy's Own Paper* (1879–1967) and the *Girl's Own Paper* (1880–1956) – that also potentially shaped young people's views of the world. Jeffrey Richards suggests, for example, that such popular fiction formed a pervasive 'sediment of the mind' that could be 'peculiarly potent', because it fed the 'imaginative life'.[26] Even so, Sunday schools and Sunday school literature were important and may, in Francis Prochaska's opinion, have contributed partly to the long-term 'formation of prejudice' among children and young people with respect to their views of non-European peoples of the Empire.[27] Philanthropic and imperial impulses, supported in large part by this literature, combined to potentially create an environment in which a 'dominant' British middle-class culture was 'centralised', and 'in this discourse of superiority, the voice of the "other" [was] disallowed'.[28] Admittedly this great slew of literature promoted the same attitudes towards working-class non-European or white children in Britain and other sending societies, who were also deemed socially lost or spiritually in need of regeneration. As such, argues Margot Hillel, the 'textual child' fulfilled a didactic role in making children 'aware of the plight of others' so that child readers in particular could 'recognize the issues and the need to do something about them'. Thus 'charity and the child, and the appeal for children to try to alleviate the plight of others, were all aligned, forming a trope that called on children to play a role in helping to right societal wrongs'.[29] Missionary magazines for the young were influential in this respect. They acted not just as imperial textual commons but also as contact zones and sites of interactive engagement, through which British world children were recruited as agents of missionary support[30] and, in the process, were potentially drawn into shared emotional and spiritual communities both within and across denominational and national boundaries.

As a specific subject of all this literature, missionary children inhabited both magazines and books in particular ways, fulfilling the range of functions identified by Hillel, for both their adult and child readers. Again, as in the newspapers, they were often nameless, occupying a somewhat marginalised space, especially in adult literature. Typical of this was a fiftieth-anniversary history of the New Zealand Presbyterian Church's (NZPC) work in the New Hebrides, from which the public learned little else about children beyond the tragically premature deaths of the first two babies born to Helen and Thomas Smaill, or the 'seven children' of the Milne family who spent their school years in New Zealand.[31] If they were named, then often the most that a reading public learned was children's births or their premature deaths. Annually published missionary reports carried these details, but so did regular magazines. The LMS *Chronicle*, for example, published such details in its monthly 'Announcements' column, recording 107 juvenile deaths by name between 1890 and 1939.[32] In a more positive light, children receiving education grants were also listed regularly by name in the published annual reports of the United Free Church of Scotland (UFC).[33] Occasionally children might also be pictured or noted interacting with local or Indigenous children, as in the case of a 1934 LMS photograph showing baby Conriss Stallan 'with his Samoan playmate' (unnamed). The photograph was deliberately part of a larger message. It was entitled 'Friends in Samoa' and accompanied by Ethel Blair Jordan's evocative verse:

In hearts too young for enmity
There lies the way to make men free.
When children's friendships are worldwide,
Let child love child, and strife will cease,
Disarm the hearts, for that is Peace.[34]

Dedicated magazines for domestic child audiences went further while avoiding details of juvenile illness or deaths which may have been deemed inappropriate for young readers. From about 1900 onwards missionary children – on their own, together with other missionary or local children, with an Indigenous carer or in their family units – were increasingly represented through stories, letters and especially photographs. Some of these were mediated by adult writers, particularly on behalf of babies or infants. One-year-old Dorothy Kirk, for instance, 'wrote' about her birthday, travelling by ship from south China to Scotland and life while on furlough in Edinburgh.[35] Missionary children also wrote their own letters which were published for other child readers, both in metropole and colonial settings.[36] Gordon and Margaret Mawson (aged eight and six respectively) wrote extensively from Canton (Guangzhou) to New Zealand in 1914, juxtaposing the familiar (family life, school, chores, anticipation of Christmas) with the unfamiliar (animals, rice fields, tropical fruit, deprivation, sickness among local people and children not able to attend school).[37] The didactic and ideological influence of a parent or editor was readily identifiable in such publications. It was seen, for example, in the Mawson children's references to their stated good fortune in having 'mothers who understand how to keep us clean and healthy', and an expressed hope that some of the Chinese children receiving missionary education 'will confess Jesus before they leave school'. That Margaret and Gordon celebrated Christmas with Chinese children in the mission's Sunday school but anticipated a second 'New Zealand Christmas afterwards', complete with Santa Claus, further differentiated them from their Chinese peers and connected them more closely with those at home expecting something similar. By the early twentieth century the cultural significance of Christmas for colonial children, like those in New Zealand, may have differed from other parts of the British metropole, thus heightening expectations of their missionary children.[38] Here is a hint of the two sides of children's narratives that will be explored later. At the same time, these magazines functioned as both cultural contact zones and vehicles for creating and sustaining emotional communities. In smaller nations like Scotland and New Zealand, the deployment of such personalised accounts or illustrations helped to build a sense of national denominational identity.

Books tended to emphasise at least three interwoven themes revolving around missionary children. One was their location within the domestic life of the companionate family unit, emphasising for readers that despite circumstances, missionaries' children were being looked after properly. Danish Protestants, for instance, expected that 'children should ideally live at home with their parents'. Therefore Danish missionary parents portrayed clear emotional labour as they sought in their public writing to reassure their supporters that they loved and cared for their children.[39] This emphasis became more common across Western societies by the twentieth century and was reflected in missionary writing. Typical in this respect is one account by Scottish Presbyterian Donald Fraser in Malawi. While his children were not centre stage in his biographical writing, they were present and their lives represented in predominantly domestic terms: celebrations of Christmas, rooms of the house that echoed with 'the shouts of happy children', outdoor meals and recreation on the veranda and extended summer holidays together in the hills.[40] At the same time, an account of the Fraser children encountering a rhinoceros while on holiday or an 1860s published photograph of a young Alexander Paterson reclining on the knee of his Indian ayah struck a discordant note with respect to how readers might further interpret these supposedly familiar domestic scenes.[41] In the process, these children were rendered both familiar – with respect to skin colour, dress, family connections and Western cultural accoutrements – and different, in terms of their environment and locale. For books, two further interwoven themes echo Hillel's wider emphasis on the didactic imperative that ran through all children's literature and on the power of missionary children to act as Christian exemplars for their readers. Novels both accentuated the dominant domestic trope while emotionally drawing in child readers to become co-participants through educated, informed and empathetic missionary support. In them missionary children performed all kinds of expected roles and ultimately exemplified lives of sacrifice, kindness, service and fortitude that an author might then hope readers would emulate in their own lives, irrespective of geography or culture.

Yet novels could also portray missionary children in more nuanced ways. E.C. Phillips's late-nineteenth-century novel *Peeps into China* was one case in point.[42] This book recounted the story of a Church of England vicar and his family going to Hong Kong, wherein the two children – Sybil and Leonard – accompanied the parents on the voyage and initial settling in before returning to England for their education. The bulk of the chapters used the voyage to narrate details of Chinese geography, culture, religions and the rationale for Christian missions in China. Children reading this novel learnt much in the process, albeit culturally configured and entered into the emotional world of the two missionary children.

Sybil emerged as more complex in her characterisation as a result. On the surface she was buoyantly happy about the prospects, exclaiming 'Oh, how very beautiful … *I like my father to be a missionary very much* [emphasis original]',[43] performing a role that might be expected by her readers. She further encouraged her father in his own concerns about going to China. Yet her anxieties were also laid bare, foregrounded by an authorial observation that

> Sybil and Leonard had as yet only learnt a part of the story. They had still to learn the rest. This going to China would not be all beautiful, all joy for them, especially for Sybil, with her very affectionate nature and dread of saying 'Good-byes', for she and Leonard were only to be taken out on a trip – a pleasure tour – to see something of China, and to return to England to go on with their education at the end of six months.[44]

Sybil expressed concerns about leaving behind a good friend, but this was easily placated.

More difficult was what she then learnt, narrated warts and all. She and her younger brother would then remain in England for schooling, at least four years for her and longer for Leonard. In her mind, she understood the reasons but apprehended the emotional cost of separation for the two siblings. At this point 'her bright eyes filled with tears', which was effectively countered by her father's response.

> [Y]ou know that it must be a dreadful trial for so very good and loving a mother as yours to part from her children; but now that a call has come to me to do my Master's work in a foreign land, and she is helping me to obey it,

you would not make her trial greater, would you, by letting her see you sad? Oh no! I know you would not; but you would help us to do our duty more bravely. Is it not so, my child?

Sybil's response was thus:

on seeing her mother coming up the garden towards them, she quickly wiped her tears away, and tried to look cheerful. Her father had gone wisely to work in giving her such a reason for trying to overcome her sorrow, and he knew that now she would set herself bravely to work to help, and not to hinder, her parents' undertaking.

E.C. Phillips then added an authorial meditation, by writing:

Mrs. Graham brought a message from Leonard for Sybil to go and see his roosts, which she at once obeyed, affectionately kissing her mother as she passed her. That was to say that she knew, and a great deal more. Another piece of news Sybil now conveyed to Leonard, and as she told it, even he could not tell that it made her very unhappy. I wonder if he believed at once this time![45]

There were clear ambiguities in the telling of this story, with the final paragraphs indicating the cost of separation for parents as much as the children and emphasising the children's ultimate positive spin on difficult circumstances.[46] Sybil's emotional labour within the private confines of the companionate family was, perhaps, a literary device used to teach children about emotional expectations in their own spheres. Yet the novel also exposed the issues that missionary children themselves faced and the mental gymnastics through which they attempted to reconcile their consequent lives. As such it foregrounds a range of important themes that will be teased out further in the following chapters.

Finally, this dual didactic and exemplary emphasis found ultimate expression through a variety of contemporary biographies and tracts in which missionary children were more centre stage. Typically, these focused on children who had died tragically and prematurely from illness or natural disaster, including Lucy Thurston in Hawai'i (1842), Charles Dwight in Constantinople (1853), Emily Lillie in Jamaica (1865), Ruth Allerton in Africa (1871), Fanny Hurd in Jamaica (1886), the Lee children in India (1899) and Carol Bird also in India (1910).[47] These publications sat within a larger corpus of religious literature that reflected contemporary Protestant literary tropes of the exemplary Christian child and death, which originated in at least the seventeenth century and were exemplified in James Janeway's popular *A Token for Children* (1671).[48] From the early nineteenth century such child-focused literature 'showed both how to elicit evidence of "the principle of faith" having taken root and how the death-bed itself could be used as a premature opportunity for exhibiting "the fruits of holiness"'.[49] It was both consolatory and didactic in purpose and, like children's hymnody, helped children to come to terms with life's 'next chapter'.[50]

Accounts of missionary children followed this line but at the same time fulfilled a slightly different function. While this is explored further in the next section, one example here is instructive. The account of Charles Dwight's illness and death in Constantinople highlighted in familiar terms a boy who previously had 'yielded to [God's] power', who had 'put his trust in the Saviour' and who 'now entered a new life'. As such, he exemplified what young readers should value – prayer, reading the Bible, right living and aiming 'to make everybody happy'.[51] However, the narrative went further in terms of pointing children to broader horizons. Readers were told that while at peace with the prospect of death, Charles still hoped to live so that he could 'do good' in his life. In particular 'his heart was set on being a missionary', to follow his father's footsteps in Constantinople; 'It was this that seemed to him even more desirable than to go at once and be with Christ.'[52] Thus it was Charles's life, as much as or more than, his death that was an important object lesson for young readers. That his death was the focus, however, underscored a deeper and pervasive literary representation of missionary children, that became calcified in public perceptions.

Difference, deprivation and danger

In 1893, ex-Premier and prominent lawyer Sir Robert Stout reported back to the New Zealand public from a visit to Samoa. One of his topics was 'Educational Institutions', with a focus on the work of the LMS. In the context of talking about missionary wives he further commented on the easily forgotten 'missionaries' children', arguing that they 'cannot be reared in Samoa any more than on the plains of Hindoostan [*sic*]' and hence, sadly, missionary parents and their children 'must be separated' – deemed to be 'one of the greatest trials of a missionary's life'. In his opinion, they could:

> remain in Samoa two or three years, but after that, if they are to be reared fairly strong children, perhaps if they are to live at all, they must be sent to a cool climate. I leave my readers to picture what that means, especially to the missionaries' wives. Some of the missionaries I met had some of their little ones in England. They hardly ever hope to see them again, and even if they did their children had been reared away from them, and had lived another life, and the charm of home is lost. What New Zealand might do not only for the missionaries in Samoa, but for all the white missionaries in the Pacific

in reference to the missionaries' children, I may point out before I close my notes. Meantime let me say that this sending of the children away from home ... seemed to me to be one of the greatest trials of a missionary's life.[53]

While avowedly parent-centric and clearly focused on the Pacific region, Stout's themes reflected entrenched attitudes and representations with respect to missionary children's health, welfare and education.

From a wider context, there were at least two main related narrative threads to such representations. Children's environment was one such thread. Addressing a crowd of 300 gathered at the farewell of the LMS ship *John Williams* from Sydney in 1862, one speaker 'trusted that they would pray for the missionary's wife', often separated from her husband, and also 'pray for the missionary's children, that they might be preserved from every taint of heathenism'.[54] Nearly thirty years later, the Rev. W.R. Fletcher made an explicit link between environment, education and family separation when defending missionary expenditure in India to South Australian LMS supporters. He remonstrated that this was dictated by the 'conditions of life in India' because, among other things, 'a married missionary with children of school-going age had to send them to England for education, as it could not, for physical and moral reasons, be imparted to them in India'.[55]

Thus, Stout's opinions meshed with prevalent and long-standing British beliefs about the impact of the physical, cultural or moral climate on European children.[56] In particular, ideas about the dangers of tropical climates for the young, especially the effect of heat on children's rate of maturation, were cemented in both scientific and popular rhetoric by the second half of the 1800s.[57] Among missionaries and their supporters, this was a widely held belief across other nationalities. It was influential, for example, in provoking the Norwegian Missionary Society to establish a Norway-based missionary home and school for the children of their Madagascar missionaries in 1887, despite pre-existing schooling and residential facilities in Antananarivo. This decision was made against the backdrop of regular child deaths in the Madagascar setting combined with the medical opinion of the day that 'advised parents to keep their children out of "tropical" areas for longer periods, as these areas could negatively affect their physical, mental and intellectual development'.[58] At the same time, not all missionary locales evoked the same sentiments, and perhaps the rhetoric was further differentiated over time. A British Association drive for white settlement in Matabeleland (Zimbabwe) in the 1890s, for example, noted that there missionaries had for many years 'reared families, and their children have married other missionaries and settled in the country'. The speaker noted that while many missionaries' children returned to England, this was for education rather than health reasons (although perhaps implying that local education was inherently inferior and thus reinforcing public perceptions of difference in the lives that missionary children lived).[59]

The second enduring narrative thread was the dual notion of deprivation and danger. On the one hand, missionary children were often construed as objects of pity,[60] due to the perception that they lived relatively deprived lives. References to 'those poor missionary children' were common. As such, they became worthy recipients of charity, feeding the heavy financial emphasis in the institutional narrative. British children were often referenced in literature as doing things like donating used toys or fundraising, each act aimed at missionary children abroad.[61] On the other hand children's lives were constantly represented as inherently dangerous both morally and physically. This perception had a long life in public memory. The Buller family, missionaries in northern New Zealand in the 1840s and 1850s, suffered the deaths of two of their nine children. A historical account of their life, written nearly a century later, still emphasised the trope of danger by noting that 'far away from any doctor or any white friend, it was often a life of intense anxiety'.[62] Newspaper headlines often leant further weight to this perception of danger and imperilled lives. But just as common were representations that drew an exotic aura around children's lives that hinted at danger or accentuated difference. In the 1920s the advent of the cinema meant that films like *The Arab* – a popular movie that cast a missionary daughter as both a love interest of a local Muslim man and someone in danger from an impending massacre – boosted such notions among religious and non-religious audiences alike.[63] Both these public narrative threads cemented a common perception that missionary children's lives were different, potentially difficult or hazardous and therefore the cause for both public concern and intervention. In turn, the public discourse helped to bolster and perpetuate both family and institutional narratives, discussed in the following chapters, that emphasised maintaining domestic stability, ostensibly for children but more particularly for the parents themselves.

A much-publicised tragedy that enveloped one missionary family in 1899 both echoed and amplified such perceptions, while at the same time perhaps quietly subverting public expectations. It was reported widely in global newspapers and further consolidated in evangelical circles by two books later written by Ada Lee, the mother of the deceased children.[64] On the night of 24 September 1899, geography and weather conspired together to wreak havoc for the north-eastern Indian hill town and region of Darjeeling. Perhaps triggered by earth tremors, but certainly precipitated by sustained torrential downpours over nearly forty hours, the slopes of Darjeeling gave way in the form of multiple mudslides. This was repeated in many other settlements across a wide area. The disaster was reported immediately in Anglo-American newspapers, but with increasing detail over time, bringing the victims into the kitchens and parlours of homes across a wide range of British and American metropole and British world urban or rural settings. Diverse newspapers both shared and replicated the details as a clear form of textual commons.

Among the hundreds of unnamed victims (local and colonial), newspaper readers encountered the names of a number of European children – mostly of missionary families – who lived in Darjeeling away from their parents at an expatriate school.[65] A greater tragedy emerged. Six of the seven children of the Lee family (American Methodists) were reported to have perished. Ada and David Lee lived and worked in Calcutta (Kolkati) while their older children – Vida, Esther, Ada (junior), Lois, Herbert and Wilbur – resided in Darjeeling. Over the night of 24 and 25 September, the tragedy was played out in two parts. First, the children were relocated from their home further up the hill, led by two of the teachers. Here they all congregated to wait out the storm in what was hoped to be a safer location. In the early hours of the morning, one side of this residence was crushed by a first subsidence, resulting in a number of deaths and injuries. Somewhat chaotically, two adults went to seek help while the two remaining adults led some of the children further up the hill. In the confusion, other children remained behind without adults. Led by older sister Vida, they tried at least three different directions of escape and were blocked each way. In an attempt to keep them all together, she took them back to the partially damaged house to wait it out – lighting a fire, saying prayers together and keeping warm. Thus, these remaining children were swept away or buried by a subsequent major subsidence. Wilbur alone survived, albeit half-buried in mud until his rescue and hospitalisation the next morning.

In the aftermath of this tragedy, various family members made their way to Darjeeling, which in itself was something of a physical and emotional feat. Ada and David Lee, with baby son Frank, made straight for Wilbur's bedside. At this stage, he was conscious, lively, talkative and sociable. He was able to inform parents and others about the night's events, before succumbing to tetanus and injuries himself on 3 October. His funeral service followed. There were many burial services conducted with solemnity. Among these, there was one notable public ceremony with a great variety of Indian, imperial and ecumenical church dignitaries in attendance. Yet there must have remained unfinished business for the senior Lees, in that some of their children were never found. Lady Curzon telegraphed Ada Lee with these words: 'Every woman and mother in India is feeling for you.'[66]

Newspapers conveyed the facts and communicated something of the pathos of these events, while occasionally opening a small window both on the religious sentiments that framed missionary families' lives and on the children's role in this tragedy. The *New Zealand Mail* carried a story in

November 1899 that reported that 'when she saw that escape was impossible Vida [older sister] made them all kneel and pray. While they were praying the house was overwhelmed.'[67] For the Christian reading public, the two books that emerged from the pen of mother Ada Lee, in 1903 and 1912, focused more concertedly on religious themes and deliberately cast the children centre-stage. The initial six chapters of *Seven Heroic Children* provided context and outlined the narrative of the tragedy, with Ada writing herself into the story in the third person. The following six chapters were devoted to telling each child's story, including a seventh child who was clearly considered a family member (and who died with them) – Jessudar 'the Bengali girl'. Jessudar was a member of the Lee household and had gone to live with the other children in Darjeeling where she also attended school. These chapters are notable in that they did not dwell on the details of the children's deaths, but rather on each child's life. The exception was Wilbur, whose survival and last days were described more extensively. At the same time, throughout the book, there was a clear and moving emphasis on how each child was valued and loved by mother and father, and the degree to which they were deeply missed. When writing about Herbert, Ada noted that

> I have many things to regret; but how I thank God now that I never felt we had one [child] too many; nor did I ever tire of their noise or of doing for them. I am glad that several years ago I wrote the lines, 'The highest honour God has ever bestowed upon me in this life is that of motherhood and the privilege of living for the children He has given me.'[68]

Seven Heroic Children worked on a range of levels: as parenting advice, as a spiritual devotional, as a popular theological treatise on the nature of God and the exigencies of living a life of faith, and as an evangelical pamphlet. Yet primarily it memorialised the children's lives, rather than their deaths. Like Charles Dwight's earlier narrative in Constantinople, the Lee children were recast as exemplars of Christian childhood and faith, warts and all.[69] Selections of their letters in a further chapter personalised this element, showcasing both their personalities and lives of faith. Adult and child readers alike were invited to take sober inspiration from the spiritual journeys of these children and to apply the lessons offered to their own lives. Thus, framed within a Protestant evangelical discourse, the children's deaths were not central, so much, as the *raison d'être* for representing their lives to a wider reading public. At the same time, the book remains a moving tribute, primarily for the way that it revealed the internal struggles of the parents to integrate deeply held beliefs and the immensity of their grief, which was real and surely almost overwhelming. In this respect perhaps it provided

Ada with a vehicle to work through her own grief. This theme emerges time and again from missionary parents' narratives and can be more broadly interpreted, especially where these narratives are reproduced in published form for a missionary reading public, as culturally circumscribed evidence of missionary parents' emotional labour.

In all of these ways, the Darjeeling tragedy heralded that while missionary children in literature were the inhabitants of dangerous or difficult places – and thus inherently different – they were also represented as children whose lives were not dissimilar to those of their readers. Furthermore, their lives mattered. True to form, this became a rallying call for children to support the Lees' Methodist 'Bengali Mission' in Calcutta. That this tragedy had an ongoing impact on wider communities of Protestant readers was evidenced well into the 1920s from places as far-flung as Newcastle in Australia, where one writer recounted how children in a local Christian Endeavour group readily contributed money to the Lees' work.[70] A final chapter in *Seven Heroic Children* outlined a plethora of projects that received philanthropic support in the following years, including a specific 'Children's Memorial' project providing accommodation and trades training for Bengali children. Of this Ada wrote poignantly that in the midst of their own grief, 'the LORD so vividly told us it was for these children who have no one to care for them that He wanted us to live; and this we are doing cheerfully and it is our joy to do His will'.[71]

Conclusion: audience and context

It is fair to conclude, then, that while contemporary literature was an important first point of contact between domestic reading audiences and the lives of missionary children, this was a complex and somewhat contested space. Missionary children, in general, appeared or were represented on adult terms, reflecting adults' agendas and priorities. As such, audience and context mattered. This comes into clearer view through the British imperial textual commons' lens, whereby these children became reading subjects for a global English-language newspaper audience that endured over many decades from the nineteenth into the twentieth centuries. As subjects, they were shared and 'known' across a spectrum of national and regional audiences and, in the process, sometimes took on celebrity status in times of war or disaster. They were further cast by adult writers as ethical or moral exemplars whose lives took on a meaning not necessarily perceived by the children themselves. Wider literature, particularly aimed at Protestant church audiences, reinforced this while also acting as a form of virtual contact zone. Adults encountered children and young people living lives often perceived to be different, disadvantaged or dangerous. Such perceptions were heightened by specific events – for example, the Darjeeling disaster, China's Boxer War and the internment of missionary children or families during World War II – and proved persistent over time.

Through literature, Western children encountered other Western children, particularly in religious magazines, who looked like them and whose lives sounded similar in terms of daily minutiae, but who also looked different (perhaps by way of their clothing or the people in their physical proximity) or who at least inhabited visibly different spaces. Magazine texts and photographs together were often ambiguous in this regard. In the New Zealand Presbyterian *Break of Day* from 1909 until at least the 1940s, for example, New Zealand youngsters read letters from missionary children that made a lot of sense and looked at photographs of children who largely looked like them. At the same time, they saw these children with exotic animals, dressed up in Chinese clothing or riding in or conveyed by vehicles pulled or carried by other people who were different. As babies or infants, they regularly appeared in the arms of a local young woman, ayah (India) or amah (China) employed or engaged as a child-minder, but who often acted as an influential child-rearer.[72] As later chapters indicate, such differences became more acute when missionary children returning home were viewed as different because of sun-burned skin or strange accents. At that point, literature and reality became mutually self-reinforcing, with many missionary children (similar to other migrant children) recounting such instances and the emotional imprint on their memories of those transition points in their lives.[73]

A broad reading of children's religious literature, across different British world contexts and over a number of decades, reveals much therefore that was common to a plethora of Protestant audiences. One broad impression from this, repeated across a spectrum of scholarship on children's missionary literature and already noted in this chapter, is that a primary outcome was the enculturation of Western child readers in imperialism and the cementing of cultural prejudices.[74] It is reasonable to argue that literary representations of missionary children helped to create a sense of identity among Western juvenile readers, through a shared Protestant emotional-theological community that was simultaneously local, national and global in its configurations. This was important for the formation of juvenile religious identity within metropole settings. In theory, it further bound together Western metropole readers and their Western missionary child subjects but, in reality, may have been more important for the former. To argue that missionary children felt a sense of belonging to that same emotional-theological community might prove more problematic. Three broader observations thus shine a light on the importance of context, helping us to think more carefully about missionary children's literary representations in terms of where, when and why.

One observation is framed by Andrew Thompson's caution about drawing monolithic conclusions about the reflexive impact of empire (at least on the British metropole). He warns that '"enthusiasm" for empire may be too global and abstract a category'; rather it 'is necessary to break down Britain's imperial experience in order to appreciate how different parts of society became caught up in the process of overseas expansion in different ways'. Therefore, for example, 'to say that the juvenile missionary movement raised children's awareness of empire does not mean it also indoctrinated them in racist or xenophobic values'.[75] What metropole children read or learnt, in this case about their Western peers in missionary settings, and how that shaped or influenced their thinking are two different things. They certainly became active in supporting missionary causes – including supporting missionary children – through the nineteenth and twentieth centuries. Yet 'we still do not really know what it all meant to them, how it was perceived, how it was felt, and to what extent it was meaningful'[76] with respect to how Western children thought about the wider world within the construct of empire.

A second observation is that the concept of 'emotional community' needs to be interrogated further both for its points of differentiation and its applicability to missionary children in particular. Mark Seymour uses a geological analogy when he argues that historians need to look for the 'fault lines' by which emotional communities are 'likely to be shot through'. Rather, the

> more historians are able to find out about the feelings of individual members, the more it becomes necessary for them to accept that historical actors, while they may appear to belong to one particular emotional community, are likely to shift their allegiances, values, and modes of expression according to the expectations they associate with a given spatial arena.[77]

This has potential for considering the different emotional communities created by the Protestant missionary movement. Jane Haggis and Margaret Allen provide important correctives, for example, to an application of emotional communities to networks of women supporting, engaged in or worked upon by foreign missions, when they highlight the racial and ideological hierarchies that existed in reality across imperial spaces.[78] For missionary children, however, the notion of a 'fault line' is not a strong enough analytical concept and emotional community might be too static when applied to particular contexts. Representations presented in this chapter point to the value to be gained from thinking about multiple emotional formations encountered over space and time, and the quite significant emotional frontiers with which children contended or struggled. This angle will be considered in later chapters.

The third observation is that, across the British Empire, missionary literature for white children served different purposes. This is clear, for example, in Christine Weir's argument that Australian Presbyterian and Methodist juvenile missionary magazines almost exclusively conveyed locally written material on the Pacific region, to emphasise Australian children's 'primary responsibility' towards their denominational work in the Pacific.[79] These magazines were much less derivative in terms of material gleaned from British or North American Protestant literary sources, especially by the early decades of the twentieth century. Thus, a more differentiated analysis of how missionary children appeared in the literature of various denominations and nations is required to properly understand their role in the literature of the period. Denominational and national identity-building was just as important a project as fostering informed and enthusiastic missionary support among the young, and it was to this end that missionary children represented in literature played their part.

One final note on context can be made here as a means of now making the transition into the following chapters. In the summer of 1910, the noted English Baptist leader the Rev F.B. Meyer extensively visited missionaries and their families in China.[80] He spent considerable time with missionaries' children at the various hill station holiday destinations. His report, clearly written for English and other Empire children, was didactic in both content and tone. There were spiritual lessons to be learnt in the stories that he here recounted. Meyer also made connections between missionary children's lives and those of his readers: the 'children enjoying themselves as you do when you are able to go to the seaside or the country for your holidays'; they 'became great friends', later writing to him with the 'fair roundhand [*sic*] of a boy, and the printing of quite a little child'. Whether or not intended, Meyer effectively rendered missionary children's lives more normal, for his juvenile readers, and in so doing he placed them as the central subjects of his report. Missionary children's lives had always mattered, but what Meyer's article signalled ten years into the new century was that they began to matter more than previously as middle-class society's view of childhood and the family evolved. This is the focus of the following four chapters.

Notes

1 Anonymous, '"God Doeth Wonders": Work of the China Inland Mission', *Poverty Bay Herald* (28 March 1927), p. 4.
2 Anonymous, 'Missionary Catechism', *The Break of Day* (March 1919), p. 4.
3 Headline, '70 British Children on Pirated Ship', *The Telegraph* [Queensland] (2 February 1935), p. 1.

4   *The Press* [Christchurch] (28 August 1937), Supplement, p. 5; (19 February 1938), Supplement, p. 2; and (11 June 1938), Supplement, p. 3.

5   Cited by Plamper, *The History of Emotions*, p. 68.

6   For example, Rosenwein, 'Worrying', 842; Rosenwein and Cristiani, *What Is?*, pp. 39–45.

7   Rosenwein, *Generations*, p. 3.

8   Vallgårda, Alexander and Olsen, 'Emotions', pp. 20–26 and further explained in Olsen, 'History of Childhood', 5–7; Haggis and Allen, 'Imperial Emotions', 691–716; Morrison, 'Settler Childhood', pp. 76–94.

9   Pratt, *Imperial Eyes*, pp. 4, 41, 43; O'Dochartaigh, 'Exceedingly Good Friends', 255–67; Martin, 'Play', p. 61 in turn citing Ganter and Grimshaw, 'Introduction', 1–6.

10 Pomfret, *Youth*, p. 1.

11 Hofmeyr, 'Introduction', 1–8; Hofmeyr and Burton, 'Introduction', pp. 1–28.

12 Note, however, the complicated nature of the so-called cablegram revolution of the late nineteenth century and the pitfalls of its historiography, in O'Hara, 'New Histories', 909–25.

13 Hofmeyr, 'Introduction', 4, 6–7.

14 Hofmeyr and Burton, 'Introduction', pp. 4, 5.

15 For a helpful introductory study of the potential of these sources for historical understanding see Vandrick, *Growing Up*.

16 *Age* (7 September 1931), p. 9; *Newcastle Sun* (20 July 1938), p. 5; *Advertiser* (9 November 1945), p. 13.

17 Anonymous, 'Some Impressions of China', *Auckland Star* (1 December 1908), p. 2.

18 *Wagga Wagga Advertiser* (25 September 1900), p. 3.

19 Anonymous, 'For the Children: The Bottle Story', *Australian Christian Commonwealth* (6 August 1913), p. 16; Anonymous, 'Sunday Circle', *Southland Times* (20 March 1915), p. 11.

20 See further, McDowell, 'Towards a History'; Galbraith, *Reading Lives*; and Grenby, *The Child Reader*.

21 Thorne, 'Religion and Empire', p. 144. This thesis also lies at the heart of Thorne's analysis of missions' impact on British middle-class culture in the nineteenth century in *Congregational Missions*.

22 Gibson, 'The Perils', p. 109.

23 Morrison, *Protestant Children*, pp. 34–54.

24 McColl, 'Imagining', pp. 77–92, especially pp. 78–79.

25 Cox, *British Missionary Enterprise*, p. 101. The influence of missionary literature for children is also recognised in Hillel, 'Give Us All', 181–82.

26 Richards, 'Introduction', pp. 1–2; Jeff Bowersox makes similar observations for children in imperial Germany, in 'Boy's and Girl's', pp. 57–69.

27 Prochaska, 'Little Vessels', 114. This is applied to the Chinese context, for example, in: Chen, *Representations*; and Chen, 'Give, Give', 5–32. For a wider synthesis of literature around this point see Morrison, *Protestant Children*, pp. 23–26, 55–63.

28 Hillel, 'Give Us All', 183.
29 Hillel, 'Nearly All', p. 176.
30 Elleray, 'Little Builders', 223–38; and for wider context Elleray, *Victorian Coral Islands*.
31 Don, *Light in Dark Isles*, pp. 30, 111.
32 'Announcements', *Chronicle of the London Missionary Society*, 1890–1939. Sampling of the LMS missionary children's register suggests that the number of juvenile deaths in the *Chronicle* were underreported for this period. 'London Missionary Society Register of Missionaries' Children up to 1940', vols 1 and 2, Archive of the Council of World Mission (formerly LMS), School of Oriental and African Studies, London [CWM].
33 NLS, Dep. 298/94, COSOC, United Presbyterian Church Missionary Children's Committees 1849–1938, Ladies' Mission Committee Minute Book 1861–1938, Minutes for 7 December 1915.
34 Anonymous, 'Friends in Samoa', *Chronicle of the London Missionary Society* (September 1934), p. 215.
35 Letter extract in *The Break of Day* (July 1914), p. 3.
36 The following example is for the New Zealand setting. Mary Clare Martin notes similar instances in nineteenth-century juvenile literature published by both the LMS *Juvenile Missionary Magazine* and the Society for the Propagation of the Gospel's (SPG) *The Children's Tidings*. Martin, 'Play', p. 63.
37 The following details come from 'A Letter from Gordon and Margaret Mawson', *The Break of Day* (March 1914), pp. 12–13.
38 For context see: Clarke, *Holiday Seasons*; Lineham, 'New Zealand Christmas', pp. 154–70.
39 Vallgårda, *Imperial Childhoods*, pp. 181–208, particularly pp. 182, 207.
40 Fraser, *African Idylls*, pp. 22–24, 56–67.
41 *Ibid.*, pp. 64–65; Ewing, *Paterson*, photograph facing p. 14.
42 Phillips, *Peeps into China*. An attached Sunday school prize certificate of the copy I read, dated Christmas 1885, suggests publication sometime after 1880 (which is cited in the novel as the date of a letter written by Sybil from China to England), p. 152.
43 *Ibid.*, p. 10.
44 *Ibid.*, p. 12.
45 *Ibid.*, pp. 19–20.
46 *Ibid.*, pp. 223–24.
47 Cummings, *The Missionary's Daughter*; Anonymous, *Charles Dwight*; Anonymous, *The Missionary's Daughter*; Lee, *Seven Heroic Children*; and Bird, *Carol*.
48 Houlbrooke, 'Death', pp. 37–38, 52; Ryrie, 'Facing Childhood Death', pp. 112, 125.
49 Jay, 'Ye Careless', pp. 112–13, here quoting further from William Wilberforce.
50 Clapp-Itnyre, *British Hymn Books*, p. 239.
51 Anonymous, *Charles Dwight*, pp. 2–3.
52 *Ibid.*, pp. 5–6.

53 Sir Robert Stout, 'A Trip to Samoa: Educational Institutions', *Samoa Weekly Herald* (18 February 1893), p. 2; Hamer, 'Stout, Robert'. Note further that the Liberal government of this period, under Sir Richard Seddon, increasingly saw the South-West Pacific as New Zealand's own sphere of empire – see Salesa, 'New Zealand's Pacific', pp. 149–72.

54 Anonymous, 'Departure of the John Williams: Valedictory Service', *Otago Witness* (11 October 1862), p. 8.

55 Anonymous, 'Congregational Union and Home Mission of South Australia: Annual Meeting', *South Australian Register* (30 October 1891), p. 6.

56 See again: Buettner, *Empire Families*, pp. 29–45; and Cleall, *Missionary Discourses*, pp. 59–60, 104–107. Such views were also held in the North American context, see: Clemmons, 'Our Children', 69–90. For broader discussions of colonial Europeans and climate see: Johnson, 'European Cloth', 530–60; and Stoler, *Carnal Knowledge*, pp. 66–75.

57 Pomfret, *Youth*, pp. 29–30. See also Pomfret, 'Imperial Rejuvenations', 939–62.

58 Tjelle, *Missionary Masculinity*, p. 180.

59 Anonymous, 'Speeches on the Lands of the Globe Still Available for European Settlement', *Birmingham Daily Post* (9 September 1890), np.

60 For a wider discussion of the tropes of 'pity' and 'hope' in representations of children see Jensz, 'Hope and Pity', pp. 259–81.

61 For example: Katherine D. McIlvaine, 'The Personal History of Polly Jay: A Story for Girls and Dolls', *Macleay Argus* (30 April 1887), p. 4; Anonymous, 'Children's Sunbeam Society: Our Sunbeam Bookshelf', *Adelaide Observer* (4 January 1902), p. 11. For a wider context for British world children's charitable literature and missions see again Hillel, 'Give Us All'.

62 J.C., 'Tangiteroria: Northern Wairoa Memories: Story of Buller's Mission', *Auckland Star* (10 April 1926), p. 18.

63 *The Arab* was seen, for example, in both Australia and New Zealand and reviewed widely in local newspapers including: *Evening Star* (19 November 1925), p. 6; *The Evening News* [Rockhampton] (20 November 1925), p. 8; *The Barrier Miner* (19 April 1926), p. 3; *Poverty Bay Herald* (9 February 1927), p. 5.

64 The following details are reconstructed from a wide range of newspaper accounts as well as from Lee, *Seven Heroic Children*. Ada also authored another more factual book on the same subject – *The Darjeeling Disaster*.

65 For example: 'English Children Killed in India', *New Zealand Mail* (30 November 1899), p. 48; *The Ballarat Star* (28 October 1899), p. 5; 'Food at Famine Prices', *Moose Jaw Herald* (6 October 1899), p. 2; and 'Earthquake in India: Hundreds Killed', *Reynold's Newspaper* [London] (1 October 1899), np.

66 *The Scotsman* (24 October 1899), p. 11.

67 'English Children Killed in India', *The New Zealand Mail* (30 November 1899), p. 48.

68 Lee, *Seven Heroic Children*, p. 77.

69 Bird's *Carol* fulfilled the same function, offering her life as an object lesson for Christian readers.

70 'A Terrible Night: Darjeeling Disaster of 1899', *Newcastle Morning Herald and Miner's Advocate* (20 August 1924), p. 10.

71 Lee, *Seven Heroic Children*, p. 155.

72 For further discussion of the combined role of text and photographs in children's religious periodicals to reinforce ideas or perception of 'self' and 'other' see Morrison, 'Colonial Archives', pp. 283–304.

73 For more generalised accounts of such cultural negotiations and imprints for migrant children, see McCarthy, *Personal Narratives*, pp. 188–90.

74 Again, see Morrison, *Protestant Children*, pp. 55–75, but also in particular Prochaska, 'Little Vessels', 114.

75 Andrew S. Thompson, *The Empire Strikes Back?*, pp. 148, 239, 241.

76 Morrison, *Protestant Children*, p. 95.

77 Mark Seymour, 'Emotional Arenas', 179.

78 Haggis and Allen, 'Imperial Emotions'.

79 Weir, 'Deeply Interested', 58.

80 Rev F.B. Meyer, 'Missionaries' Children in China', *The Methodist* (8 January 1910), p. 8. Among other things Meyer was an enthusiastic supporter of ventures among children and youth, including acting as President of the British National Christian Endeavour Union. See: Ottewill, 'The Early Years', 300.

2

Parental narratives

Between 1930 and 1935 English woman Phyllis Long wrote annually and warmly to her friend Doreen Ross in New Zealand (where Phyllis had taught during the early 1920s) telling of her new life in Srinagar, Kashmir.[1] In 1928 she married Eric Tyndale-Biscoe, a teacher returning from England to work in Kashmir for the Church Missionary Society (CMS), and subsequently moved there with him. In turn, Eric was the missionary son of CMS educationalist Cecil Tyndale-Biscoe, who established a number of schools in Kashmir between 1890 and 1947.[2] In 1929 Phyllis and Eric had their first child, Hugh, the third generation of that family to live in India in a missionary context. While Hugh did not completely dominate Phyllis's letters, he loomed large, as did his sister Ann born in 1932. From the start, they were not cosseted. Phyllis stated that Hugh was raised 'on Truby King methods', which included sleeping on the veranda during a snowy winter, and she enthused that at seven months he was 'wonderfully good', 'entertaining' and 'attractive'.[3] Both children were regularly described as 'marvellously healthy', enjoying the outdoors especially through summer holidays, riding donkeys and ponies, playing in the water and spending time with young adults visiting from England on temporary work projects. All of this was not without its critics, with other people 'horrified' for example that Hugh rode his donkey at age two, saying that he would become 'bandy-legged' as a result. By age six Hugh was swimming and rowing a boat, and three-year-old Ann revelled in the water. In 1934–35 Phyllis and Eric took the children back to England while on furlough. There, too, Phyllis indicated that their parenting style was their own, writing that the children slept 'equally in a car, in a garage, & in a barn' while on holiday. Hugh and Ann were, she wrote approvingly, 'very adaptable'. They took the children to a Welsh offshore bird sanctuary and put them into a nursery home in Dorset for seven weeks while Phyllis cared for her sick mother.

On their return to Srinagar in 1935 Phyllis's letter struck a slightly different tone, indicating potential underlying anxieties about the children as they grew older. She wrote,

Our family is very flourishing & we have now a friend of mine living with us, who helps to look after the children & is trying to start a school in Srinagar for English children up to 10 years old ... There is nothing of the sort at present & people don't seem to bother much about their children's education in India, so I expect it will be bound to be a slow business, but Mary is very efficient & keen & the children love her, so we hope very much it will be a success. We want at any rate to be sure of being able to keep them with us for this five years & at the same time to give them as good a chance as they would have in England ... After the next five years we don't know what we shall do – at present everything seems to be working out extraordinarily well & pleasantly for us – so 'why worry' is what I say.

At this point, the correspondence ends, with no further indication of the children's or family's trajectory throughout the following years. Longer term, Hugh, at least, went on to education and a scientific academic career in New Zealand and Australia.[4]

These narrative fragments of an English family living in northern India frame this chapter. It focuses on the narratives around missionary children that were constructed primarily by parents and in family settings, especially as they emerged through the early decades of the twentieth century. Therefore, it asks two questions: how were children's lives described and represented by their parents and why was this significant? After outlining the demographic shape of missionary families – utilising indicative data from three selected British world missions – the chapter considers the religious underpinnings of parents' narratives. It then examines these narratives further, arguing that while domestic details were to the fore, a deeper set of anxieties lay at their core: the maintenance of family life, keeping healthy and attaining a good education for their children. These were emotionally framed and were further bolstered by a religious rationale. As a result, missionary children became caught up in a perpetual set of negotiations over the best places to live, how to stay healthy and especially where to be educated. Therefore, from the perspective of missionary parents' narratives about their children, dislocation and separation emerge as important themes, because they caused parents much anxiety. As such missionary parenting, both its realities and its representations, can be conceptualised as a particular form of emotional labour.

Conceptualising the missionary family

Early Protestant missionary societies, like the LMS in Tahiti, were initially ambivalent about the missionary family, and their subsequent accommodation of it tempered by the pragmatics and politics of location or context.[5] Yet by the end of the nineteenth century the notion of family, and of the missionary family in particular, had become one of the foundation pieces of Protestant missions, to the extent that 'missionary projects were theologically and rhetorically embedded in concepts of kinship' wherein the 'language of family and universal brotherhood permeated their writing'.[6] This notion of family was wide-ranging. Geographically, theologically and mentally, it broadly linked missionaries and local Christians (in theory at least) within regions and across denominational boundaries; missionaries with their home-base constituencies; and their constituencies with non-missionary Christian peoples abroad. By the 1900s this wider construction of kinship was a key marker of home-base women's missionary support networks.[7] More specifically it linked single and married missionaries within their respective organisations. In the Basel Mission, for example, 'the "mission family" included all members … who lived in a certain geographic region, who became a substitute for one's extended family in the European homeland'.[8] The same was true for other Protestant missions. While there were obvious constructions of difference within, through and across these family variants, the notion of family increasingly became central and constitutively important to definitions or understandings of mission across the nineteenth and twentieth centuries.

Missionary children like Hugh and Ann Tyndale-Biscoe experienced all of these variations of family and they also lived in other kinship contexts including their extended families, schools and residential homes for missionary children. At the heart of their experience, however, was the Western domestic family unit which, by the early 1900s, was increasingly 'shaped by affection, based on companionate marriage, and centred on the nurturing of children'.[9] The Protestant missionary family, home and household was a complex nexus which historically evolved over the long nineteenth century and which increasingly reflected modernising trends well into the twentieth century. As such, argues Alexandra Walsham, it reflected a wider tradition in Western Christianity whereby

> [t]he family and the household have been regarded as microcosms of the social and political order, basic building blocks of the state and society. Hovering on the boundary between the public and the private … [t]hey have simultaneously been seen as sources of sedition, corruption and moral degeneration and as key arenas in which to educate, nurture and indoctrinate the next generation.

Christian families and homes 'have both buttressed and subverted the ecclesiastical status quo', operating historically as 'symbols of stability and danger'.[10]

In mission contexts, the family and household reflected some of these paradoxes, in that it served both as a domestic unit for the sake of parents and children and as a theological or ideological exemplar for missionary subjects. The notion of the missionary household as an exemplary 'object lesson of a civilised, Christian home' for Indigenous or non-Christian people connected missions to a wider civilising project and is now well documented. It was deployed as a missiological ideal and strategy in a diverse range of settings across the nineteenth and early twentieth centuries, albeit not everywhere the same.[11] Indeed, in some cases, the late nineteenth-century trend towards creating physically separated missionary compounds 'removed from the midst of the people' could inadvertently act to 'reduce the value of the very desirable object lesson of a Christian home'. This was a problem that endured well into the twentieth century and was a point of criticism by the extensive and ultimately influential 1932 American 'laymen's inquiry' (titled *Re-thinking Missions*) into missions.[12]

For missionary families, there were inherent tensions in this construction of ideal domesticity. The Rev Irwin Correll, an American missionary to Japan speaking to the theme of 'environment and home' at the 1900 New York Missionary Conference, argued that the missionary home fulfilled a dual role. It was first a 'constant object-lesson' that proved 'clearly that the teaching of the meek and lowly Jesus … redeems its promises and brings to its believers untold comfort and joy'. At the same time the 'sacred confines of the Christian home' should offer a place of rest and restoration for the often male missionary: an 'atmosphere purified by the presence of the Divine Spirit' and a 'haven of rest to the weary soul, where the hungry soul is fed and strengthened for better service'.[13] Correll left unresolved the implicit tension between the missionary home's public and private functions and how this might impact its other inhabitants.

That tension might not have been such a concern in earlier decades, in that routinely 'public and private remained intermingled in the nineteenth-century middle-class home', especially the juxtaposition of 'servants and masters' and their uses of domestic space.[14] Yet by the 1930s, the impact of wider thinking about childhood and the family was patently obvious. Dana Robert cites an influential American text, *Christian Home Making* published in 1939, which focused on 'the major characteristics of a Christian home as a place of physical and spiritual well-being and support'. It should primarily be 'a "democracy" where each individual could thrive', a 'place of rest and comfort', as well as the 'beginning point of responsibilities to the wider community'. Overall 'Christian homemaking included a neat, orderly, hygienic home, with well-tended children'.[15] This was the aspirational ideal at least. The realities cohered more often around 'the missionary struggle to establish and maintain' such a household in given contexts.[16] The important point here, however, is that children and their welfare were as central to that ideal as they were to the family discourse more generally framed by the early twentieth century, and this development both shaped parental narratives and laid a foundation for the anxieties hinted at in Phyllis Long's letters.

Reconstituting the missionary family

Thus, the concept of the missionary family and household is now well-documented, and its nuances are much better understood. However, to date, little has been written about the demographic shape and constitution of missionary families. Statistics are often episodic or embedded in other scholarly narratives, for example, the nine children of the Crooks family in 1820s Tahiti (LMS) contrasted with Hugh and Ann as the sole children in the Tyndale-Biscoe family of the 1930s; or the fifteen LMS children who died out of sixty-five born in Papua up to 1914.[17] Systematic statistics are a rare commodity, forcing the historian to be innovative in terms of thinking about what sources exist and how they might be used to reconstitute families. The following brief discussion is one attempt to do this. It draws on indicative data gathered from three different Protestant missionary points of origin between about 1860 and 1940: LMS families in India and the South Pacific (as a representative sample of the overall LMS population for this period);[18] families from the most populous branches of Scottish Presbyterian missionary work (COS and UFC) in various geographical locations; and families from New Zealand Presbyterian missions (Synod of Southland and Otago and the Presbyterian Church of New Zealand) in the New Hebrides, south China and northern India.[19] There is enough congruence in trends across all three to suggest that missionary families from other British Protestant groups may have looked similar or experienced the same kinds of changes over this period. Here questions revolve around the character of the companionate missionary family (with a focus on the number of children), how it changed from the late nineteenth into the twentieth century and how changing size related to emerging family narratives in this period.

As such this is not a full-blown exercise in family reconstitution. In making the following observations, it is noted that the historical demography of the Western family is the subject of extensive scholarship and that there are important nuances to consider. Discussions of family size, for example, need to be set against such broader issues as social change, differentiated influences (class, race, religion and geography), emerging birth control technologies and marital age among others. For Britain, the 1870s to the 1920s was a period of 'profound social and demographic changes' and therefore was equated to 'the dawning of a new era in the nation's family life'. This, in turn, was reflected in such British settler colonies as New Zealand.[20] For the missionary context, both household and family also need to be differentiated further, in that the household could be made up of any combination of immediate kin, extended family, Indigenous peoples (especially students, adopted children or domestic workers) and other mission personnel.[21]

Between about 1860 and 1940 at least 363 separate families, incorporating some 1,539 children, can be counted for the three groups. The year or exact dates of birth are known for 54 per cent of the Scottish families, 90 per cent of the New Zealand families and all of the extant Indian and Pacific LMS families (represented in Figure 2.1). These included children born prior to their parents' departure as missionaries and those born *in situ* at various points from first arrival onwards. In Figure 2.1 the solid line represents annual birth numbers and the dotted line is the overall extrapolated trend. For each of the sampled missions there were no recorded birth data for 1872.

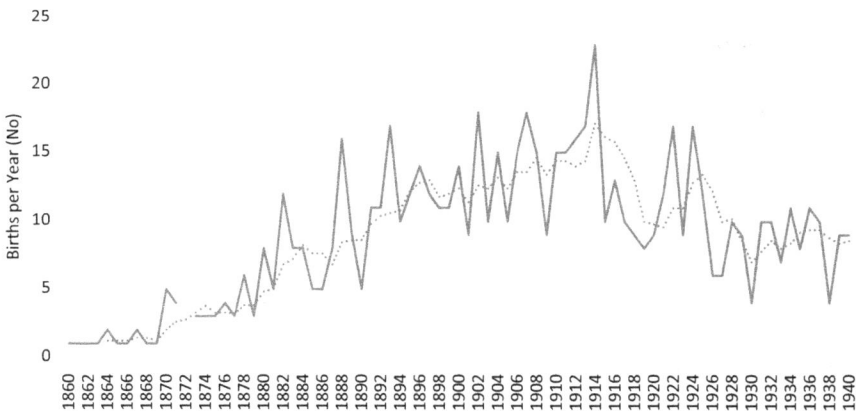

Figure 2.1 Annual missionary children's births, 1860–1940. Graph based on data for LMS families derived from Volumes 1 and 2 of the 'London Missionary Society Register of Missionaries' Children up to 1940' and from copies of the *LMS Chronicle*, both held in the Archives and Special Collections, School of Oriental and African Studies, London. Data for Scottish and New Zealand Presbyterian missionary families are compiled from the following sources: (1) Scotland – annual reports to the General Assemblies of the Church of Scotland, the Free Church of Scotland and the United Free Church of Scotland 1860–1940, and from both Scott, *Fasti*, vol. 7 and Lamb, *The Fasti*; and (2) New Zealand – annual reports to the General Assemblies of the Synod of Southland and Otago 1866–1901 and of the Presbyterian Church of New Zealand 1869–1940, monthly issues of *The Break of Day* children's magazine, individual missionaries' staff files and 'Register of New Zealand Presbyterian Ministers, Deaconesses & Missionaries'.

While the numbers of children born varied annually the overall trend line clearly indicates sustained growth up to World War I, particularly from the 1880s to the 1910s. This growth in children's presence in missionary contexts reflects an explosion in missionary numbers in this period across the Protestant and geographical spectrum. Kenneth Scott Latourette noted that by the end of the nineteenth century, there had been 'an expansion of unprecedented extent from both the newer bases and the older ones' which underwent a further 'brave surge' in the interwar decades.[22] This was certainly true of British missions in this period but was exemplified in the astonishing growth of American missionaries abroad. Between 1880 and 1915 American missionary numbers grew from 2,716 to over 9,000 in total. By 1925 there were an estimated 29,000 Protestant missionaries worldwide, with around half from the North American continent.[23] There was a demonstrable rise in the numbers of younger and single missionary recruits, especially women.

At the same time, married missionaries at departure and families later constituted within mission settings were also significant components. For example, of the twenty-three New Zealand Presbyterians working in the New Hebrides, between 1868 and 1900, eighteen were married couples who contributed seventeen children to the missionary population.[24] It is possible that those married stayed longer *in situ* as missionaries. One survey of American Protestants in the late 1920s and early 1930s, for example, suggested that the average service of married missionaries was just over thirteen years compared with nine years for those single.[25] The burgeoning numbers of children were a direct outcome of this growth in missionary numbers and longer sustained service of married missionaries. They also mirrored a wider trend for the imperial era, for French and English juvenile populations in places like Hanoi, Saigon, Singapore and Hong Kong.[26] The trajectory of missionary births also reflected wider demographic changes that may have amplified the family's role as a locus of companionship and nurture for all members.

At issue here is family size and child spacing. First, the numbers of children born partly reflected Western demographic processes of increasingly smaller family sizes evident from the late nineteenth century onwards. Across all three representative missions, median family size hovered between four and six children until the 1890s, while the number of children consistently ranged between one and seven children per family up to the 1900s. These figures were consistent across geographic locations. Larger families were not unknown. Both William and Fanny Lawes in Papua (LMS), with ten children between 1868 and 1890, and Mary and James Shaw in India (COS), also with ten between 1870 and 1888, may have been statistical outliers; yet there were at least another eight families with between eight and ten children in total.[27] In several cases, sets of twins boosted total numbers. While one child died during childhood in five of these larger families, in none of the families above the median was child mortality a significant barrier to having more children. What is tragic, from the compiled statistics, was the number of smaller families devastated by child mortality rates of 25 per cent or more. Altogether there were no unusual patterns of gender, with almost equal numbers of girls and boys at birth. From the 1910s, however, the median number of children born to missionary parents quickly settled at two or three per family, irrespective of geographic or national context. At least one other independent survey of American Methodist missionary families in this same period indicated similar average figures.[28] By the 1930s this was a noted point of concern for some commentators. American scholar and eugenicist Ellsworth Huntington argued, referencing what he saw as the high calibre of missionary children, that it was 'highly desirable that there be relatively large families among missionaries, among whom both parents have been chosen through a process of strenuous selection'.[29]

Declining missionary family size was consistent with broader demographic changes in Western societies from the late-nineteenth century onwards. Census data for England and Wales, for example, suggest that when married women born in the mid-1800s are compared with those born at the beginning of the 1900s, each cohort had quite distinctive birth experiences. For the mid-1800s cohort, up to one-third experienced seven live births each, while this pertained to only 5 per cent of the early 1900s group. Conversely about half of the latter routinely had one or two children and perhaps 20 per cent remained childless.[30] Similar patterns pertained in such settler societies as New Zealand, where the average number of children per European settler family declined from nearly seven in 1880 to just over two by the 1920s. There 'migrants replicated their marriage cultures' which resulted in 'demographic patterns that were very similar to Britain'.[31] Thus these trends translated across to British world missionary families regardless of their point of geographical origin.

Second, the spacing of missionary children's births reflected the declining number of children born per family. Median birth spans (the number of years from first to last birth) across the three missionary groupings indicate an emerging trend, from a high of fourteen years (for LMS parents in the Pacific and India in the 1860s) to typically a span of between two and five years by the 1920s. In essence, parents increasingly spent fewer years focused on infants and young children, albeit with minor fluctuations across locations or decades. Closer analysis of the LMS figures indicates an expected but very clear positive correlation between children per family and birth span right across the period. Further close analysis of the two national Presbyterian missions also indicates very clear patterns of child spacing. For both Scottish and New Zealand families, two years was consistently the median spacing between one child and the next, irrespective of family size or mission location and across the whole period. There is the merest hint that New Zealand missionary parents may have spaced their children marginally longer than Scottish parents, particularly in the first two decades of the twentieth century. The factors underlying this pattern are not at all clear, and any connection to self-imposed fertility limitation or environmental factors remains entirely speculative.

These figures do, however, give pause for thought in the context of considering missionary parents' narratives concerning their children. In their exploratory study of family size in late Victorian and Edwardian England and Wales, Eilidh Garrett et al. argue that national 'complex patterns of employment, class, place and religion … can be understood only when taken in the context of communities, not of occupational or social groups. People modelled their behaviour on and acquired their beliefs from their parents, friends and neighbours.' This extended, inter alia, to 'their expectations of marriage and the number of children they were likely to have'.[32] As other historians readily note, the family by the 1900s was beginning to change significantly with respect to size, structure, emotional underpinnings and ties, and in terms of roles and relationships.[33] Missionary families reflected these changes, with perhaps middle-class values or expectations having a greater impact as the missionary workforce became increasingly professionalised and better educated. Religion may have been an additional factor for these families. Canadian research for the period 1871–1901, for example, indicates that declining fertility was a marked characteristic of Protestant women regardless of province or rural/urban distinctions. Exploratory analysis of infant mortality in early twentieth-century Dublin similarly points to different experiences for Roman Catholic and Protestant families, further linked to socio-economic status and patterns of urban deprivation.[34] At the same time, wider research indicates how religion might have an impact on families. Religious values operated variously to emphasise 'positive norms of obligations and assistance to family members'; and 'provide specific guidelines for the performance of marital and family roles that shape role behaviors [*sic*]'. Religious settings 'constitute environments in which participants can sanction and reinforce valued behavioral [*sic*] norms'. Of more specific relevance to missionary families, echoing Garrett et al., further research needs to focus on 'religion/fertility links in their context', specifically asking if a 'concentration of coreligionists in social locations and variations in the religious climate may have an effect on the link between religion and fertility'.[35]

As the next section outlines, religion was indeed a central factor for these families, but the direct connection between belief and family size/structure remains less well drawn. More detailed and inflected research at the micro level needs to occur, focusing particularly on the relationship between religious denomination, ethnicity, geographical origins and education, and the influence on these of wider modernisation. Yet it is likely that, by the early twentieth century, a combination of shared Protestant religious values intersecting with wider demographic and social trends combined to create missionary families that were generally smaller, with less time now spent on child raising, potentially more family resources and certainly the ability to direct and therefore expect more care at an individual level. In this context, British missionary families, as in wider middle-class Western societies, were well advanced towards 'completing the "sacralisation" of childhood, in which children became economically "worthless" but emotionally priceless'.[36] In such circumstances, the health, welfare and education of each child became foundationally important foci for parents, and the pursuit of these a source of great energy and anxiety as a result.

Parents' religious motivation

Religion was fundamental to the constitution of these families and lay at the heart of missionary parents' narratives, even if this was but one of several evident themes to be discerned. Hugh and Ann Tyndale-Biscoe were typically born into a family whose geographical location was shaped by religious considerations and convictions. Their grandfather, Cecil, came from an English gentry family in which religion was taken seriously. Cecil cemented those convictions through a childhood pledge of missionary service, volunteer work for the Children's Special Mission Service while at Cambridge University and eventual ordination as a Church of England priest in 1887. At this point, he applied to the CMS and was sent in 1890 to the school in Srinagar, Kashmir, where he would make his name as an educational missionary.[37] Sport was high on his agenda as a strategy for effecting change. His approach, work and life certainly need to be interpreted within discourses of manliness, eugenics and empire. At the same time, he had 'practical objectives in mind' when engaging Kashmiri boys with sports. Specifically, he sought to 'introduce the local youth to a new code of ethics' predicated on Christianity; 'it was his profound desire as a Christian to introduce his pupils to HIM who taught all men to love one another and show it by practice'.[38] Christianity shaped Cecil's own life trajectory, that of children like Eric who returned to India for religious reasons as a married adult, and thus determined that Hugh and Ann (a third generation) would likewise be born and grow up in India for the same reasons.

However else missionary families fitted into the 'empire family' trope, religious motivation serves to differentiate their narratives from other imperial participants.[39] Likewise, missionary children were who and where they were because of religiously framed convictions or decisions made by their parents, either before or after marriage. Where they ended up living and the manner of that lifestyle were in all cases shaped by their parents' motivation towards and decisions about missionary service. Thus, parents' missionary or religious vocations were central to any definition of children's lives, while at the same time often framed or facilitated by the imperial or colonial contexts in which they lived. From their perspective the religious factor was important, and missionary involvement was integral to Protestant religious identity throughout the nineteenth and twentieth centuries.

The decisions that parents made to pursue a religious vocation, as 'foreign' or overseas missionaries, need to be taken seriously on their own terms, irrespective of the ways in which motivation was undeniably a complex mix of the 'religious' and the 'secular'.[40] Idealism, religious convictions or imperatives, spiritual fervour, life circumstances, pity, romantic and heroic imaginations, gendered notions of service and duty, new opportunities, nationalism and imperial citizenship were all a part of this motivational mix. An answer as to what motivated them lies within this complex and that space should be one in which productive dialogue can occur. Manktelow, for example, argues that LMS missionaries in the South Pacific were often 'colonial actors' whose controversial actions (when viewed from hindsight) were intertwined with 'a more placatory side of benevolence, philanthropy and a genuine desire to do good'. Yet we are left with a subject that often sits uncomfortably alongside modern-day sensibilities. With respect to missionary families, this 'discomfort with the past and continuing calls for public heroisation has led us to ignore the role of the intimate, the personal and the emotional in the history of Christian mission'.[41] This 'discomfort', however, should not limit further discussion. The religious factor thus complicates a secular hermeneutic for missionary motivation. Missionary children's lives were defined and framed in significant ways by their parents' religious dispositions, decisions and actions.

How were these decisions conceived by the adults involved? Two representative family examples are instructive. One was the Marwick family. William and Elizabeth (née Hutton) Marwick were Scottish missionaries, first for the United Presbyterian Church (UPC) of Scotland at Calabar in Nigeria throughout the 1890s (separately and together) and then in Jamaica (at Falmouth) for the UFC from 1901 to 1911. They had six children in total, including a baby girl who died. The family was together in Jamaica from 1902 to 1906, when Elizabeth returned to Edinburgh to care for the children in various stages of their education. William remained in Jamaica until 1911 and then served as a colonial chaplain in India before finally re-joining the family in 1916.[42] The other was the Gray family. James and Marion (née Scott) Gray were Scottish-born missionaries for the NZPC from 1921 to 1941 in the northern Indian Punjab region. James had migrated to New Zealand with his family around 1901 and Marion joined him there after marriage at the end of World War I. In India they had five children; the two eldest returned to New Zealand for high school in 1934. Marion returned to Auckland in 1939 with the other children and was finally joined by James in December 1941 on the eve of the war in the Pacific.[43]

For the Marwick parents, the evidence is indirect, gleaned more from letters to children and their extended family. This material indicates two adults whose lives were theologically suffused in ways that flowed naturally out into everyday life and relationships. William was a well-educated man of faith whose correspondence demonstrated a noted ability to integrate both reason and faith. At the same time, faith was highly personalised, with an emphasis on both its relational aspects (the believer in a relationship with God and others) and its high obligatory and ethical demands. Character and faith went hand in hand to the extent that the formation of life-long Christian character became foundationally central, irrespective of the contexts in which these ideals were lived out. The details of this were neatly captured in a letter from William to his eldest son Willie in 1898, which accompanied a Bible sent from Calabar as a present for his fourth birthday. He wrote extolling the Bible as the 'best of books' which was superlative in its ability to talk about

> God & His love in sending His only Son Jesus Christ to save us all & make us good, & about Jesus Christ Himself, & His life in this world & His death on the Cross for our sins, & about His life in heaven as Mediator & Intercessor & the Holy Spirit's work & saving men & making them holy.

William expected that his children would take time to understand it fully, but also anticipated that this was not beyond their reach. He finished by saying to his 'darling Willie' that 'if you try to follow Jesus & to learn of Him while you are young – which just means giving your heart & your mind to Him – you will grow up a good boy & become a good man. That is the best birthday message I can give you'.[44]

The path that James and Marion Gray took towards missionary work can be more fully reconstructed from their application records.[45] James grew up in a typically evangelical Presbyterian family environment, describing his childhood faith in terms of 'growth' rather than personal crisis. This naturally flowed on to him receiving 'Christ as my Saviour' at age fourteen. As a young adult he further 'learned the truth about the Indwelling of the Spirit and was led definitely to yield my whole life to his control', an experience to which he attributed a 'new power and reality, a new restfulness in service'. This translated into a life pathway that took him from school to university, Presbyterian ministry training and two years as a YMCA travelling secretary.[46] After World War I service with the Medical Corps, he completed his theological study in Glasgow, where he met Marion and applied for missionary work, initially to work in China. His desire to 'serve God' in the 'Foreign Field' emanated from a strong sense of 'duty' and of other peoples' perceived 'need', and he iterated that 'as far as I know my own heart it is for the glory of God'. These sentiments were common to the application narratives of many New Zealand Presbyterian missionary parents of this period.

Marion also came from a family of active faith but her decisions were, in part, predicated on those of James. She candidly related in her application that 'until 1½ years ago – when I met Mr Gray – Christ was rather a vague personality, not as now – a Vital necessity; and since Christ has become an essential part of my being I am consumed with the desire to give up the rest of my life to His work'. She articulated her missionary motivation in terms of a 'great wish to do something really useful in trying to tell others of the great thing I have found'. At the same time, there was a clear sense that Marion was her own person. Second son Ian later offered the view that his mother 'was a very powerful character' and he suggested that his father's reputable career as a missionary and minister was due in no small measure to 'having my mother behind him'.[47] She was, it seems, an indomitable character.

Missionary parents' religious actions and motivations were thus formative for their children. Christian beliefs and sentiments initially propelled William and Elizabeth Marwick separately towards missionary service and later sustained them as parents. These same beliefs and sentiments continued to drive William's sense of ongoing vocation and sacrificial service, separated further from his wife and children over a decade. In these terms, theologically constructed missionary motivation provided the rationale for family separation, albeit with torn parental emotions and during significant years of growing up for the children.[48] As such, religious activities framed many of the daily routines that shaped their lives. Both parental conviction and personality also framed the Gray children's lives, although not entirely without problems. James Gray alluded to this in a letter home in 1932 concerning the children's education, noting that 'we don't feel it right that the children should be deprived of parental influence during their most crucial years' and that 'one is torn betwixt conflicting duties'.[49] Similar sentiments of regret or concern over separation are also found in the Marwick correspondence. Over the longer term, however, despite this tension, both sets of parents' theological conviction and force of personality combined to undergird a strong and enduring commitment to the missionary task before all else, initiating and straddling periods of both short and prolonged family separation for both sets of children.

Maintenance of family life

While religious rhetoric remained fundamentally important, another reading of the sources also indicates that parents' narratives typically emphasised two common elements (the maintenance of family life and anxiety over children's welfare), with one feeding into the other. First and naturally, parents' narratives were replete with domestic details typically focused on the life cycle and family life. These were key defining features of Phyllis Long's letters in the 1930s, with Hugh and Ann's domestic lives caught in amusing and sometimes moving detail. However, source types dictated to a degree how children were written about and were clearly gendered with respect to both content and focus. Fathers' official letters are one entry point, wherein domestic details had an oftentimes perfunctory place. Manktelow notes that such brevity or indeed silences 'reflect more the inability of the male missionary to find space in his *writing* [emphasis original] for children, rather than a difficulty in finding them space in his life'.[50] Birth announcements regularly proliferated in fathers' letters to their mission secretaries. Herbert Davies (New Zealand Presbyterian – hereafter NZP), writing from Hong Kong in 1912, somewhat eloquently advised his committee of

> the arrival of another missionary, – master John Butler Davies [Jock], – who … made his advent into the world with a piercing yell, which aroused the whole neighbourhood … His militant ways foreshadow a man of much combative force, & judging from the fact that he obeys the prophetic injunction to 'cry aloud & spare not', I think he should make a good preacher of the John Knox type.[51]

More typically fathers' letters emphasised two things: either baby and mother doing well at birth and then over subsequent years, or they only referred to children when illness or death intruded on the family's fortunes. In many fathers' published autobiographies or biographies, there is a ringing silence around their children.

Mothers also wrote official letters (less frequently but often with more domestic detail) and they also wrote more formally for missionary magazines at home. In 1920 Margaret Davies (NZP) noted in more detail that seven-year-old Jock 'is fine and strong … a real Chinese – he loves them really better than foreign children'. The local environment gave him opportunities to learn: 'watching tadpoles develop into frogs' and 'the development of mosquitoes, moths & silk worms. To-night we have a fire-fly under observation.' As a youngster Jock had 'a dog, a cat (a beautiful Siamese-brown face, tail & paws, & cream body), a canary & some mud fish all presents to him'. After seeing two of the Rome to Tokyo planes refuelling at Canton in 1920, Jock and 'the children have been playing aeroplanes all week'.[52] At the same time, in some circles at least, mothers perceived in these domestic details something of wider didactic value. As late as 1909 Dorothy Teichmann (BMS) wrote to her English readers that missionary wives could 'make their homes a place to which Indians are welcome'. Furthermore, possibly reflecting her own practice, she suggested that when visiting Indian homes, 'if … she takes one of her children with her, all parties are well pleased, and the English children learn before leaving for England to take a loving and intelligent interest in their India friends'.[53] While obviously invoking the rhetoric of the 'ideal' missionary home, the 'object lesson' to be gained from domestic experiences such as this was as much for the children as it was for other readers.

Domestic details are also found in family letters, memoirs and diary entries, as exemplified in the correspondence of Phyllis Long. Throughout her first year of life in China, Jean McNeur's father George (NZP) recorded her progress, noting: a 'wee girlie' weighing in at '8½ lbs' at birth in 1907; her first trip back to New Zealand; being weaned at eight months old; and her first birthday with the wider family before returning to China.[54] Anna Malcolm (CIM) regularly noted details of only son Ronald's progress as an infant born in China's Anhui province in 1910: 'a sunny, happy little chap'.[55] From Bolivia, George Allan (Bolivian Indian Mission – hereafter BIM) recounted to his sister instances of his son Joe's sense of humour and commented on Joe's ability to see through the guile of other missionary children feigning sickness for their own benefit.[56] Donald Fraser (FCS), writing later about family life in Nyasaland (Malawi), invoked warm memories of his children when he re-conceptualised the now relatively empty family home as: 'haunted by ghosts … rowdy little ghosts, whose feet run from room to room, and whose shouts and calls allow no peace'; as a shrine 'sacred for the memory of these fierce struggles' (referencing times of sickness and death); and as the site of seasonal celebrations like Christmas when the children 'danced and yelled … when Santa Claus descended so successfully from a man-hole in the ceiling'.[57] William Marwick simply told his Edinburgh family that young Willie was 'getting on nicely at school' at Falmouth (Jamaica), that he 'plays well on his own' and 'enjoys himself a good part of the day'.[58]

Occasionally parents wrote more extensively about their children's lives. One such instance is the unpublished autobiography of English BMS missionary Ernest Burt.[59] In Shantung Province (Shandong), China from 1892, Ernest married Helena Tetley in 1894 and they had four children (Harold, Margaret, Lucy and Winsome) before Helena's premature death in 1904 from influenza. While he focused mostly on his work, Ernest also devoted significant space to domestic details. Children's births, death and occasions of illness were all noted. There were pets, birthdays and holidays. Indeed, holidays featured often, accentuated because these were the times when the family came together again after multiple separations. Travel with children also featured and was remembered warmly: locally, to other parts of China (especially to the children's school at Chefoo), once to Japan and several times to Britain on furlough overland through Russia or by sea. The children also figured prominently in Ernest's second marriage in 1910 to Helena's sister Ethel (with whom the two youngest girls resided in England after their mother's death). Ernest's reminiscences also extended to the children in their adult years, touching at points on tragic events both global and domestic.

In Ernest's account, there are strong resonances with the content of children's narratives encountered in later chapters. Furthermore, there was a clear emotional thread running through his writing that focused on the children's happiness. A general and defining association between childhood and happiness was well-established by the early twentieth century and was readily applied to religious contexts.[60] Here it seems to have found a niche in parents' thinking, where it dovetailed with the emerging expectation that missionary family life would be convivial, nurturing and sustaining for its constituent members. Happiness also emerged as an important facet of the institutional narrative that developed in response to parents' concerns and anxieties (see extended discussion in Chapters 3 and 5). In effect, then, this rich focus on domestic details reflected parental concern for their children's welfare and the overall maintenance of family life.

Anxiety, health, education and separation

There emerged, then, a formative emotional narrative thread that reflected these underlying parental concerns over children's welfare. This was signposted in Ernest Burt's memoir. He wrote poignantly about their second daughter 'Margaret, a sweet child, born in Taunton in October 1901, but dying in the following July and now resting in the little plot of burying ground two miles south of Tsowping city [Zouping] on the slope of a hill commanding a magnificent view over the plain and towards the mountains'. He then reflected:

[the] children were very dear to us but gave us much anxiety. Harold had diphtheria, dysentery & measles, but after he was eight years old enjoyed good health. Lucy nearly lost her life from dysentery in the summer of 1903 and was only saved by the most drastic of remedies. How vividly her father remembers sitting up with her night after night, ministering to her needs. When Harold was a small boy he had a white donkey of his own which it was his pride to ride. There were other children in the place and their childhood was a happy one.[61]

The potential for children to be debilitated by illness or to die prematurely was equally inclusive of places like China and the British metropole.[62] Ernest hinted at this when he further noted that his wife Helena's death in 1904 was 'the first great bereavement I had known',[63] suggesting that an infant's or young child's death was less unexpected. However, it is possibly significant that this litany of his children's potentially life-threatening illnesses was juxtaposed with descriptions of his son Harold riding a donkey or of happy children. If happiness and emotional or physical security were taken as the expected norm for children – as evidenced by the weight of domestic detail in parents' accounts – then parents' decisions to geographically relocate their families elsewhere, albeit for religiously altruistic reasons, gave rise to both explicit and implicit concerns about things like health and educational prospects. These in turn came to dominate what they had to say about their children. Phyllis Long wrote 'why worry', but her expressed concerns about Hugh and Ann's longer-term education revealed that such issues were not far below the surface for many parents. As one New Zealand father, himself a doctor, wrote referencing another family's struggle with illness: 'bringing up children in India is no joke'.[64] British world and American missionary parents certainly bought into the dual rhetoric of the exemplary missionary family and the home as a place of 'physical and spiritual well-being and support' described earlier by Dana Robert.[65] The narrative emerging here, however, indicates that by the early twentieth century, the maintenance of family life and concerns for children's health and education all pre-empted the ideal imperatives around exemplary homes and families.

It seems apposite, therefore, to think further about the emotional dimensions of parents' narratives about their children. This coheres particularly with the notion of parental anxiety. Anxiety is a commonplace human emotion,[66] historically evident but perhaps more obviously a focus of the twentieth century, post-Freud, and the subject of recent historical analysis particularly in the American context.[67] It is a complex notion, described by different names over the centuries and, often, entangled with 'fear' as a cognate and enduring emotion.[68] While it is possible that by using the notion of anxiety we impute a modern preoccupation onto the past,[69] words like 'anxiety' and 'worry' (and cognate terms) are present in historical accounts enough times to warrant further examination. This is especially so with reference to children's health, as well as exigencies of travel or warfare.[70] To date, the literature on missionary parents' anxiety is limited, with an emphasis on parent–child separation, whether for missionary or wider empire families, and a more recent focus on theological and socio-political influences specific to modern contexts.[71] While separation was certainly an important element, here the sources suggest that, for missionary families (especially by the early 1900s), there were at least three dimensions whereby anxiety was configured more complexly: concerns for children while in the mission context; anticipating longer-term separation; and coping with or rationalising actual separation.

Both the health and education of children loom large in missionary parents' discourse. Firstly illness, and sometimes death, were perpetual issues across the period, particularly so in tropical African settings. There were still many instances, well into the first half of the twentieth century, wherein missionaries' children died *in situ* – tragedies such as the apparently unexplained demise of six-year-old Nancy Miller (NZP) while on summer holiday in Hong Kong with her parents in 1926. Nancy was one of nine New Zealand Presbyterian children who died in mission contexts between the 1860s and the 1930s (out of a total of about ninety-four children) – four in the New Hebrides, one in China and four in India.[72] LMS records suggest that such hazards were not confined to mission settings, in that of the 107 child deaths recorded in the *Chronicle* between 1889 and 1939, two were at sea and nineteen while children were in locations like Australia, England or Scotland for education.[73] References to illness, rather than deaths, were more widespread, wherein parents and children expected illness as the norm. Margaret Davies (NZP) wrote somewhat tellingly that her husband's illness in the summer of 1928 meant that she could not visit her son Jock at school in Chefoo, noting that 'Jock will be disappointed but he is so used to being sick himself that he understands'.[74] George Allan's (BIM) description of his son's illness in Bolivia was also typical. Joe succumbed to typhoid fever while at school and was later treated with a combination of 'massage treatment', a 'hot-pack at the back, and cold over the intestines & liver, enemas night and morning, & a warm bath daily, & careful dieting'. George hoped that 'he will be soon over it'.[75] While children's illness was obviously a cause for concern, in neither case above was it construed as a reason for returning to New Zealand. George was perhaps typical, too, in expressing his frustration that 'I didn't come along here to nurse sick folk'. This indicated that while he was glad to give Joe his time and attention (and Joe thought it 'all right to have Daddie [*sic*] all to himself all the time'), illness was more an annoying interruption to the main focus of missionary work.[76] At the same time, there were other instances when concern about a child's health was the catalyst for missionary parents deciding to return definitively to their home countries.

Up to the early 1900s, narrative data tend to corroborate Esme Cleall's broad contention that while 'determining what was distinctive about the *missionary* [emphasis original] experience of sickness in the empire from a demographic perspective is difficult', in missionary writing the 'experience of sickness was often filtered through an exclusive lens of particularity whereby illnesses were constructed as a specifically *missionary* experience. Illness became reflexive of and contributory to a specifically missionary identity.'[77] Sometimes this was expressed through family separation, depending on location or circumstances and perhaps more prevalent up to the late nineteenth century. In 1877 LMS missionaries William and Fanny Lawes had to abandon their post at Port Moresby (Papua) because of a particularly virulent season of malarial fever, which tragically claimed the lives of several of their Polynesian teachers as well as their young son Percy. After temporarily relocating to northern Australia, Fanny returned to England with the surviving children for their health's sake while William remained on site in Papua.[78] From the 1900s, however, illness was not typically a strong motivating factor for such family separation in parental narratives. Rather, it was seen as a problem mostly to be endured or dealt with while children lived in missionary contexts. Indeed, in some instances, illness in the mission field could be perceived as less serious or debilitating than 'at home'.[79] Missionary children's experience of illness and death is a much larger topic that requires further research, and it certainly needs to be thought about more carefully as to its gendered representations and geographical occurrences. This health and welfare rhetoric became increasingly more professionalised so that by the 1930s, missions and churches clearly had higher expectations for their missionary families.[80]

Secondly, anxieties about education did emerge as a more typically motivating factor for family separation. Parents' narratives were marked both by repeated concerns over children's education – particularly for the high school years – and by the emotionally taxing combination of resignation and acceptance about sending children away or home for those years. In some instances, especially in such early nineteenth-century contexts as the LMS and the ABCFM in the Pacific,[81] circumstances dictated that schooling had to be on site or at least regionally based. From the 1850s, however, it became either a policy or a stated preference for many British and European missions, such as the Basel Mission in India and the LMS, to routinely repatriate children home for their education.[82]

In the Indian context, Buettner correctly observes that British adolescents were often sent home to avoid 'physically and culturally threatening contacts with India's climate and indigenous and mixed-race populations', an observation that also stood for children in other geographical settings.[83] Yet there were also other reasons, reflecting specific cultural biases or the changing cultural politics of the mission field, especially in the interwar period. The Scottish and New Zealand Presbyterian cases are instructive here. William Marwick valued highly both the Scottish high school system and Scottish literary/linguistic traditions and so in his mind the only proper education was a Scottish one. For New Zealanders, there were other tensions. George Allan betrayed a distinctly British-centric prejudice, through his criticism of apparent American favouritism when it came to academic honours for their children at school in Bolivia. He lamented that 'they may blow about Americans and American cleverness, etc, as they like, but they fall far short of the Britisher in that fine sense of honour which is the glory & strength of the British character'.[84] Ada Harvie in northern India struck a note of concern about her daughters at Woodstock School, when she noted that they were 'fast acquiring American accents & vocabulary & to some extent outlook'.[85] More candidly, James Gray was concerned that Woodstock was 'frankly & wholly an American [school] in aims & methods' which did not give an 'adequate grounding' for 'New Zealand requirements'. This in turn raised 'the question in our minds of the wisdom of bringing [Scott and Ian] back' to New Zealand. James's concerns were also gendered to a degree: India was not 'helpful or healthy for young boys'.[86] This was a veritable minefield for missionary parents, sometimes resolved on site but more often one that forced them to contemplate either family dismemberment or a return home.

For some parents, family separation did not necessarily lead to anxiety. Many letters home mention these separations matter-of-factly without apparent concern. Yet the historical record indicates that it was also difficult for many others. However, for all the emotional and financial difficulties that separation posed, it was the default position of a large grouping of parents by the end of the nineteenth century (if not earlier) and therefore the logical focus of institutional policies and the resulting public discourse that normalised it more widely. At that point, parents' anxieties were further compounded by both the anticipation and the actuality of family separation. Sometimes separation was anticipated and confronted while families were on furlough in their home countries. More problematic were the decisions faced in mission contexts. Here the anticipation of children returning to the realities of 'home' – where they were often culturally and emotionally estranged – sometimes caused acute parental anxiety. Following the tragic death in northern India of sixteen-year-old Tom Riddle from diphtheria in 1934, his father Thomas (NZP) wrote movingly that:

[t]he separation [to go to senior high school in New Zealand] that would have come in Jan.[uary] was one that we dreaded. The [American Presbyterian]

missionaries are really afraid to send their young folk back to the conditions of America. Three of them have in the last few years taken their own lives in America. One a splendid young woman lived next door to us in the hills last year. She was a leader in her college societies in America, but some depression got her and she deliberately planned and took poison. The fear of modern conditions for a boy not accustomed to them was real but now he is in the Father's keeping.[87]

Separation had many spatial and temporal permutations. This was not always experienced as problematic by the children themselves and, in some respects, worked to redefine what was 'normal' for families in imperial or missionary contexts.[88] However, it was the longer-distance and more final separations necessitated by children's education that engendered the strongest parental emotions including anguish, anxiety, loneliness and possibly guilt. From Calabar in 1898 William Marwick wrote to his mother and sister in Edinburgh that while reading aloud the children's letters, 'I could hardly control my voice sometimes & the tears flowed in my eyes as I read about our little ones'. Early on he and Elizabeth sent their four-year-old son Willie 'many happy returns' and wrote poignantly 'it is the first you will spend separated from [us], & we shall be yearning ... to miss you & give you our presents & to see your bright happy face & to hear you & Margaret talk & play together'.[89]

Family bonds were certainly maintained through regular letter writing.[90] Faith Cook, daughter of English CIM parents in China and later Malaysia, writes that she had a 'postal relationship' with her parents that 'would form the bedrock of my security and development from a young teenager to womanhood and beyond'.[91] However, this did not diminish the physical and emotional distance between family members and indeed, as Poul Pedersen speculates for one Danish missionary family in India, frequent letter-writing may well have heightened parental anxieties even further.[92] In Manktelow's words, the 'painful difficulties of separation leap out from missionary letters and journals, and speak most eloquently to the bonds of love and affection' between parents and children.[93] While she was writing of the early nineteenth century, this was no less true of missionary families later on. For all concerned separation was at heart an emotional issue.

Anxiety, separation and emotional labour

As such, it is possible to argue more broadly that missionary parents' anxieties were constitutive of what is referred to as emotional labour. This derives in the first instance from the work of American sociologist Arlie Hochschild, based on her earlier notion of 'emotional work' and developing the dramaturgical social theories of Erving Goffmann.[94] It was 'coined by Hochschild in a study that focused on the work of American flight attendants'. Emotional labour, that is work that 'requires one to induce or sustain the outward countenance that produces the proper state of mind in others', was typical of post-industrial society, wherein an 'increasing number of people interact with other people as part of their job'. At heart, it involves 'the management of feeling to create a publicly observable facial and bodily display'.[95] Hochschild referred to this further as the 'commoditization of feeling', focused on the 'capacity to manage meanings', and which highlighted distinctive class and gender configurations.[96] In this regard, Vallgårda further notes the 'highly productive capacity' of emotions, to 'shape and reshape individual identity, social relationships, and different kinds of communities'. In so doing she aligns the idea of emotional labour with political power, the idea of emotional practices and also emotional communities.[97]

Vallgårda's study of Danish missionaries in South India is the most significant application of this concept for the history of missions. She uses it in a more 'figurative sense', in order to 'denote the efforts of the missionaries to manage … their feelings and, in the process, to define themselves as individuals and as a community'.[98] Her focus is on published sources, with a double emphasis on how parents represented themselves to their Danish audience at home and how they publicly coped with the impact of children's deaths. On the one hand, separation was represented as a form of painful 'emotional duress' which was arguably 'harder on the parents than on the child' but which also served, in a similar way argued by Cleall, to bolster a sense of collective missionary identity and to reassure their domestic audience that they valued 'the close-knit nuclear family'.[99] On the other hand, referencing children's deaths, a 'specific religiously informed ethos of sacrifice and faith figure as vital' in parents' 'portrayal of personal bereavement'. More particularly, utilising the notion of 'religious sacrifice', Vallgårda argues that children's deaths and family separation served to intensify missionary parents' relationship to God which in turn 'helped describe the missionaries as neither ungrateful nor as pitiable subjects'. Rather they could be seen as 'particularly worthy servants of God'.[100] The overall effect was that in the process '[b]y emphasizing love, tenderness, pain, faith, and even happiness and joy instead of, for example, anger, doubt, relief, or frustration in relation to familial separation, the narratives named, enhanced, and sought to elicit certain emotions while downplaying or silencing others'. Thus emotional labour helped, among other things, 'to define missionary identity and connect the missionaries to a broader circle of missionary supporters'.[101]

Vallgårda's observations for one cultural context, while limited mostly to published or public sources, ring true for the wider diversity of British world missionary families considered here for the same period. Yet two further things can be said, again drawn from a broader collection of missionary contexts but also from a range of sources both public and private. First, the religious or theological dimensions of missionary parents' emotional labour need to be brought more to the forefront, to acknowledge the deep importance of the religious contours of their narratives. In a general sense, there is a strong resonance between Vallgårda's findings for Danish missionary families and Buettner's observations about British imperial families in India. Buettner argues that a 'discourse of family sacrifice runs through countless family letters, fictional works, and other contemporary commentary on British life in the empire'.[102] Vallgårda rightly highlights, however, that this discourse of sacrifice was significantly re-articulated by missionary parents in specifically theological terms as 'religious sacrifice', with respect to how they communicated with their home audience.

This is fundamentally important, because it was through a predominantly religious or theological lens that they variously experienced, viewed, constructed and re-constructed their worlds. It was more than simply a reconfiguration of reality for a perceived domestic audience, although that was important. It was also a profound expression of missionary self-identity and experience. Herein lay the unresolved tension between faith, religious vocation and parental responsibilities. As such, parents understood that there was a real cost to their decisions and many suffered emotionally as a result, with anxiety as a key marker of such suffering. The evidence points to the reality of that struggle, rather than simply its representations. Put simply, separation was emotionally painful in the most literal sense. Privately written sources suggest that this was so, albeit rationalised or justified through a theological lens. Faith Cook recalls a letter that her father wrote semi-apologetically to her in adulthood in which he tellingly betrayed both his feelings and his earlier adult assumptions about children's emotions:

> I guess you feel life has been pretty tough on missionaries' children. It has, and on missionary parents too, but their children didn't choose the sort of life they had to live and their parents did. I remember going back to our empty room fiddling about tidying the room with a heart as heavy as lead ... There was nothing we could do about it. We had already lost our little Godfrey. You were too young to feel that much.[103]

Faith and her brother Christopher experienced prolonged periods of significant separation within and beyond China, both for education and because of the long-lasting conflicts with Japan. Here Faith's father privately articulated both feelings of remorse and a spiritually constructed means of self-justification that, as Faith admits, was entirely congruent with both his character and his deeply engrained sense of religious vocation. He admitted his own sense of anguish and guilt, readily echoed by missionary parents from other Protestant groups, and offered a theologically framed rationale in which he mused that

> We can only say that we know that suffering, for the Christian, is not the terrible thing the world thinks it to be. I don't mean that we don't feel it as badly. What I do mean is we know it comes to us from our Father's loving hand and somehow he has purposes of love in permitting it. And I'm sure that is true of the things you find difficult and still do.[104]

Faith suggests that, in reality, a blend of her father's driven personality and theological imperatives need to be accounted for. Still, she also observes insightfully that for her parents the emotional cost of separation from their children was tantamount to a 'second bereavement'.[105]

Second, therefore, emotional labour was used variously to express both public and private anxieties and responses to separation, or may have been turned inwards as parents struggled with the realities of their decisions. In public documents directed at the home base, as Vallgårda indicates, there was an emphasis on affirming the social status quo and on building connections between the mission field and home. Private documents, however, reveal a greater depth of emotional distress and exertion, and perhaps a greater degree of honesty. Here emotional labour provides one further way of understanding missionary family relationships.[106] Two examples will suffice. One is the different ways in which Thomas Riddle (NZP) communicated the tragic loss of two of his and Isobel's children in India: infant daughter Helen accidentally drowned in 1921 while severely ill, and teenage son Tom who died from diphtheria in 1934. In his published biography Thomas devoted no more than two pages to each incident, recounting the details with a brief theological reflection.[107] This reflection was personalised, in that Riddle pondered the reflexive impact of each tragedy on his own spiritual understanding and character development, as well as how each incident formed in him a greater sense of empathy for the sufferings of those among whom he worked. This was the stuff of devotional books ubiquitous in contemporary Protestant circles, wherein the spiritual life conveyed biographically became an object lesson for the reader's benefit. At the same time, in this instance, the pain of loss was turned inwards in a productive sense. In the process, he 'got deeper into the meaning of life' and simultaneously found that he was 'one of a great unrealized brotherhood of sorrow'.[108]

In his private letters to the New Zealand Presbyterian office, there was unexpected candour alongside the expected religious rhetoric. At Helen's death, there was a greater congruence between the letter and the published account.[109] It was different in response to Tom's later death, perhaps reflecting the longer and sustained mutually respectful relationship between father and son. There Christian hope was juxtaposed with 'the sense of utter defeat and irreparable loss', of 'pain' and acknowledgement of the 'deprivations of life'. The book's reflexive comments were clearly made in hindsight, dating from a letter written at least a year after Tom's death. In that later letter, too, were the very private observations about Thomas and Isobel's anxieties over Tom's imminent departure to New Zealand, in the light of tragedies befalling American young adults adjusting to America from India.[110] Here were missionary parents engaging more intimately and privately with trusted friends within the wider missionary family, confiding, confessing and divulging the complex emotional impact of real and tragic loss.

The second and final example comes again from the Marwick family of Scotland. Despite the deeply internalised theological imperative that drove William as a missionary, early parenthood provoked moments of unanticipated crisis. Separated from their first two children in 1899 he confided to his mother and sister from Nigeria that now he was 'sometimes tempted to wish I had never come back, & sometimes to make up my mind not to come back if I am asked to finish this term'.[111] Shortly thereafter they returned to Scotland with their other children. Within two years the whole family relocated to Jamaica for another appointment; barely two years later the two oldest children returned to Edinburgh, as did Elizabeth with the remaining children in 1906. Therein ensued ten years, barring furloughs in Scotland, in which William lived separated from his family. Here the normal separation experience was inverted. It was William who felt keenly his physical dislocation within the family and who continued to struggle with the dual pressures of vocation and parenthood.[112]

Through these years he wrote voluminously to his family and others. One possible reading of these letters suggests that he was attempting to theologically rationalise his continued separation from the family. Writing in 1911 to Sir J. Alexander Swettenham (a past Governor of Jamaica), William linked his own circumstances to the letter's focus on developing a theology of 'childlike obedience' to God. Here he sketched out the imaginary impact of a child's father having to leave family or children to the sole care of the mother, wherein it 'would be the mother's aim to [inculcate] a principle of love, & thus to prepare the child for the performance of filial duties'. He further wrote that

[i]t so happens that I am in the position of that imaginary father … The youngest who cannot remember her father has yet been taught to love him & even obey his wishes [by?] the simple undogmatic ways referred to above. In

the same simple childlike ways even an adult can be taught to love & obey his heavenly Father.[113]

This internal turmoil was possibly expressed further through a seemingly fraught epistolary relationship with his third son George. Writing on his thirteenth birthday, William thanked George for sending him a scheme of current Sunday school lessons and hoped that he would excel in upcoming examinations.[114] To prepare for twentieth-century adulthood he insisted that George 'must try and make the best' of both his schooling and church involvement. This sentiment was bolstered by reference to a recent speech by Edinburgh University's 'Lord Rector' who had talked about being 'patient, painstaking & diligent in acquiring knowledge'. William thought this to be 'good advice for school-boys as well as for University students'. Then he grounded his comments with advice aimed at helping the young George further:

> There are a number of mistakes in your letter to me which you need not have made if you had watched each word & sentence as you wrote it, or that you could have corrected if you had read it over before giving it to Mother … You can write correctly if you just use a little care, & it is worth while [*sic*] to do your best when you write to me as well as [for?] your exercises at school. I want to see myself from your letters that you are improving, & because you love me you will do your best, & it is because I love you that I tell you about these mistakes.

The whole letter ended sentimentally with repeated birthday wishes and 'warmest love & kisses & all good wishes' from a 'loving father'. William was certainly caught between familial and vocational obligations.[115] These later letters were more sober epistles of censure, correction, moral guidance and theological expectations shot through with a confusion of feeling. They expressed William's frustrations over George's struggles at school and, at a more fundamental level, of being an absentee father. Perhaps they also reflected the nature of this father–son relationship, regardless of the distance. Nevertheless, here was a complex interplay of parental and filial emotions not easily disentangled. If children like George were 'casualties of Empire',[116] then so too were their parents. Parents like William and Elizabeth Marwick were separated from their children by internally and culturally driven religious obligation, but at the same time were plagued by doubts or feelings of guilt and by heartfelt and oftentimes intense feelings of anguish. This, then, was a seemingly unavoidable and oft-repeated expression of missionary parents' emotional labour.

Conclusion

In this chapter, Protestant missionary children's lives from the late nineteenth into the early twentieth centuries have been viewed firstly through the lens of parental narratives, with a primary focus on the companionate family as a key organising principle and formative reality. It has addressed two underlying questions: how were children's lives described and represented by their parents and why was this significant? By the turn of the twentieth century missionary families increasingly reflected a demographic and societal shift towards smaller, emotionally framed family units wherein value was placed on each member, including children. As such, children like Hugh and Ann Tyndale-Biscoe became the norm, and the ways in which their lives were individually and affectionately represented by their mother Phyllis were typical of the wider missionary community. While children's lives were not necessarily self-referenced in religious terms, underlying religious motives and imperatives clearly shaped their parents' vocational choices and the necessary relocation of families to mission field locations. In turn, religious or theological imagery could be employed in some parents' articulation of their children's position in the greater scheme of things. Thus, religion differentiated them from other Empire families and it also partially shaped how parents rationalised their living contexts to or on behalf of their children.

Phyllis's letters also reveal a predominant and wholly expected focus on children's domestic lives and their relationships with their families. This covered the full spectrum from birth, through infancy and early years, and on into older childhood and adolescence. This detail was not unique to missionary parents – embracing the experiences of many imperial or colonial families of the period – and it accentuates children's views of their own lives that life was 'ordinary'. In the context of missionary families, however, parents either implicitly or explicitly understood that their children's lives were not ordinary. This focus reflected clear and abiding parental concern for their children's physical and emotional welfare and the overall maintenance of family life. In turn, this emerged as a formative emotional narrative thread for parents, particularly expressed as anxiety over such issues as children's happiness, health and education. Anxiety both fed into parents' consequent decisions to break up the family (especially for education) and was exacerbated through the resulting exigencies of child–parent separation. As such, this chapter has employed the concept of emotional labour as a way of conceptualising and nuancing the resulting parental narratives constructed around their children, especially with respect to the religious imperatives underlying such narratives and their publicly or privately differentiated representations.

This parental lens, however, is simply a starting point. Partly in response to these expressed concerns, churches and organisations in the home-base constituencies took up the cause, developing policies and establishing institutions to alleviate parents' anxieties and to ameliorate the impact of separation on parents. However, as the next chapter indicates, a child-centred approach to the impact of lifestyles and family separation on children only began to be addressed in the 1930s. Therefore, this parental lens, while revealing a rich narrative around children, is deficient on its own. Chapter 3 examines the institutional lens, which helps to explain the consolidation of denominational and organisational views of childhood more broadly. At the same time, both lenses leave unexplored, for example, what 'emotional labour' looked or felt like for children and what they consequently thought of their own lives. The third, child-centred lens thus becomes pivotally important for a holistic and integrated understanding of missionary children's lives.

Notes

1 The following details are extracted from letters written for the Christmas mail in 1930, 1931, 1932, 1933, 1934 and 1935. Alexander Turnbull Library, Wellington (hereafter ATL), MS-Papers-11956–07, Doreen Ross Papers, Phyllis Long outward correspondence to Doreen Ross 1927–1935.
2 Bellenoit, *Missionary Education*, pp. 169, 179, 186; Studdert-Kennedy, 'Christian Imperialists', p. 134; Majumdar, 'Tom Brown', pp. 105–20; Mangan, *The Games Ethic*, pp. 177–91; Murray, 'Tyndale-Biscoe', p. 686.
3 Another New Zealand missionary, Elva Jackson (CMS) also resorted to the 'Truby King schedule' when raising infant daughter Kamala in southern India in the early 1940s. Jackson, *Indian Saga*, p. 73.
4 Walker, 'Tyndale-Biscoe'.
5 Manktelow, *Missionary Families*, pp. 96–99.
6 Cleall, *Missionary Discourses*, p. 29.
7 See for example: Haggis and Allen, 'Imperial Emotions', 691–716; Prevost, *The Communion of Women*; Robertson, 'Girdle'.
8 Konrad, 'Lost', 219.
9 Marten, 'Family Relationships', p. 19.
10 Walsham, 'Introduction', p. xxi.
11 Langmore, 'The Object Lesson', p. 85, in turn quoting LMS Secretary Ralph Wardlaw Thompson in 1893. The evolution of this concept is outlined in Robert, 'The "Christian Home"', pp. 134–65. Further examples can be found, inter alia, in: Manktelow, *Missionary Families*, p. 99; Cleall, *Missionary Discourses*, pp. 290–73; Grimshaw, 'Faith', pp. 260–80; Ross, *Women*; Choi, 'The Missionary Home', pp. 29–55; and Maxwell, 'The Missionary Home', pp. 428–55.

12 Angus Library and Archive, Regent's Park College, Oxford (hereafter Angus Library), Baptist Missionary Society Archives (hereafter BMS), BMS Reports of Committee and Abstracts 1890–1891, Alfred Henry Baynes, 'Report on the Indian Mission by the General Secretary, Baptist Missionary Society, 1889–1890', p. 79; Hocking, *Re-Thinking*, p. 295.

13 Editorial Committee, *Ecumenical Missionary Conference*, pp. 320 and 318–19.

14 Hamlett, *Material Relations*, p. 61.

15 Robert, 'The "Christian Home"', p. 163.

16 Maxwell, 'The Missionary Home', p. 455.

17 Manktelow, *Missionary Families*, p. 96; Langmore, *Missionary Lives*, p. 75.

18 Up to 1945 there were 349 missionaries in India and 155 in the South Pacific, comprising 45 per cent of the total LMS missionary complement in this period. Goodall, *London Missionary Society*, pp. 595–623.

19 Data for LMS families are derived from Volumes 1 and 2 of the 'London Missionary Society Register of Missionaries' Children up to 1940' and from copies of the *LMS Chronicle*, both held in the Archives and Special Collections, School of Oriental and African Studies, London. Data for Scottish and New Zealand Presbyterian missionary families are compiled from the following sources: (1) Scotland – annual reports to the General Assemblies of the Church of Scotland, the Free Church of Scotland and the United Free Church of Scotland 1860–1940, and from both Scott, *Fasti*, vol. 7 and Lamb, *The Fasti*; and (2) New Zealand – annual reports to the General Assemblies of the Synod of Southland and Otago 1866–1901 and of the Presbyterian Church of New Zealand 1869–1940, monthly issues of *The Break of Day* children's magazine, individual missionaries' staff files and 'Register of New Zealand Presbyterian Ministers, Deaconesses & Missionaries'.

20 England and Wales: Garrett, Reid, Schurer and Szreter, *Changing Family Size*, p. 1; New Zealand: Montgomerie, 'New Women', 38.

21 To better gauge the complex relationships within missionary households see: Semple, 'Making Missions', pp. 23–40.

22 Latourette, *A History*, vol. 4, p. 2 and vol. 7, p. 16.

23 Cox, *British Missionary Enterprise*, pp. 213–15; Anderson, 'American Protestants', 102, 105.

24 'Register of New Zealand Presbyterian Ministers, Deaconesses & Missionaries'.

25 Lennox, *The Health and Turnover*, p. 19.

26 Pomfret, *Youth*, pp. 2–3, 23.

27 The Lawes' entry is in the 'London Missionary Society Register of Missionaries Children', vol. 1, p. 45, SCM/LMS, SOAS; and the Shaw entry in Scott, *Fasti*, pp. 580–81.

28 Brummitt, 'The Fate', p. 37.

29 Huntington, 'The Success', 75.

30 Garrett et al., *Changing Family Size*, pp. 1–3.

31 Olssen, 'Towards', p. 258; Wanhalla, 'Family', p. 459.

32 Garrett et al., *Changing Family Size*, p. 399.

33 For example see Barrett and Kukhareva, 'Family Relationships', pp. 22–24.

34 Gauvreau, 'Religious Diversity', pp. 235–58; Connor, 'Poverty', 625–46.

35 Van Poppel and Derosas, 'Introduction', p. 9.

36 Marten, 'Family Relationships', p. 29; in turn referencing Zelizer, *Pricing the Priceless Child*.

37 Mangan, *Games Ethic and Imperialism*, pp. 178–80.

38 Mangan, *Manufactured Masculinity*, p. 897; in turn quoting from Tyndale-Biscoe's *Fifty Years*, p. 20.

39 Introduced, for example, by Buettner, *Empire Families*, pp. 110–14 in relation to the Indian context.

40 See further: Morrison, *Pushing Boundaries*, pp. 95–120; Proctor, 'Scottish Missionaries', 43–61; Hill, 'Women', pp. 170–85; and Samson, *Race and Redemption*, p. 25, in turn quoting from Piggin, *Making Evangelical Missionaries*, p. 125.

41 Manktelow, *Missionary Families*, p. 206. The same point is emphasised in Thurlow, review of *Missionary Families*, 236–67.

42 National Library of Scotland (hereafter NLS), Acc. 4886 (33–38), Marwick Papers, Marwick Letter Books 1890s to 1917. See also: Orr, *Bones of Empire*, p. 175; 'Papers of William Hutton Marwick'; and 'Rev. William Marwick'.

43 'Rev. Henry Begg Gray' and 'Mr George Tasker Gray', 'Register of New Zealand Presbyterian Church Ministers, Deaconesses & Missionaries'; Gray, *We Travel Together*.

44 NLS, Acc. 4886 (36), Marwick Papers, Marwick Letter Books 1890s to 1917, William to Willie, 10 September 1898.

45 Presbyterian Research Centre, Dunedin (hereafter PRC), GAO149 Punjab Mission Archive (hereafter PM), Staff Files, 'James Gray' (6.06) and 'Marion Scott' (6.08), Folder 1.

46 'Very Rev. James Lundie Gray', 'Register of New Zealand Presbyterian Church Ministers, Deaconesses & Missionaries'.

47 Ian Gray, interview, New Zealand, 29 December 2014.

48 The tensions between a missionary father's domestic versus professional responsibilities and priorities is further examined, in the context of Lutheran Norwegian missionaries in late-nineteenth-century Africa, in Tjelle, *Missionary Masculinity*, pp. 166–88.

49 PRC, PM, 'James Gray' (6.06), Folder 1, James Gray to Rev. Mawson, 12 January 1932 and 11 August 1932.

50 Manktelow, *Missionary Families*, p. 147.

51 PRC, GAO148 Canton Villages Mission Staff Files, Series 6, 1901–1940 (hereafter CVM), Herbert Davies to William Hewitson, 16 August 1912.

52 PRC, CVM, Margaret Davies to Alexander Don, Box AA 16/5, 28 April 1920.

53 Angus Library, BMS, 'Alfred Theodor Teichmann', IN/60, Dorothy Teichmann, 'Free to Serve', extract from *The Herald*, December 1911.

54 Hocken Library, Dunedin [hereafter Hocken], George Hunter McNeur Papers, MS-1007, ARC-038, Diaries of George McNeur, 1907–1908.

55 Hocken, Ron Malcolm Papers, AG-775–001/001, Anna Malcolm's Notebooks and Letters, 1899–1914, Entry for 21 February, 1911.

56 SIM International Resource Centre, Fort Mill, South Carolina (hereafter SIM), Bolivian Indian Mission Archives (hereafter BIM), George and Mary Allan Personal Collection, Box 11, George Allan to Jean Allan, 3 June 1911.

57 Fraser, *African Idylls*, pp. 21, 22–23.

58 NLS, Acc. 4886 (37), Marwick Papers, Marwick Letter Books 1902–1903, W. Marwick to Mother, 27 January and 18 March 1902.

59 Angus Library, BMS, 'Ernest Whitby Burt', CH/56, 'Autobiography of Rev. E.W. Burt (China 1892–1933)'. This consists of 113 typed pages of unpublished material held loosely in a manila folder.

60 See further: Stearns, 'Defining', 165–86; Morrison, 'Settler Childhood', pp. 81–82.

61 'Autobiography of Rev. E.W. Burt', pp. 30–31.

62 For the English context in this period see, for example: Pooley, 'All We Parents Want', 528–48. For New Zealand see Olssen, 'Truby King', 3–23.

63 'Autobiography of Rev. E.W. Burt', p. 32.

64 PRC, PM, Dr Adam Harvie to Rev. George Jupp, 26 December 1927.

65 Robert, 'The "Christian Home"', p. 163.

66 Crocq, 'A History of Anxiety', 319–25.

67 Stearns, *Anxious Parents*; Stearns, *American Fear*.

68 Ingram and Lawlor, 'The Gloom', pp. 55–78; Bourke, 'Frightened', pp. 55–78; and Bourke, 'Fear', 111–33.

69 Bourke, 'Fear', 120–21.

70 Examples include: New Zealand Presbyterian: PRC, CVM, Margaret Davies to Barton, 14 February 1925; PRC, PM, Ada Harvie to Rev. Mawson, 7 August 1932; PRC, PM, James Gray to Rev. Mawson, 29 July 1934; James Gray to Rev. Budd, 3 July 1936; Angus Sutherland to Rev. Mawson, 18 April 1930; Scottish Presbyterian: Christie, *Dugald Christie of Manchuria*, p. 99; London Missionary Society: SOAS, CWM/LMS, Papua New Guinea, Incoming Correspondence 1905–1907, Box 11, Charles Rich to Rev. Thompson, 11 February 1906; SOAS, CWM/LMS, Papua Incoming Correspondence 1905–1907, Box 11, C.W. Abel to Rev. Thompson, 10 May 1905.

71 Buettner, 'Parent-Child Separations', pp. 115–32; Pedersen, 'Anxious Lives', 13–17; Ward, 'The Anxious Climate', 11–13.

72 PRC, CVM, Andrew Miller to Henry Barton, 4 August 1926.

73 *LMS Chronicle*, 1889–1939.

74 PRC, CVM, Margaret Davies to Henry Barton, Box AA 16/5, 14 July 1928.

75 SIM, BIM, George and Mary Allan Personal Collection, Box 11, George Allan to Brother, 13 November 1914.

76 *Ibid.*

77 Cleall, *Missionary Discourses*, pp. 111–12.

78 SOAS, CWM/LMS, W.G. and Fanny Lawes Papers, Personal Papua New Guinea, Box 1, Folder 10, W.G. Lawes to 'My Dear Sister in Christ', 18 September 1877; King, *W.G. Lawes*, pp. 91–94.

79 NLS, Scottish Foreign Mission Records 1827–1929, MS.7610, Church of Scotland: Incoming Letters, George Mill to Rev. McLachlan, 19 February 1924.

80 A concern for missionary families' health was signalled as early as the 1910 World Missionary Conference in Edinburgh. See further discussion in Chapter 3 and also Morrison, 'It Is Well', 306–29.

81 See again Manktelow, *Missionary Families*, pp. 100–107; Schulz, *Hawaiian by Birth*, pp. 69–92.

82 Konrad, 'Lost', 219, 221; Manktelow, *Missionary Families*, p. 124.

83 Buettner, *Empire Families*, p. 110. Note again that the detrimental impact of environment on missionary children was a focus of academic writing on missionary children across a range of mission contexts (Chapters 1 and 3).

84 SIM, BIM, George and Mary Allan Personal Collection, Box 11, George Allan to Brother, 13 November 1914.

85 PRC, PM, Ada Harvie to Rev. Mawson, 11 September 1934.

86 PRC, PM, James Gray to Rev. Mawson, 12 January 1932; PRC, PM, James Gray to Mr Budd, 15 February 1938.

87 PRC, PM, Thomas Riddle to Rev. Mawson, 4 November 1934.

88 Buettner, 'Parent-Child Separations', p. 117.

89 NLS, Acc. 4886 (36), Marwick Papers, Marwick Letter Books 1898–1901, William to Mother, 22 May 1898, and William to Willie, 10 September 1898.

90 See for example: Duff, *Changing Childhoods*, pp. 50–51, 54–56; Cleall, 'Far-Flung Families, 174–75.

91 Cook, *Troubled Journey*, pp. 100–101.

92 Pedersen, 'Anxious Lives', 9, 13–17.

93 Manktelow, *Missionary Families*, p. 149.

94 Plamper, *The History of Emotions*, pp. 119–22; Hochschild, 'Emotion Work', 551–75.

95 Landahl, 'Emotions', 105; Vallgårda, *Imperial Childhoods*, p. 12; both in turn quoting from Hochschild, *The Managed Heart*, p. 7.

96 Hochschild, 'Emotion Work', 569–70; Plamper, *The History of Emotions*, p. 121.

97 Vallgårda, *Imperial Childhoods*, pp. 12–13, particularly p. 13.

98 *Ibid.*, p. 13.

99 *Ibid.*, pp. 193, 194.

100 *Ibid.*, pp. 184, 196.

101 *Ibid.*, pp. 199–200.

102 Buettner, *Empire Families*, p. 112.

103 Cook, *Troubled Journey*, p. 117.

104 *Ibid.*

105 *Ibid.*, p. 97.

106 For further application of 'emotional labour' to private communications within a domestic family setting see Morrison, 'Reimagining', 465–88.

107 Riddle, *The Light*, pp. 148–49, 192–93.

108 *Ibid.*, p. 192.

109 PRC, PM, Thomas Riddle to Rev. Don, 18 June 1921.

110 PRC, PM, Thomas Riddle to Rev. Mawson, 4 November 1934, 4 July 1935 and 4 August 1935.

111 NLS, Acc. 4886 (2), Marwick Papers, Marwick Letter Books 1898–1901, William to Mother and Lizzie, 13 October 1899.

112 Similar sentiments emerged from the letters of Norwegian Lutheran missionary David Jakobsen, Madagascar, to his children domiciled in Norway, between about 1892 and 1902. Ask, *Dear Rikard*.

113 NLS, Acc. 4886, Marwick Papers, Letter book, 1911–c.1917, William to Sir J.A. Swettenham, 23 February, 1911.

114 The following quotes are from: NLS, Acc. 4886(30), Marwick Papers, loose letter in the back of Letterbook 1890–c.1892, William to 'My Dear George', 11 December 1912.

115 For the issues raised around the role of 'father' in the late Victorian and the Edwardian eras see: Olsen, 'Daddy's Come Home'; and Olsen, 'The Authority', 765–80.

116 Brendon, *Children*, p. 212.

3

Institutional narratives

Two missionary conference papers and two sets of correspondence between missionaries and their home committees encapsulate the central issues that linked parental and institutional narratives about missionary children. At the same New York conference in 1900, where the missionary household was touted as an important exemplary 'object lesson' for non-Christian peoples, a less ebullient and more anxious note was struck. In an emotionally charged address, Evangelical Lutheran missionary Rev L.B. Wolf posed a dilemma when he asked:

> when … we do get married, what then? I stand here after sixteen years of service in South India. I do not know at the present time which way to turn. I had a Christian home, which I believe under God, was as powerful in India as my own work. But that home is broken up. Why? Because I dare not keep my children on the plains of South India; and if I go back as a missionary now, I must go back alone. That is the other side of the shield. What are we to do, then?[1]

Central to this cry for help was the assumption that the separated family, and the consequent loss of intimacy and attendant lack of familial companionship, was abnormal. A reply of sorts was made by another panel speaker, the Hon J.B. Angell, President of the University of Michigan. Addressing 'three great trials' faced by missionaries, Angell offered a general response that raised more questions than answers. The first trial was

> that which comes upon the father and mother when that sad day arrives that they must send their children home for education when they so need the companionship of father and mother, and when father and mother even more, perhaps, need the companionship of their children. We can do something to help in this matter by caring in all ways possible to us for the comfort and help of the children at home.[2]

These were well-worn concerns. As early as 1822, LMS missionary James Hayward lamented that 'nothing effectual' was being done officially for missionaries' children.[3] By the 1900s such questions remained unresolved for many parents.

In 1901, what 'caring in all ways possible' practically meant was tested through a letter opened by Alfred H. Baynes, the BMS Secretary in London. It was from John Whitewright, resident in China since 1881 (joined by his new wife Martha Allen in 1883) and who, from 1887, was the principal of a training institute for pastors and teachers in Shantung.[4] They had four children (Elsie, Ethel, Alfred and John) and in all that time had only been back to England twice. Now returning to China and about to leave their children in England for the next eight years, Whitewright sought permission for a short mid-term furlough to reunite the family and thus mitigate a lengthy separation.[5] He framed his request rationally, presenting both parents' and children's perspectives. He had rendered sustained and exemplary dedication to his task – it was an 'honour' and a 'privilege' to be 'an ambassador of Jesus Christ' in China – and meant no disrespect in writing. Rather, he outlined how he had forfeited furloughs in the past for the sake of the BMS, thus reinforcing his sense of commitment and duty. However, his duty was also to his children who were God's gift and a divine responsibility. In this instance not only were parents to be separated from the children, but the children were to be separated from both the place that they called 'home' and from the Chinese people who they 'loved' and to whom they were 'intensely loyal'. His request was intensely emotional in places. He referred to eleven-year-old Alfred, a 'manly little fellow', who

> opened his heart the other night to his mother. I think any father who saw him, as shaken with sobs, he clung to his mother and told her how he had begun to count the days till we go and had too begun to count the time till we come back, would feel that, if it be at all possible, that we should see him and his sisters in four or five years' time, it should be so.

Whitewright wrote that he could similarly 'tell sad stories of parents who have come home after many years to find their children strangers, and alas have gone back with saddened heart to their work leaving them strangers still'. By this, he appealed to contemporary norms of family cohesion and stability. Here he was thinking of other Baptists but could have been speaking on behalf of others like COS missionaries Mr and Mrs Paterson in India. In a similar fashion, they petitioned their committee in 1895 for a short furlough to see their children, but to no avail.[6] Whitewright hoped that 'those who have the joy of their children with them in their own land' would look favourably on his request.

The outcome was ambiguous. The BMS China sub-committee agreed to Whitewright's request but put on hold his suggestion that such mid-term furloughs should become future policy.[7] Subsequent meeting minutes are silent as to a final decision. While his own circumstances were unique, Whitewright's plea was not isolated or atypical. He appealed on behalf of other Baptist missionaries and to other precedents in the wider Protestant missionary community. Yet despite all the emotional and financial difficulties that separation clearly posed for parents like Martha and John, it was firmly established by the early 1900s as the default position of parents and therefore the logical focus of institutional policies and the resulting public discourse that normalised it.

Some three decades on, and in a completely different geographical setting, family separation continued to be a contested issue between missionaries and their committees, expressed through sustained and significant parental anxiety. A second set of correspondence, between James Gray in India (NZP) and the New Zealand office, revealed a father who sought to do his 'duty by the Church which sent us out and by our children as well'.[8] Between 1932 and 1938 Marion and James first wrestled with secondary schooling options in New Zealand for their two eldest (Scott and Ian), and later with the welfare and schooling of the remaining children (Robert, David and Patricia). They felt strongly that it was not 'right that the children should be deprived of parental influence during their most crucial years'.[9] Boarding school was too expensive and placing children with wider family too unfair a responsibility. Therefore, they asked their committee to consider establishing a missionary children's home in New Zealand, similar to one in Edinburgh, where 'under sympathetic and wise control children could have the advantages of a Christian home and education at a good institution'.[10] To this end Gray also tentatively enquired about housing his sons in Edinburgh for their further education there, at least while on furlough in Scotland.[11] The idea of a children's missionary home never caught hold in New Zealand, due to the smaller numbers involved and the vexed question of location. Scott and Ian eventually attended boarding school in Christchurch. This proved to be emotionally costly for one boy and a financially unsustainable option for the whole family. For Marion and James, the tension became too much as they sought to heed 'the claims of the children'.[12] In 1938 James wrote again asking to stagger the family's return over the following two years and for further financial help. By 1941 the entire family came together again in Auckland. Yet the degree to which missionary parents were emotionally compromised and the extent to which their committees failed to fully comprehend such torment was summed up plaintively by James:

> I suppose there are some good folk – mostly those who have never had to face the problem – whose dictum would be that a missionary should hand his children over to his relatives, and stick to his job on the field. Well, we feel

there <u>ought</u> [emphasis original] to be another way, whereby we can be faithful to the call and yet not neglect our bairns. That is all, I think, I need to say.[13]

This chapter thus turns to the institutional narratives around missionary children that emerged in response to parents' concerns and demands. It addresses three underlying questions: how did churches respond to parental concerns; how far did parental and institutional narratives converge, and to what effect; and to what extent had this narrative begun to change by the end of the period? The chapter argues that there was a clear, but not always exclusive, convergence between family narratives emphasising separation or disadvantage and institutional narratives focused on mitigation of these problems. It is in this convergence that we can perceive further the dilemma that parenthood posed for adults motivated towards missionary service, and how this impinged on both mission policy and pragmatics. Institutional narratives reveal primarily a discourse that stressed the impact of separation on parents. In particular, the chapter considers three key elements. First, it outlines how children were variously thought about and represented in policy making, using selected British or Anglo-world examples and building on literary representations previously considered. Second, it examines the phenomenon of children's missionary homes as an expression of the institutionalisation of separation, indicating how an emotional discourse of domestic stability and happiness was used to represent these homes to church constituencies. Third, it indicates how institutional narratives began to change. The 1930s marked a partial turning point in official rhetoric, with the emergence of an academic and professional discourse that moved towards a more child-centred approach to missionary children's lives.

Missionary children in policy making

To date, this aspect has received little scholarly attention and there still remains the need for a nuanced and comparative analysis of missionary children in policy making. The discussion that follows is therefore indicative. What the material reveals is that the journey towards effective children's support was long and tortuous, that its progress and outcomes were often context-specific, and that an understanding of children's needs was often an afterthought. Some organisations – like the ABCFM, Basel Mission, CMS and the LMS – got to grips with this by the mid-nineteenth century or possibly in a shorter time frame than other groups. The early establishment of schools for their children was evidence of this.[14] Yet this was a slow and uncertain pathway for other groups, revealing an underlying tension between two different sets of demands or expectations faced by mission leaders: theology versus pragmatics. On the one hand, the first ABCFM missionaries in the Hawaiian Islands were reminded that the 'kingdom to which you belong is not of this world' and that their mission was primarily 'to the native race'.[15] As Manktelow notes, missionary organisations were at heart 'ideological' institutions whose 'ultimate objective was a religious one: the spiritual transformation of non-western peoples'. On the other hand, a theological imperative had to be balanced alongside 'fiscal responsibilities, and the constant need to juggle millennial haste with the realities of a crowded philanthropic marketplace'.[16] In many cases, such as John Whitewright, practical realities caught up with high ideals and good intentions, forcing committees to focus on the pragmatic aspects of making missions work. This included the welfare of their children. Diverse missionary committees and leaders wrestled with these concerns, and did so well into the twentieth century. For instance, it was still explicitly an issue in 1910 for the Foreign Mission Boards of both Canada and the USA, pondering the issue of how to provide suitable children's schooling in China as opposed to sending them home.[17] Likewise, as late as 1936, Woodstock School's principal Allen Parker remarked that '[o]ne great difficulty which remains is that of the education and development of the children and the pain of separation from them'.[18] The emerging narrative, forced often by circumstances or practical realities, thus sought to mitigate the problem by relieving parental anxieties and fostering denominational support on their behalf.

Starting points

From the early nineteenth century, there were two common starting points for policy making which set the tone for the institutional narratives. First, provision for children often emerged as missions grew and were compelled to develop increasingly complex administrative systems and more clearly defined employment conditions. Children's welfare was a by-product of this process and financial concerns dominated the resulting narrative. As such children were seen and treated as dependents, with little regard to their agency. A perfunctory note that the ABCFM resolved to make 'provisions for Widows, Children, and Invalid Missionaries' in early nineteenth-century Ceylon (Sri Lanka) was typical.[19] In a similar way for the LMS from 1818 onwards,[20] evolving policy centred initially on establishing a 'Fund for Widows and Families of Deceased Missionaries'. This fund was initiated after the much-publicised death of one male missionary in British Guiana (Guyana) and the pressure from resulting public agitation. By 1851 the LMS Fund had become self-sustaining, thus 'dramatically evidencing the missionary public's collusion in the missionary family's ascendancy'. While there was already a school for LMS children in Tahiti, education did not become a bigger issue until the 1830s and 1840s, with the establishment of dedicated schools in London (see next section). At the same time, these developments served to integrate missionary wives and, by association, their children into LMS 'institutional mechanisms of control' and ultimately 'shaped the terms of engagement between family and mission'.[21]

Similar developments were evident in the denominational missions of the various Scottish Presbyterian churches. In 1849 the UPC was the first to make explicit 'provision … for the widows and children of missionaries of the Church labouring in Tropical Climates' – namely families living in the Caribbean and Nigeria.[22] This fund was essentially an insurance scheme for wives or children in the event of a missionary father's death, paid into by both the missionary and the denomination, and which required the missionary (but not the wife or children) to submit pre-existing medical information. Unless stated otherwise, wives or children would be remunerated by the UPC for up to five years after the father's death. By the 1860s this focus was broadened with the inauguration of a denominational scheme to support missionary families for their children's education.[23] Likewise, in 1886, partial provision for COS missionary children resulted from a more general move to tighten up employment conditions for ministers and missionaries. In this case, provision was similarly made for a 'widows and orphans' fund, but also for travel costs of children returning home for education.[24] Case-by-case administration of such schemes, however, exemplified the complications thrown up by different field locations and by the economic burden of missionary families split often between field and metropole (maintaining two households).

From about the 1880s onwards, more comprehensive policies across all Scottish Presbyterian branches helped to consolidate both children's welfare and its public narrative. These were linked to tighter missionary employment conditions and typically focused on families' ability to support their children through education, including travel. When the mission work of two Presbyterian branches was amalgamated, through the creation of the UFC in 1900,[25] there was already an 'Education of Missionaries' Children Fund', managed through denominational budgets and available to every missionary family with school-aged children. By 1920 it had an annual income of nearly £1500 and had supported a total of 265 children.[26] It was one way of focusing church members on targeted giving. In the NZPC (which tended to copy or parallel Scottish Presbyterian developments in this period), a similar scheme was referred to as the 'children's allowance' and was reported as such in annual salary schedules. Longer-term financial statistics indicate that missionary children represented a substantial investment for denominational committees.[27]

As a second starting point, policy responses were often made within the first generation of missionary activity and were forced primarily by the growing numbers of wives and children. This became particularly acute in the last two decades of the nineteenth century. Here there was a clearer connection to parental concerns which was more explicitly narrated through denominational reports and publicity. For the ABCFM, operating in Ceylon and the Hawaiian Islands in the early to mid-nineteenth century,[28] the resulting pressure of numbers meant that the 'economy of childrearing' became a 'distracting and familiar topic' for the mission's board in Boston. Parents adopted an 'economic argument' that focused on the support required for children's education and re-settlement back in America. Betraying their cultural expectations, they lamented the perceived lack of appropriate educational or employment opportunities for their children *in situ*. In response the board first offered one-way passages to America for children's schooling and, finally, provided annual stipends for their education. By 1846 some 100 children had been repatriated under this scheme. In the Hawaiian setting, however, frustrated ABCFM missionaries took matters into their own hands in 1841 by establishing a preparatory school at Punahou, near Honolulu, for their own children's education.[29] Ultimately pressure from parents and some children prevailed. In 1848 ABCFM missionaries were allowed to purchase private property, enabling them to develop educational infrastructure for their children on site and in the process contributing to the American colonisation of the Hawaiian Islands.

Presbyterian women and missionary children's policy development

With respect to the British Empire, different settings had different dynamics or demands, particularly towards the end of the nineteenth century. For instance, education was more specifically the catalyst for policy set by colonial Presbyterians in New Zealand. In this case, both rhetoric and practice were also intimately related to the emergence of women's support of missions and their participation in settler-society religion. By the early 1890s, the first generation of New Zealand missionary families in the New Hebrides (Vanuatu) faced the issue of their children's education. Across the Australasian colonies, comprehensive primary education had been available since the advent of compulsory schooling in the 1870s,[30] providing viable alternatives for parents. As a result, one option for late-nineteenth-century British LMS missionaries in Melanesia was to send their children to nearby Australia. For New Zealand, education *per se* was not the problem; rather missionary families faced the issue of how to relocate their children in ways that would be least disruptive to children's domestic lives. This was made more acute because most of their early colonial Presbyterian missionaries to the New Hebrides originated from Scotland or Norway, and therefore had no close family to depend upon in New Zealand. Longer-term schooling options *in situ* remained non-existent.

In 1891 settler Presbyterian women responded to seven such children who required support and residence in New Zealand. A Ladies' Mission Aid Association was constituted to assist 'our New Hebrides missionaries in maintaining and educating their children when required to leave the Islands, on account of the climate and other causes'.[31] The Association sought to foster public awareness of the children's needs throughout the colony, primarily through women's networks, and to raise funds for their support. Within seven years, up to £180 was received annually from southern Presbyterians.[32] Such support, however, was episodic. A more definitive church-wide policy was eventually established, initially replacing the scheme with a per capita allowance system, financed out of Presbyterian budgets but with the expectation that parents would secure 'suitable residence and guardianship' for their children.[33] This reflected growing numbers of missionary children and anticipated the expansion of colonial Presbyterian projects in southern China and northern India in the 1900s. It also coincided with a changing focus for Presbyterian women's groups on supporting women's work for women. Within a decade children's support was guaranteed and enshrined in both missionary employment conditions and annual budgets.

While women did not exclusively define missionary children's lives, they were important in shaping the institutional narrative in British imperial settings.[34] The nineteenth century was the crucible in which an enduring link between gender and children's welfare was perpetuated, specifically the perception that children were part of 'women's work' in both church and society.[35] For the missionary context, the New Zealand case exemplified this, as did the Scottish UPC Ladies Mission Committee, formed in 1861 to 'aid ... in working out the scheme for granting assistance to foreign missionaries in the education of their children'.[36] In both cases, women became the key motivators and drivers of financial schemes to sustain denominational support. Their immediate focus on children in the 1890s then shifted to a focus on women's work and, longer term, both formed stepping-stones towards women's formal participation in church structures as deaconesses, elders and eventually as ordained clergy later in the twentieth century.[37]

Presbyterian women in Scotland and New Zealand thus helped to set the rhetorical parameters for public discourse about missionary children which, in turn, helped lead to policy responses and infrastructure development. This discourse echoed or reinforced parents' narratives, with a double emphasis on family separation (and its implications for children's emotional welfare) and on children's health and education. Initially the Scottish UPC Ladies Committee, for example, was charged with 'enlisting the services of

[Church] Ladies & showing kindly attention to the female children of missionaries who are receiving education & the wives of missionaries who are in this country'.[38] While UPC records indicate that education was central, there was a clear focus on children's domestic and emotional welfare. This notion of 'caring' for missionary children, commonplace by the end of the nineteenth century, was also evident in colonial New Zealand rhetoric.[39] 'It is very desirable', wrote Jane Bannerman to New Zealand women in 1891, 'to have the children of each Mission family kept together, so that they may grow up maintaining their brotherly and sisterly relations and affections, which could not be the case were they placed under separate guardians'.[40] This was as much an issue for the domestic churches as it was for the missionary families:

> [w]ere fathers and mothers amongst us to consider this, and from time to time imagine themselves similarly situated as our Missionary parents are … there would be a readiness and a willingness to render the aid needed … to make good to our Missionaries' children the absence of a father's and mother's presence, love, and care, and to gladden the hearts of our Missionary parents by bearing to them the assurance that loving hearts were directed towards their children.[41]

Women's public and institutionally framed discourse also paralleled parents' concerns about children's health, education and future careers, echoing the widely held contemporary cultural and scientific views about the impact of environment on expatriate children. UFC women spoke for many others when they reminded their Foreign Missions Committee that the 'missionaries of the Church, specially [*sic*] those labouring in tropical climates, are under the necessity of sending their children home, with the view of preserving their health and providing them with a good education'.[42] Similarly, Bannerman noted that for children in the New Hebrides,

> [f]rom the climate, the want of means of education, and the surroundings to which the Missionaries' children are exposed, it is necessary that they should be removed from the Islands at a very early age; otherwise, they are certain to contract disease, fail to be adequately educated, and in other ways be unfitted for future, useful active lives. It is thus necessary that, while yet young in years, they be removed to the Colony.[43]

By the early 1900s, missionary children were the focus of policies aimed at stabilising the welfare of all families. This was an evolutionary, uneven, circumstantial and gendered process that, oftentimes, fed and reinforced the public stereotypes or perceptions around missionaries and their children discussed previously. Despite obvious differences across various settings, the overall institutional narrative sought to mitigate the issues of separation for both adults and children and to draw wider church or denominational constituencies into a collective sense of responsibility and ownership. The following section outlines how this dual project of mitigation and public support was promoted, through an emotionally framed discourse about missionary children's homes in England and Scotland.

Missionary children's homes

In 1930 some 300 people attended a garden party in Edinburgh to celebrate thirty years of the Duddingston 'Home House' for the 'sons and daughters of Church of Scotland missionaries'.[44] As reported to the wider public in the *Scotsman*, under the telling rubric of 'The Overseas Sacrifice', the celebration acknowledged the seventy-eight children who had lived in the home, sent there by their parents 'to be brought up in a Christian atmosphere, and not surrounded by the immorality [of] non-Christian lands'. The account noted that this was 'not an institution, not an orphanage, but a home' overseen by local women who 'had been mothers indeed to the missionaries' children'. Between 1900 and 1916 two such homes were established in Edinburgh for Presbyterian missionaries' children: first the Duddingston Home House (COS) followed later by Cunningham House (UFC).[45] Other dwellings were periodically gifted by interested individuals for the same purpose, such as a smaller one at Stranraer in southwest Scotland in 1918 and a house at North Berwick, on the coast near Edinburgh, for UFC missionary children over the summer holidays.[46]

By the 1900s similar institutions existed in diverse home-base and mission-field settings, with residential and educational functions either separated or combined. A precedent was set by the opening of the LMS South Seas Academy on the Tahitian Island of Moorea (Mo'orea) in 1824, the only one of three planned regional residential schools for the South Pacific, India and South Africa to see the light of day.[47] Over subsequent decades this model of field-based residential school was replicated by both North American and British societies, for example: the ABCFM school at Punahou (1841); the non-denominational Woodstock School in India (1872); and, most famously, the CIM Chefoo schools in China (1880).[48] Other European organisations did likewise, including residential schools established by the non-denominational but largely Lutheran-based Norwegian Missionary Society in South Africa's Natal province and in Madagascar.[49]

As early as the 1820s, however, LMS missionary parents increasingly argued 'that children should be sent "home" for their education'.[50] In 1838 the coincidental opening of the Institution for the Education of the

Daughters of Missionaries, at Walthamstow north of London, and subsequently a school for boys at Blackheath in 1842, fortuitously began to
meet this need. Both were readily adopted by the LMS Board of Directors.[51]
These institutions were independent philanthropic projects that, over the
longer term, provided residence and schooling for children of a wide cross-
section of British Protestant missionary families (but especially used by the
LMS, BMS and some Scottish Presbyterians). As such they represented a
trend that would become increasingly normative, replicated in a range of
geographic settings. The CMS established a similar residence and school
first at Islington (1850) and then at Highbury in London (1853), replaced
by a larger institution at Limpsfield in Surrey (1887).[52] Other Western
missions established purely residential homes on a smaller scale – providing something of a model for the Scottish churches – exemplified by: the
Basel Mission home in Switzerland (1859); the Walker Missionary Homes
of the ABCFM in Massachusetts, USA (1870); the NMS Solbakken home
in Stavanger, Norway (1889); the American Presbyterian Westminster and
Livingstone homes, Ohio, USA (c.1893); and the Baptist Missionary children's home in Washington State, USA (1895).[53] While missionary parents
were often quick to criticise the running of these institutions, evidenced by
correspondence for the CMS Highbury home,[54] such criticism simply served
to underscore how critically important this strategy for children's support
and education had become by the 1900s.

Again, as with missionary children's policy making, there is to date limited consideration of these institutions. Existing secondary literature suggests at least two important avenues for ongoing scholarship. First, these
institutions constituted important sustaining sites of empire. This was made
explicitly clear in the report of the Blackheath School's annual prize giving
of 1899. There boys sang songs that linked missions to the existence, if not
the cause, of empire. These included specially written songs like 'Sons of the
Empire' as well as a selection from T.M. Pattison's cantata 'Britannia and
Her Daughters'.[55] The domestic provision of institutional care and education, both for missionary and other Empire children, was an important component of both what Catherine Hall and Sonya Rose elsewhere have referred
to as being 'at home with the Empire', and of the 'webs of empire' with their
'shifting linkages' explicated by Tony Ballantyne.[56] To date, this connection
with empire has been best represented by Buettner's and Brendon's focus
on British children from India domiciled in the Walthamstow complex of
residential schools, and by Semple's analysis of how English middle- and
upper-class schooling patterns were translated into the CIM's approach to
educating missionary children in China.[57]

Second, children's missionary homes also need to be considered within
the wider purview of children's institutionalisation, both in the British

metropole and across various British imperial and colonial settings. Their establishment from the mid-nineteenth century onwards coincided exactly with and gave expression to 'increasing charitable or governmental intervention, leading to a more systematic approach to residential provision and a huge increase in the number of individuals living in institutions'.[58] As Shurlee Swain recently noted, how this has been narrated and interpreted, across various imperial sites, has demonstrably changed over time. Moreover, concerns about child abuse – residential and other – and resulting commissions of inquiry for a range of geographical and postcolonial contexts continue to give the issue much-needed prominence in both new- and old-world settings.[59] Therefore, well beyond the scope of this book, a more comprehensive treatment of children's missionary homes is required which, among other things, should pay careful attention to the discursive role of place, space, adult–child relationships and colonialism among others. By way of introduction, this chapter adopts a comparative approach.[60] Selected examples help to focus on public representations of these homes and the significance of these representations for the consolidation of institutional narratives about missionary children.

Public representations

Who were the target audiences, what were they told and why? Public representations were primarily aimed at a twofold audience: domestic adult and child missionary supporters in their respective denominations, and missionary parents. In turn, these representations were most readily found in a range of print materials produced by each denomination for public consumption – namely annual reports and denominational or organisational periodicals for all ages – as well as accounts in regional or urban newspapers, especially covering annual meetings or prize-giving ceremonies. Likewise, from the beginning, their purpose was crystal clear: to galvanise public support and thus ensure the longevity of the homes. From its inception in 1850, the directors of the initial Islington home placed the responsibility for this on CMS supporters by requesting their sustained financial and prayerful support. This intention remained operative for each of the relocations to Highbury and Limpsfield.[61] Similarly, the manifesto for the Edinburgh COS home laid the responsibility for funds and maintenance on Presbyterian women and men, for whom it should be a 'duty' and a 'pleasure' both to give and to pray.[62] Because fees paid by missionary parents were in all cases subsidised, then the burden to make up the difference and provide funds for infrastructure development was ongoing. Pleas in 1931 for more funds to maintain Cunningham House, although understandable during the Depression, were typical of annual reports replicated over the longer life of all these homes.[63] Missionary children were considered to be 'Children of the Church' who legitimately had 'every claim upon our interest and help'. Where they lived also deserved to be places of 'beauty and grace'.[64] Yet the fact that quite detailed articles on these homes continued to appear in various church publications, from the 1850s to the 1940s, indicates that this was a message that needed repeated emphasis.

There were two important points of differentiation with respect to why these homes were publicly reported. One was didactic and practical, focusing on readers' spiritual welfare as much as on those of the child subjects. Alongside their informative function, magazine articles drew attention to missionaries and their children as spiritual and practical exemplars for the reader. For child readers, this was made more explicit and was turned regularly into object lessons about personal faith and active prayer. In the CMS context, the familiar format of children's sermons or children's newspaper columns (a story followed by a moral or expected action) was employed to foster other children's prayers for the homes. Typically, the Limpsfield Home matron Mrs Thornhill described the home's environment and infant inhabitants at length, finishing by asking:

> I wonder what you would do if you had no father and mother to tell all your little troubles to. I am sure you will ask God to comfort the children at Limpsfield, and their parents who leave them for our Lord's sake. It makes us very happy to think how many in all parts of this great world are praying for us, and we always believe that God loves our children, and we do want to put Him first in all things.[65]

For adult readers, the object lessons were more subtly, if no less pointedly, drawn. In reporting on both Scottish homes to Presbyterian readers in 1934, the writer mused:

> one wondered how some people could be so blind to the value of missionary work. That men and women should go out to the far corners of the earth, voluntarily separating themselves from their children, is surely a remarkable instance of the power which the message they carry exerts on them. It is in that power, as it radiates outward, that the peace, the prosperity of the world depends.[66]

Such reports had a polemical value, certainly to rally adult financial support but, just as importantly, for the wider cause of overseas missions.

The other point of differentiation was that missionary parents were also a key target audience. Articles constantly affirmed the 'pain and anxiety'[67] experienced by parents through the sacrifice of family separations. Therefore, reporting aimed to reassure them of their children's physical, emotional and spiritual welfare whilst separated. That this was expected by parents was made clear by Donald Fraser (FCS) for Cunningham House. In a post-World War I advertising leaflet, quoting a letter he wrote to the committee, he noted that 'I deeply appreciate all that the Home has done for my children. It was a constant delight to us to know how happy they were.'[68] A later article reinforced this sense of expectation when the writer thanked the matrons in charge of each of the two Scottish homes, whose efforts 'an increasing number of missionaries all over the world recognise ... with gratitude'.[69] More explicitly Beatrice Sawyer wrote that 'It is always ... of the parent one thinks.' She was mindful of the 'anxious parental heart' she addressed and, accordingly, edited her writing in order to provide comfort to distant readers.[70]

Literature for the CMS homes struck this same note of reassurance. When the new Limpsfield home opened in 1887 published reports argued that the new rural setting would greatly benefit their children. The location was chosen for its 'healthiness' (and proximity to London), with extensive open grounds and situated well above sea level. It was architecturally designed to let in light, provide spacious living areas separated from the educational spaces and accommodate different age groups and the sick. It was designed to 'secure ... the application of all the latest improvements known to be necessary for sanitation, for ventilation, and for the warming of the building'.[71] At the same time, especially from the 1900s, reporting tended to emphasise the children's educational progress. This was not surprising given the CMS institution's dual function as both residence and school. Parents were constantly reassured that high educational standards were maintained. Boys in particular were well prepared to progress on to public school education.[72] By the 1930s education was a dominant theme in representations. In 1933 the CMS Limpsfield institution was more commonly referred to as 'St Michael's' school rather than as a 'home'.[73]

Domestic stability and children's happiness

Such reassurances to parents indicate both the content of the representations and how these changed. Further, then, what were the underlying emphases and why were they significant for institutional narratives of missionary children? Primarily discussion here focuses on tropes of domestic stability and children's happiness. Elements of these have already been noted in earlier discussion. However, while an educational emphasis was evident from the beginning, so too was a focus on domesticity and well-being. The Walthamstow girls' institution proposed to 'provide for the daughters of

Christian Missionaries a thoroughly good and liberal education adapted to their talents and future prospects', and to place them in a setting which should have an 'entirely paternal character' and 'be the home of the children while under its care'.[74] This reflected wider trends as well as middle-class fears that missionary children, separated from parents and other siblings, were bereft of the benefits of family or home life. As Jane Hamlett notes for girls' private boarding schools the design and use of their residential space 'remained modelled on family life' throughout the nineteenth century.[75] Buettner makes the same observation for the Walthamstow girls' school, outlining further that the Blackheath school for boys replicated this pattern, irrespective of gender. She argues that by 'portraying itself primarily as a domestic space, only secondarily as an educational facility, and placing little emphasis on sport, [Blackheath] set itself apart from the vast majority of British boys' boarding schools' of the period.[76] This emphasis still persisted going into the twentieth century, as exemplified by the Scottish homes with their sole focus on the domestic function, to enable children to attend local day schools. Mrs Catherine Charteris, co-founder of the COS Edinburgh home, spoke for many when she stated unambiguously that the aim was to provide 'a real true home for our missionaries' children – as like as possible in warmth of love and piety to those natural homes of which their parents ... have had to deprive them'.[77] Likewise, matron Lily Wilkie narrated to parents and readers the daily routines for children living at Cunningham House, from a conviction that 'if that feeling of home could be maintained the ideal of the Church [on behalf of parents] would be attained'.[78]

The domestic home continued to be the dominant 'reference point' with respect to both conceptions and representations of British children's institutional spaces throughout both the nineteenth and early twentieth centuries. Across a wide range of institutional types, including children's homes, public representations were 'suffused' with the 'rhetoric' of domesticity.[79] In the process, such institutions 'helped to construct ideas and practices that reinforced particular social identities'.[80] This is particularly apposite when we next turn to consider how missionary children themselves viewed their place in such homes. Here, however, we need to note the second dominant trope in the homes' public representations, wherein their inhabitants were primarily construed as happy children.

Scholarship on happiness as a historicised emotional construct indicates that this was not just a modern preoccupation. Evidence of social expectations that childhood and happiness were connected is found, for example, among early modern European Jewish families and in the writings of eighteenth-century French military deserters.[81] On balance, however, happiness featured more prominently in the modern period, accompanied by an increasing connection between 'happiness' and 'pleasure' and an emphasis on happiness as a marker of 'one's effectiveness as a parent'.[82] Peter Stearns notes that this 'association' had 'gained headway in the nineteenth century … as part of the new celebration of childish innocence. By the 1890s vague ideas were increasingly focused into claims that children should be urged to be cheerful as part of a pleasant emotional demeanour that would make family life more rewarding' and that it was adults' responsibility to inculcate this through nurturing the right environment. By the 1920s this had become an embedded cultural expectation in Western societies, to the extent that this 'new adult responsibility to assure happy childhoods was a close companion to the modern responsibilities for emotional oversight'.[83] This emotional turn was linked to such factors as demographic changes in the family, the professionalisation of childhood, consumerism, changing cultural values and compulsory schooling. As such it prevailed across a range of English-speaking societies, albeit with some variations.[84]

The two tropes of domestic stability and children's happiness certainly went hand in hand with regard to missionary children's public representations. However, while missionary parents were the main focus of the emphasis on domestic stability, along with the home-based constituency,[85] the dual emphasis on happiness served to bring children and their needs more clearly into view. We have already noted that happiness emerged as a key theme in relation to missionary parents' anxieties over their children's welfare. This translated directly into the institutional narrative concerning children in the various homes. In the public rhetoric of the CMS homes, for instance, children were variously described in emotional terms as either to be 'pitied' or 'sorrowful' (accentuating both their physical and emotional dislocation) or as 'happy' or 'bright'. In this regard English Anglican children were reminded that while the Limpsfield house parents

> do everything possible to make [the missionaries' children] happy, and to take the place of father and mother to them, there must be lonely times in their little lives now and then when they long very much to fly far over the sea and have once more a big hug from the real father and a good-night kiss from the dear mother.[86]

From about the 1870s onwards, however, happiness emerged as the dominant emotional descriptor, often predicated on children's physical appearance and state of health.[87] This acted as a further reassurance for parents and emphasised to English CMS supporters that these children lived in conditions expected of the culturally prevalent affectionate or companionate modern family. The language also indicated that happiness was both an identity marker of children's character or welfare and also something that could be induced, for example, through the provision of cakes or games on special occasions.[88]

This emphasis on happiness was made much more explicit in the publicity for the Scottish homes, with the sense that children were as central to adults' concerns as their parents. The Scottish Presbyterian discourse focused on promoting happiness and maintaining a sense of normality. The stated focus of the homes was to provide a surrogate family within which children, separated from their own families, would experience companionship and emotional security among their peers. Repeatedly the wider public read that these were not just institutions but instead constituted 'a home – with just a small "h"'.[89] As such they were ideally represented as 'happy' homes or as places which fostered the pre-requisites for a 'happy family'. Closer scrutiny of the language used for the interwar period reinforces the themes to be found for the CMS home.[90] Happiness, health and environment were linked together. Likewise, being happy was evidenced in things like children's play, general dispositions towards being cheerful and shared laughter. Articles made it clear that children's happiness resulted from close attention to the physical condition, spaces and routines of the homes, as well as the little daily details normal to home life.

At the same time, children's happiness was not guaranteed. It was paired with other emotions consequent on family separation and therefore it had to be nurtured and nourished. This was clearly evident, for example, in an account written by Lily Wilkie, whose long term as matron at Cunningham House enabled her to paint a much more complex picture for her Scottish readers.[91] She described the children as having made significant sacrifices, for which she admitted candidly that 'all the love and care and sympathy we can give them does not make up for the loss of companionship of father and mother'. Hence happiness was intrinsically wrapped up with other emotions or emotional practices: sorrow and sadness, loneliness, 'desolation' and crying. Certainly, in her writing, there was an expectation that the children might achieve a degree of emotional self-control through such hardships and that 'absorbing interests' could serve to deflect such emotions. However, her account also points to children's altruism towards one another, as a result of a 'great bond of sympathy'. Happiness was thus also expressed through sympathy, compassion and empathetic kindness towards one another. In this respect, happiness, at least from an adult perspective, was tied to character building as much as a disposition, experience or practice.

This emphasis on children's sacrifice was picked up a decade later in the 1933 report for the CMS home at St Michael's. Violet Vodden suggested to a wider reading audience of English Anglican boys and girls that the home's children could rightly be 'proud of being sons and daughters of missionaries and of giving their parents gladly for the service of the Kingdom'.[92] Here the notion of sacrifice, so dominated by parental perspectives over previous decades in public discourse, was turned neatly on its head in the same way that Wilkie had done for the Scottish setting. Children, like their parents, also made a significant sacrifice. This was clearly an adult's perspective and children had other ways of articulating this. Children's perspectives will be considered further, in Chapter 5, where the concepts of emotional navigation and emotional management together provide a further critique of the happiness discourse. What is significant here, however, was an acknowledgement in adult rhetoric that children were central and that their thoughts and feelings were important.

Interwar missionary children in professional and academic discourse

This more child-centric thread began to appear more concertedly in the institutional narrative from the 1930s onwards. In 1936, American Bible Society secretary Carleton Lacy noted that the missionary in China was now variously perceived to be 'a freak, a hero, an imperialist, a martyr, a colossal trouble-maker or an ambassador of international understanding and goodwill'. However, he argued that such generalisations were misleading, citing the growing number of missionary children attending the residential Shanghai American School as evidence that 'the American missionary and his family is not to be a rapidly disappearing aspect of the Chinese landscape'.[93] Lacy's article indicated a swirl of new thinking around missions and the changing relationship between Western and emergent Indigenous Christianity in the interwar period. Questioning and critical inquiry were integral features of these years, epitomised in William Hocking's broad-ranging *Re-thinking Missions* critique of 1932.[94] Children were not central to this wider critique, nor did they feature in Hocking's recommendations. However, his narrative indicated a potential turn in how missionary children were institutionally conceived and represented and it is this turn that we are interested in here. In tune with other institutional rhetoric Hocking acknowledged that education was the key issue, which burdened both parents and organisations with 'the expense of tuition and travel'. Likewise, family separation could impact particularly on children. He wrote that separation often occurred 'at a time when children are going through difficult periods of adjustment to different modes of living, to different countries, and to different peoples. The anxiety and strain of these separations and the financial responsibilities incident to them are very great.'[95]

The early twentieth century was marked by an increasingly child-centred focus, evidenced by the growing emphasis on child welfare and protection but also by an interest in child psychology and how this played out in educational practice and civic policies.[96] Likewise, missionary children in the institutional narrative became more clearly obvious in their own right, both on the pages of newspapers, magazines or denominational reports and in university research theses that reflected the changing intellectual milieu. Although mostly American in provenance, such was the nature of Protestant missions that this literature reflected and spoke collectively to the broader spectrum of Western missionary contexts. At the same time, it indicated a growing differentiation of missionary children's perceived needs based on nationality. While this emerging discourse has been briefly commented on in the literature,[97] here this chapter more extensively outlines indicative ways in which missionary children began to be represented institutionally through a more professionalised lens.

Initially, this discourse focused on children's health, albeit often predicated on parents' ability to remain in the mission field or the missionary family's well-being. Children's health was one key element of parental narratives and therefore remained an ongoing concern in the institutional narrative. By the 1920s, however, the common-place public expectation was that a wide range of illnesses could largely be mitigated by advances in medical knowledge and should no longer count as a missionary problem. At the same time, health itself was defined in broader terms, more than just physical illness, and was linked to missionary well-being, longevity and trans-generational sustainability. This change was more than hinted at in New Zealand missionary Thomas Riddle's privately communicated concerns about the mental health of teenagers returning to America from India in the early 1930s (Chapter 2).

Nowhere was all this clearer than in a series of publications penned by American physician William Lennox between 1920 and 1933 which, in turn, were referenced by various writers over the period.[98] Known for his pioneering work on epilepsy at Harvard University, Lennox previously spent four years as a medical missionary in China[99] and as such was called upon to report on missionary health. Lennox's focus was pragmatic. In 1920 he challenged churches, through co-opted military rhetoric familiar to that period, to use 'all the up-to-date measures of preventative medicine to preserve the health of its expeditionary forces'. To do otherwise was 'wasteful' of both missionaries and their children.[100] Children were also to the fore in his 1933 commissioned report for the Foreign Missions Conference, with a dedicated chapter comparing missionary children in China and Japan with contemporary children in America. Here children appeared as statistical representations through numbers, graphs and generalisations. By his estimation child mortality was little different between mission and 'home' contexts, at least for East Asia. The only differentiation was a slightly higher mortality rate for children in China and from continental European missionary families. Where it was higher, this was primarily in the first three years of life.[101] Lennox thought that parental care and medical knowledge were fundamental to children's well-being. In his mind, children's health was as much about broader issues as it was about the children themselves. While Lennox noted that '[n]o study of conditions dealing with the lives of missionaries would be complete if their children were not taken into account', he observed that:

> In most fields children remain with their parents, and many a capable missionary has been forced to leave his assignment because of the ill health of a child. Further, these children are an important source of new recruits. Finally, in most communities the health of the children is a barometer of the health of the community.[102]

More significantly, however, Lennox's approach prefigured a nascent trend – both in institutional reporting and the emerging social sciences – that signified missionary children as a unique category. This trend was represented by a series of surveys focused on children *in situ*, their education and their adjustments between the mission context and America.[103] They included: American missionary children's life trajectories (1927) by Dr Ellsworth Huntington; American Methodist children in India (early 1930s) by the Rev Dan Brummitt; and at least two University of Chicago theses focused on American students who attended Woodstock School in Landour, India (one in 1936 by the Rev Allen Parker and the other in 1947 by the Rev Robert Fleming).[104] Here the 1947 study is especially relevant because it considered ex-missionary children who had lived in India between 1929 and 1938 and because it was conceived as 'follow up' research to that of 1936.[105] The surveys' authors represented a range of home-base, mission field and academic constituencies. Huntington was a noted sociologist at Yale University and a prominent member of the American Eugenics Society. Brummitt was active in editorial roles for the Methodist Church and Epworth League. Parker was the principal of Woodstock School and Fleming also taught there.[106] Taken together three broad observations can usefully be made from these surveys with respect to the children in their purview.

Observation: future potential or future problem?

First, they presented two apparently contradictory views: one positively portrayed missionary children as great potential for the future; the other took a more deficit view by casting them or their contexts as a problem. Missionary children were perceived to be an advantaged group when compared with their American peers, who collectively represented a 'conspicuous, persistent, and resourceful figure'.[107] Huntington pointed to their 'unusually high character' and their 'unusual ability' to 'achieve notable success', quoting from both a speech by missionary statesman Robert Speer and a survey of Yale and Harvard male graduates.[108] He cited evidence from post-high school educational statistics and the many missionary children who as adults graced the pages of *Who's Who in America*. Furthermore, he drew attention to 'cosmopolitan' interests[109] formed by their varying geographical and cultural contexts. Writing of the Indian setting, Parker noted the implications of this, albeit through a male lens:

> All of this gives him a broader outlook upon life, and his knowledge of human nature ... will be far more penetrating than that of his companions. He has seen and been associated with poverty as no westerner can ever conceive it. He has been entertained in the home of the very wealthy, witnessed gorgeous pageantry, and enjoyed the sumptious [*sic*] hospitality which can only be experienced in the Orient.[110]

Yet more negatively a substantial litany of problems was associated with missionary children's lives and experiences. Primarily these were factors that marked a child as 'different ... were he to spend his early years in the United States and receive the average training for later life'.[111] America, not the mission settings, was the *de facto* norm. This reinforced the trope of difference and deprivation already noted in public representations of missionary children. For Parker's study group of ninety-six ex-students from Woodstock School (all American), these problems were both attested to in the questionnaire responses and extrapolated from wider anecdotal evidence.[112] They included: varying degrees of isolation from other Western children; restricted mobility, especially for girls; the impact of being overly dependent on servants; exigencies of climate; clothing styles out of touch with contemporary American trends; and children's religious development.[113] Added to this list was a further grouping of problems that revolved around education (in its varying permutations), family separation and eventual cultural adjustment to America.

This latter group of issues highlighted an emerging view that missionary children's experiences, while often generic, should be further differentiated with respect to national origins. Parker argued, for instance, that the status quo of British children returning home from India for education was understandable in terms of geography, history and the 'splendid system of boarding schools' available.[114] For American children, however, this was different. Such schools either did not readily exist in America or were elitist and too expensive. He wrote that

> [m]any of the difficulties met by missionary children of former generations and much of the bitterness they have held toward their parents and the

circumstances of their early life can be traced directly to the failure of these [British colonial] schools [in India] to give children the background and training which they especially needed.[115]

Parents, therefore, expected solutions better fitted to perceived cultural needs or expectations. This pattern of rhetoric and cultural assumptions was still operative after World War II. In outlining his study rationale in 1947, Fleming acknowledged both the positive and negative scenarios above.[116] However, he broadened the scope of the issue further when he observed that his subject either 'implies that American children with a foreign background may have to face some problems of adjustment which are not in the experience of children reared in America' or that 'such children may go through phases of adjustment very similar to those of American youth'.[117] As such, he set his study within a wider body of post-war research examining American adolescents' adjustment from school to further study or work. Significantly, he also argued that his study group was not unique, in that issues of adjustment also pertained to 'many Americans abroad whose children were educated in primary and secondary schools outside the United States', and who faced the same issues of how to reintegrate their children back home again.[118] Here, perhaps, was the true starting point for the wider field of third-culture children's studies that began to emerge after World War II.

Observation: parents' critical role

In a sense, these two sets of views were simply mirror images of one another. Second, then, missionary parents were deemed to be critically pivotal within this discourse with respect to both the perceived problems and their solutions. Attributions of missionary children's success were seen as the result of parenting and home environment. Lennox's 1933 survey made this explicit by tying children's health to the 'intelligent care' shown by parents through their own medical knowledge and training.[119] Other surveys broadened the argument from health to other characteristics of children's lives. Brummitt explicitly linked successful children to 'missionary parents who ... have given their children the finest educational preparation that comes to any group of American boys and girls, rich or poor'.[120] Huntington also stressed this point but proceeded to lay more emphasis on what he termed missionary children's 'fine biological inheritance'.[121] While missionaries' selection was done rigorously and holistically, he suggested that

the most important point of all is that among foreign missionaries ... the *same rigorous selective processes apply to both fathers and mothers* [emphasis original]. Selection on both sides of the family seems to be one of the great secrets of the success of missionaries' children. All this means not only that the missionary child is very carefully trained, but that the biological material to which the training is applied is of high quality.[122]

Huntington thus made an unmistakable appeal to social Darwinism in his use of the word 'selection', outlined through an explicit eugenicist rationale. Nineteenth and twentieth-century eugenics is a complex subject, with increasingly well-documented evidence that how it played out differed between the USA and Britain on the one hand and other national or Empire-wide contexts on the other.[123] By invoking 'biological inheritance' Huntington very clearly aligned himself with the American focus on environment and parenting. In this respect, as Martin Pernick notes, '[w]hat made a trait hereditary was the parents' moral responsibility for causing it, rather than the technical mechanism of its transmission. On this view, eugenics meant not simply having good genes, but being a good parent.'[124] As such, Huntington saw missionary children as proof of his belief that 'able leaders are born as well as made', and that missionary families were exemplars of how 'high grade parents tend to produce children of high grade'. It was imperative, then, that 'there be relatively large families among missionaries, among whom both parents have been chosen through a process of strenuous selection'. For the world's sake, he argued, there was 'no greater need than that of high-grade children in high-grade homes'.[125]

Parents also bore the burden of providing solutions for missionary children's perceived problems *in situ*. Parker reiterated, in his thesis, the views of people like Speer and Huntington, which echoed the same underlying eugenicist tropes. He noted the stringency of missionary selection and 'the high quality' of the parents of whom the majority understood 'the peculiarities and problems which face them and use the best in their powers to resolve them'.[126] Yet parents were also problematic in their responses to these issues, depending on a range of dispositions. Parker clearly differentiated between 'faith missionaries' and those representing denominational boards, perceiving in the latter a higher quality of missionary parent due to mission selection processes.[127] Furthermore, he noted that parents tended to respond variously to problems and posited that this was potentially detrimental to the longer-term trajectories of children's lives. For example, parents tended to fall into one of three groups when responding to children's isolation. One group was 'only vaguely aware of their children's inherent need for companionship' and limited opportunities to play with local Indian children. They tried to 'make their children happy' by providing multiple toys and books or by emphasising relationships with adults. A second group did not take 'the problems of childhood very seriously' and gave full licence to interact with others as they wanted, including local or Indigenous children. As a result, a child might potentially become a 'little Sahib' who learnt to 'boss every situation' with serious implications for later life. The third group, in his mind the 'large majority' of parents, 'consciously set themselves to the solution of this problem' with 'varying degrees of success'.[128] Parker's thesis can be read as both a defence and a promotion of the field-based missionary boarding school. At the same time it presented a clear rationale for why parents required support through the best of contemporary knowledge and ideas about education and human development and how they might enact these ideas in their own settings. As such the research findings were aimed equally at missionary parents and their 'committees and boards in America'[129] – whose duty was to support parents and who had to consider policy implications.

Observation – missionary children as an emergent focus

In many respects, then, children were more evident in this rhetoric but still not necessarily central. In large measure, they were represented in reference to both parents and families and they existed variously as numbers, a category or a concept. The third and final observation, however, is that even so, they were now being taken seriously as a group with perceived intrinsic qualities, unique circumstances and definable issues to face. In this respect, the early research examined here demonstrated that it was drawing on contemporary empirical and philosophical understandings of education that reflected the growing interest in child or adolescent developmental psychology.[130] Furthermore, children and young people came into sight as individuals in their own right as well as a broadly defined category.

Parker and Fleming's research was arguably the first attempt to carefully talk to or learn from missionary children, albeit as survey participants at some distance from that experience. Here were the recorded memories, thoughts and feelings of 184 ex-missionary children. Certainly, they existed largely as statistical representations or as anonymously cited examples of a range of experiences and perspectives.[131] But I would argue that this was inherently significant, in that both researchers liberally used direct quotations from the ex-children's survey responses throughout their writing, thus giving their respondents a voice. It is unclear whether or not the original survey forms still exist, but if so they would constitute a valuable historical source.

Also significant were the principles underlying or informing the research. While Fleming noted that '[o]ne should see the individual in relation to the sum total of his experience', he then proceeded to argue that two equally important principles were to '[a]pproach the individual from his own point of view' and to understand that '[s]everal personality types seem to exist'.[132] It was important to him that younger people were allowed to speak for themselves without fear of being spoken for by older adults and to recognise their often widely differentiated experiences. To facilitate this, he paired macro analysis with the presentation of individual case studies, moving from the general to the case-specific. As a result, children's lives were described not just in terms of things like health or education, but also by more affective elements: speech, clothing, sexuality, relationships, leisure and religious identity among others.[133] In essence, the research added colour and diversity to public representations of missionary children's lives. It gave them an identity and allowed their experiences to be differentiated from adults and from one another.

Conclusion

In this chapter, Protestant missionary children's lives from the late nineteenth into the early to mid-twentieth centuries have been viewed through the lens of institutional narratives, focusing on the evolution of policy, missionary children's homes and the emergence of missionary children as a distinct category of concern for professionals and academics. It has addressed three underlying questions: how did churches respond to parental concerns; how far did parental and institutional narratives converge, and to what effect; and to what extent had this narrative begun to change by the end of the period? While policy developments were intermittent from the earliest decades, missionary children were more central to organisational concerns by the turn of the twentieth century. Missionary committees were forced to respond to the growing complexities of their operations and to the fact that missionaries kept having children, and in increasing numbers from the 1890s. Initially, churches made provision for the welfare of bereaved wives and children and then built children's travel or education costs into missionary employment conditions. Significant pressure for children's welfare came from denominational women at home, who were instrumental in organising on behalf of children or their parents and in representing their cause to wider Protestant constituencies. Ultimately missionary children became most visible as residents of various institutions established for them in home countries like England and Scotland, linked to parents' perceived anxieties and concerns over education. It was here that institutional and parental narratives converged most discernibly. Missionary parents' expectations of accountability from their denominations and of their children's welfare meant that most official representations of those homes continually focused on parents' sacrifice or on maintaining domestic stability, as a measure of the official response to parents' demands.

While that focus remained well into the interwar years, at the same time another thread began to develop in the institutional narrative. Through the official rhetoric of the homes there also emerged a concern about children's emotional welfare, signified most clearly in the emphasis on children's happiness. This was clearest for Scottish homes by the 1920s and 1930s, but also for English homes in the late-nineteenth century. Again, this was used to help boost the homes' profiles for domestic constituencies, accentuating the need for the infrastructure and living conditions that would provide children with the best means for as normal a life as possible. In the 1930s, reflecting the wider milieu of contemporary educational and psychological thought, this move towards child-focused rhetoric also began to appear in professional reporting and academic research. Missionary children increasingly became a focus for study and research-informed interventions in their own right, as well as this being a further response to parental concerns. Such institutional narratives were also clearly adult-led or conceived, but their significance lay in the attempt to either integrate children more centrally within the discourse around their welfare or to divine from children their experiences and concerns. In terms of this book, this latter focus is significant for the next three chapters. On the one hand, as exemplified in Parker's and Fleming's research, the intimate details of children's experiences and their perspectives on dislocation or adjustment became just as critically central to the discourse of their lives as the contours we have discerned within parents and institutional narratives. On the other hand, while children as research participants were often faceless and lumped together as a category, this was not wholly so. Case study and anecdotal evidence brought forth children's individuality. Therefore, hearing their voices, on their own terms as far as possible, is critical to the task of bringing all three narrative lenses together.

Notes

1 Editorial Committee, *Ecumenical Missionary Conference*, p. 314.
2 *Ibid.*, pp. 320–21.
3 Manktelow, *Missionary Families*, pp. 103–104.
4 Myers, *The Centenary Volume*, pp. 127, 134–36; A Correspondent, 'The Rev. J.S. Whitewright', *Times* (14 January 1926), p. 14; *The Baptist Handbook for 1927*, p. 352.
5 The following details are taken from Angus Library, BMS, BMS China Sub-Committee Minutes, Minute Book No. 4, 1901–1904, 16 December 1901, embedded letter, John Whitewright to Alfred H. Baynes, 14 November 1901.
6 NLS, Dep. 298/9, Church of Scotland Overseas Council (hereafter COSOC), Church of Scotland Foreign Mission Committee Minute Books 1869–1940 (hereafter COSFMC Minutes), Minutes for 19 November 1895.

7 Angus Library, BMS, BMS China Sub-Committee Minutes, Minute Book No. 4, 1901–1904, 16 December 1901 and 20 January 1902.

8 PRC, PM, James Gray to Mr Budd, 15 February 1938.

9 PRC, PM, James Gray to Rev. Mawson, 12 January 1932; James Gray to Mr Budd, 9 February 1938.

10 PRC, PM, James Gray to Rev. Mawson, 12 January 1932.

11 National Records Scotland (hereafter NRS), CH1/5/246, Church of Scotland Archives (henceforth COSA), Home House for Missionaries' Children Reports, 1923–1933, 25 October 1932.

12 PRC, PM, James Gray to Mr Budd, 9 February 1938.

13 PRC, PM, James Gray to Mr Budd, 15 February 1938.

14 Konrad, 'Lost', 219; 'Church Missionaries' Home, Islington/Limpsfield Common'; Goodall, *London Missionary Society*, p. 546.

15 Schulz, *Hawaiian by Birth*, p. 18.

16 Manktelow, *Missionary Families*, pp. 39–40.

17 Anonymous, 'Schools for Children of Missionaries', *The Chinese Recorder and Missionary Journal* (1 November 1910), p. 698.

18 Parker, 'An Analysis', p. 1.

19 Mullens, 'Previous Conferences', p. 370.

20 The following comments are based on Manktelow, *Missionary Families*, pp. 39–44.

21 *Ibid.*, pp. 40, 41.

22 NLS, Dep. 298/93, COSOC, United Presbyterian Church Missionary Children's Committees 1849–1938, Committee on Missionaries' Widows and Children 1849–1874, Minutes for 10 May 1849; see also Hewat, *Vision*, pp. 14–33, 193–208.

23 NLS, Dep. 298/94, COSOC, United Presbyterian Church Missionary Children's Committees 1849–1938, Ladies' Mission Committee Minute Book 1861–1938, Minutes for 26 December 1861 and 27 March 1862.

24 NLS, Dep. 298/9, COSOC, COSFMC Minutes, Minutes for 2 March 1886.

25 Hewat, *Vision*, p. 303.

26 NLS, Dep. 298/6, United Free Church of Scotland Foreign Mission Committee Minute Books 1900–1929 (hereafter UFCFMC), Minutes for 17 February 1920; NLS, Acc. 7548, Church of Scotland Foreign Missions Committee 1929–1964, Register: Education of Missionaries' Children 1901–1931.

27 NLS, Dep. 298/6, UFCFMC, Minutes for 28 February 1905; PRC, GA1 Foreign Missions Committee Series 12.3, Outwards Correspondence (Rev W. Hewitson and Rev A. Don), Outwards Letter File 1919, 'Salaries of Foreign Missionaries from January 1, 1919'; NLS, 298/6, UFCFMC, Minutes for 23 January 1906.

28 The following comments are based on Schulz, *Hawaiian by Birth*, pp. 18–30. For Hawai'i further context is given in Grimshaw, 'Christian Woman', 489–521; and *Paths of Duty*.

29 For Punahou School see further: Schulz, *Hawaiian by Birth*, pp. 69–92.

30 For the New Zealand context see: Ewing, *The Development*; and McGeorge, 'Childhood's Sole Serious Business', 25–38. For Australia see: Jackson, *Constructing National Identity*.

31 'Report of Ladies' Mission Aid Association, 1892', *Proceedings of the Synod of the Presbyterian Church of Southland and Otago*, 1866–1901 (hereafter *PSPCSO*), p. 63. This meeting was also reported to the wider public by the likes of the *Nelson Evening Mail* (3 November 1891), p. 2 and the *Otago Daily Times* (29 October 1892), p. 2.

32 Annual reports of the Ladies' Mission Aid Association, 1892–1897, *PSPCSO*.

33 'Foreign Missions Committee Report, 1898', *PSPCSO*, p. 107.

34 For wider context see such as Haggis and Allen, 'Imperial Emotions', 691–716 and Prevost, *The Communion of Women*.

35 See further: Prochaska, *Women and Philanthropy*; Macdonald, *A Unique and Glorious Mission*; Wilkie, *Weaving Vision*, pp. 47–56.

36 NLS, Dep. 298/94, COSOC, United Presbyterian Church Missionary Children's Committees 1849–1938, Ladies' Mission Committee Minute Book 1861–1938, Minutes for 27 March 1862.

37 For how this worked out in one British settler colonial context (Australia) see: Pitman, 'Our Principle'.

38 NLS, Dep. 298/94, COSOC, United Presbyterian Church Missionary Children's Committees 1849–1938, Ladies' Mission Committee Minute Book 1861–1938, Minutes for 27 March 1862.

39 Anonymous, 'Presbyterian Women's Missionary Union', *Otago Daily Times* (3 November 1898), p. 8.

40 'Report of Ladies' Mission Aid Association, 1892', *PSPCSO*, p. 64.

41 'Report of Ladies' Mission Aid Association, 1895', *PSPCSO*, p. 84.

42 NLS, Dep. 298/6, UFCFMC, Minutes for 23 January 1906.

43 'Report of Ladies' Mission Aid Association, 1892', *PSPCSO*, p. 64.

44 Anonymous, 'The Overseas Sacrifice', *Scotsman* (12 June 1930), p. 11.

45 Records for the two Edinburgh houses come primarily from: Church of Scotland, *Home-House*; NLS, Acc. 12398/78, Church of Scotland Board of World Mission (hereafter COSBWM), Cunningham House for Missionaries' Children 1919–1973; NRS, COSA, CH1/38/10/2, Home House for Missionaries' Children Reports, 1900–1947; NRS, COSA, CH1/5/245, Home House Council Minutes 1914–1922; NRS, COSA, CH1/5/246, Home House for Missionaries Children Reports, 1923–1933; NRS, COSA, CH1/5/247, Home House for Missionaries Children Reports, 1934–1947. Note further that both Edinburgh homes had a regular presence in the pages of the *Scotsman* from at least the 1900s to the 1930s.

46 NLS, Dep. 298/6, UFCFMC, Minutes for 19 November 1918; Anonymous, 'Wills and Estates: Stranraer Lady's Bequests', *Scotsman* (14 November 1918), p. 4); NLS, Acc. 12398/78, COSBWM, Cunningham House for Missionaries' Children 1919–1973, Annual Reports, 1923 and 1925.

47 Manktelow, *Missionary Families*, pp. 100–107. Also see further: Manktelow, 'Rev. Simpson's', 159–81; and Manktelow, *Gender, Power*, especially pp. 97–99.

48 Schulz, *Hawaiian by Birth*, p. 69; 'Woodstock School'; Semple, *Missionary Women*, p. 167; and Semple, 'The Conversion', 29–50.

49 Tjelle, *Missionary Masculinity*, pp. 172–73; Ask, *Dear Rikard*; and for broader context see Hovland, *Mission Station Christianity*.

50 Manktelow, *Missionary Families*, pp. 113–15.

51 *Ibid.*, p. 115; Buettner, *Empire Families*, pp. 154–55. For wider context see: Martin, 'Women and Philanthropy', 119–50; and Martin, 'Children and Religion'. The school moved to its Sevenoaks site in 1882.

52 Anonymous, 'The Church Missionaries' Children's Home', *Church Missionary Intelligencer* (August 1887), p. 505.

53 Konrad, 'Lost', 221; 'Church Missionaries' Home, Islington/Limpsfield Common'; 'The Home That Eliza Built'; 'Baptist Missionary Children's Home Association'; Anonymous, *Presbyterian Homes*; Ask, *Dear Rikard*; and Tjelle, *Missionary Masculinity*, pp. 180–82.

54 Cadbury Research Library Special Collections, Birmingham (hereafter Cadbury), Church Missionary Society Archives (hereafter CMS), G/AMc11 Miscellaneous Reports and Papers, Folder 11/1: Correspondence from Parents about Education at Home, Mrs Clark to Miss Norris, 30 December 1871; and CMS missionaries to 'Members of the Committee of the C.M.S.', 12 February 1872.

55 'Blackheath School. For the Sons of Missionaries. Imperialist Songs', *Daily News* (13 July 1899), p. 3.

56 Hall and Rose (eds), *At Home*; Ballantyne, *Webs*, pp. 14–15.

57 Buettner, *Empire Families*, pp. 154–62; Brendon, *Children*, pp. 189–93; Semple, 'The Conversion'.

58 Hamlett, Hoskins and Preston, 'Introduction', p. 2. See also: Swain and Hillel, *Child, Nation*.

59 Swain, 'Introduction', 2. For further context see: Crane, *Child Protection*; Musgrove and Michell, *The Slow Evolution*; and Sköld and Swain (eds), *Apologies*.

60 Referencing Hamlett, Hoskin and Preston's belief – contra the 'total institutions' approach of Erving Goffman and the surveillance approach of Michel Foucault (each of whom set an early agenda for analysing institutions but were too monolithic in their analysis) – that a 'comparative' and 'cross-institutional' approach helps to nuance the complexities within and between residential institutions. Hamlett et al., 'Introduction', pp. 3–6.

61 Cadbury, CMS, G/AMc10 Regulations for the C.M. Children's Home, 'Missionaries' Children's Home. Extracts from the Regulations adopted by the Committee, April 2, 1850'.

62 Church of Scotland, *Home-House*, p. 7.

63 'Missionaries' Children. Church of Scotland Home', *Scotsman* (24 November 1931), p. 6.

64 Christine Orr, 'The Home for Missionaries' Children', *Missionary Record of the United Free Church of Scotland* (January 1921), p. 366; Beatrice Sawyer, 'Happy Family: Pakistan, Africa, Arabia Missionary "Juniors"', *Life and Work* [nd], p. 56.

65 Mrs Thornhill, 'At the C. M. Children's Home, *The Children's World* (November 1891), p. 113.

66 Anonymous, 'Two Happy Homes: The Home-House, Duddingston, and Cunningham House', *Life and Work* (March 1934), p. 122.

67 This trope was commonly employed from at least the 1850s. Anonymous, 'The Missionaries' Children's Home', *Quarterly Token* (January 1859), p. 4.

68 NLS, Acc. 12398/78, COSBWM, Cunningham House for Missionaries Children. 'United Free Church of Scotland "Cunningham House"', advertising leaflet 1921.

69 'Two Happy Homes', p. 122.

70 'Happy Family', p. 56.

71 'The Church Missionaries' Children's Home', p. 506. For a broader discussion of space and materiality in residential institutions for adolescents and young adults see Hamlett, *Material Relations*, pp. 144–79; and Hamlett, 'Space', pp. 119–38.

72 The Reverend Prebendary Fox, 'Prize-Giving Day', *Church Missionary Gleaner* (December 1908), pp. 191–92.

73 Violet A. Vodden, 'St Michael's', *The Round World* (December 1933), pp. 182–83.

74 From an article in the *Evangelical Magazine* of July 1837, quoted in Pike, Curryer and Moore, *The Story*, p. 14.

75 Hamlett, *Material Relations*, p. 147.

76 Buettner, *Empire Families*, p. 159.

77 Church of Scotland, *Home-House for Foreign Missionaries' Children* (Edinburgh: Church of Scotland, [1897]), pp. 3, 6–7.

78 Lily F. Wilkie, 'The Home That Is Like Home', *Other Lands: The Magazine of the Overseas Work of the United Free Church of Scotland* (January 1922), p. 62.

79 Hamlett, Hoskins and Preston, 'Introduction', p. 11. See further: Fisher, 'Viewing', pp. 17–33; and Cottam, 'Small and Scattered', 175–92.

80 Hamlett Hoskins and Preston, 'Introduction', p. 12.

81 Berner, 'For the Pleasure', pp. 29, 30; Seriu, 'Deserters', p. 181.

82 Grant, 'Parent-Child Relations', p. 117.

83 Stearns, 'Childhood Emotions', pp. 169–70.

84 Stearns, 'Defining', 165–68; Morrison, 'Settler Childhood', p. 82. See also Hatfield (ed.), *Happiness*.

85 Replicated in other non-British locales such as Denmark, Vallgårda, *Imperial Childhoods*, pp. 181–208.

86 A.E.B., 'Prize Day at the C.M. Children's Home', *The Children's World* (November 1894), p. 166.

87 E.D., 'Our Missionaries' Children's Home', *Church Missionary Society Juvenile Instructor* (July 1870), pp. 99–106; Anonymous, 'A High Day at Highbury', *Church Missionary Society Juvenile Instructor* (August 1872), pp. 131–36; Anonymous, 'A Day at Limpsfield', *The Children's World* (November 1891), pp. 171–72.

88 'Prize-Giving Day', pp. 191–92; 'Young Folks' Corner', *Other Lands* (July 1922), p. 139.

89 For example: Anonymous, 'Missionaries' Children', *Scotsman* (19 November 1929), p. 7; Anonymous, 'The Overseas Sacrifice', *Scotsman* (12 June 1930), p. 11.

90 This section references: 'The Homes for Missionaries Children', *Missionary Record of the United Free Church of Scotland* (January 1921), p. 47; 'The Home for Missionaries Children', p. 366; 'The Home That Is Like Home', pp. 62–63; Untitled column, *Other Lands* (April 1922), p. 85; 'Young Folks' Corner', pp. 139–40; Untitled column, *Young Scotland* (January 1933), p. 110; 'Two Happy Homes', pp. 121–22; and 'Happy Family', pp. 54–57.

91 All quotes here are from 'The Home That Is Like Home', pp. 62–63.

92 'St Michael's', p. 183.

93 Dr Carleton Lacy, 'New Demands Made on Modern Missionary to China Field', *The China Press* (4 July 1936), p. B13.

94 Hocking, *Re-Thinking*.

95 *Ibid.*, p. 297.

96 See for example: Crane, *Child Protection*, p. 3; Kagan, 'Child Psychology', pp. 167–70; Peat, 'Child Development', pp. 85–87; Jones, 'Child Guidance', pp. 87–88.

97 Austin and van Jones, 'Re-entry', 315–25; Bretsch, 'A Study', 609–610; Hollinger, *Protestants Abroad*, pp. 16–17; Mason, 'Missionary Conscience', pp. 2–4; Moessener, 'Missionary Motivation', 189–200.

98 William G. Lennox, 'Wasted Lives', *The Chinese Recorder* (1 September 1920), p. 608; Lennox, *The Health of Missionary Families*; Lennox, *A Comparative Study*; Lennox, *The Health and Turnover*; W.W. Peter, 'Guard Your Health: How to Avoid Dysentery', *The Chinese Recorder* (1 July 1921), p. 495; Reginald M. Atwater, 'What Place Does Hygiene Deserve in the Christian Missionary Enterprise?', *The Chinese Recorder* (1 July 1925), p. 421; J.G. Vaughan, 'Missionary Health', *The Chinese Recorder* (1 April 1929), p. 244.

99 Obituary, 'William Lennox, Physician, 76, Dies', *New York Times* (23 July 1960), p. 19.

100 Lennox, 'Wasted Lives', p. 608.

101 Lennox, *The Health and Turnover*, pp. 176–78.

102 *Ibid.*, p. 175.

103 Note that a further commissioned study written in 1936 by Dr J.G. Vaughan ('Missionary Children: A Study of Their Problems') was not able to be accessed for this current study. For details see Mason, 'Missionary Conscience', p. 3.

104 Huntington and Whitney, *The Builders*; Huntington, 'The Success', *The Missionary Review of the World* (February 1935), pp. 74–75; Brummitt, 'The Fate', pp. 37–38; Parker, 'An Analysis'; Fleming, 'Adjustment'. A third thesis on missionary children's education was not able to be accessed for this current study: Van Evera, 'A Study'.

105 Fleming, 'Adjustment', pp. 11, 2.

106 'Ellsworth Huntington Papers'; 'American Eugenics Society – Members, Officers and Directors Database'; Baketel (ed.), *Methodist Yearbook 1921*, p. 260; 'Guide to the Parker Family Photographs'; 'Fleming, Robert Leland (1905–)'.

107 Brummitt, 'The Fate', p. 38.
108 Huntington, 'The Success', pp. 74, 75.
109 Brummitt, 'The Fate', p. 38.
110 Parker, 'An Analysis', pp. 34–35.
111 *Ibid.*, p. 28.
112 Of the ninety-six respondents, fifty-five were girls and forty-one were boys. They ranged in ages from eighteen to twenty-eight, all having been in the school in the previous decade (1924–34). All were American in origin. Note that for the total school population, typically the majority (77 per cent) were North American (with a range of other nationalities represented) and the majority (79 per cent) were from missionary families. Parker, 'An Analysis', pp. 8, 5–6.
113 *Ibid.*, pp. 28–35.
114 *Ibid.*, p. 59.
115 *Ibid.*, pp. 59–60.
116 Note that Austin and van Jones' survey of writing on missionary children 1934–86 erroneously dated Fleming's study as '1974', not '1947'. Austin and van Jones, 'Re-entry', 318, 323.
117 Fleming, 'Adjustment', p. 1.
118 *Ibid.*, p. 10.
119 Lennox, *The Health and Turnover*, p. 179.
120 Brummitt, 'The Fate', p. 38.
121 Huntington, 'The Success', p. 75.
122 *Ibid.*
123 See further Paul, Stenhouse and Spencer, 'Introduction', pp. 1–19.
124 Pernick, 'Eugenics', pp. 328–29.
125 Huntington, 'The Success', p. 75.
126 Parker, 'An Analysis', pp. 36, 37.
127 *Ibid.*, p. 36.
128 *Ibid.*, pp. 39–41.
129 *Ibid.*, p. 101.
130 See Lassonde, 'Age', pp. 219–24.
131 Fleming, 'Adjustment', pp. 84–103; Parker, 'An Analysis', pp. 10–27.
132 Fleming, 'Adjustment', pp. 5–7.
133 *Ibid.*, pp. 13–19, 23–24, 25–41, 44–50.

4

Children's and young people's narratives: life as ordinary

Rose still has the certificate that she received as a six-month-old baby, cross-ing the Equator in 1931 with her family, *en route* from Scotland to Kenya.[1] Born in Edinburgh in late 1930 while her parents were on furlough – her mother previously a nurse and father a joiner, both employed by the Church of Scotland – she spent the next fifteen years of her life in Africa as one of five children. These years involved various transitions: to Blantyre in Nyasaland where her father took up longer-term construction and trades training responsibilities; back to Scotland for a furlough in 1936; to East London in South Africa at the start of World War II; to boarding school in Cape Town for two years; and eventually a definitive return to Scotland in 1946, when international travel finally resumed after the cessation of conflict. It is clear, from her narration, that in hindsight the return to Scotland was personally premature. Southern Africa was home and Scotland, initially, was a foreign land. She fondly recalls the freedoms of Africa 'playing and the sunshine and um ... the songs of birds and it got quickly dark at night and then mosquito nets', as well as 'the sunshine and the outdoor activities'. Life in Africa was 'very nice'; 'I loved it ... but I was very sorry when I had to leave Africa ... because I loved the life in Africa and the heat and everything.'

Rose understood the inevitability of returning 'home' to Scotland. Previously she had contended with different languages and different ways of life, yet Scotland was no easy step. At school 'I could hardly understand what some of the children were saying because of their accent and up in Montrose, I mean there's a lot of them were very broad and the girl sitting next to me ... sometimes I just didn't know what she was speaking about.' She now had to learn Latin and French rather than compulsory Afrikaans ('I didn't like languages'). Furthermore, she had to adjust to 'boys in the class', experiencing coeducation for the first time. Eventually she did adjust and forged a new life (senior high school, working in a local bank, marriage and her own family). She pondered how far childhood experiences afforded her a later degree of resilience – particularly earlier adjustments to boarding school and the sense that change was the norm. Family or church rites and rituals provided continuity. Overall, Rose felt that she was 'very lucky that I had the upbringing that I did'. Her story was typical of many of those narrated orally through the Scottish and New Zealand interviews, juxtaposing daily life and a series of larger-scale adjustments or disruptions across time and space. In turn, many of the same themes emerge from other published and unpublished memoirs of adults narrating their missionary childhoods.

While Rose's view was generally positive, with a hint of lament about what she left behind, other voices emphasise negative aspects. In a moving reflection on identity, Church of Scotland minister Catherine Hepburn writes that being simultaneously 'a daughter of the missionfield, of the church and in particular the Church of Scotland' is a 'fundamental fact of my life' that 'has been a source of both joy and pain. It is highlighted every time I am asked where I come from or where I belong. The answer is complicated: I belong and I don't belong.'[2] Like Rose, growing up in Nyasaland from 1955 to 1964 was a positive experience, interpreted through 'rose-tinted spectacles' as 'the gift of my missionary childhood'.[3] Conversely her memories of coming to Scotland 'are seen through a very dark glass':

> Instead of vast expanses of sunlight, there was the learning of the word 'dreich'. Instead of the excitement of tropical storms, there was drizzle. Churches kept their doors closed, lively children were frowned upon and not a baby was to be seen being fed anywhere. It didn't feel right that congregations were mostly made up of people who all looked the same with their white-skin colour, and above all there was that great and solemn affirmation of the faith: 'We've aye done it this way!' … Settling into my father's first charge in Scotland, it seemed as if his dog-collar enclosed not only his own neck but his children too and we were thereby marked as a different order of humanity from others; and being a daughter of the missionfield as well as the manse was only an added cause of suspicion to those of my peer group who had never travelled across Scotland.[4]

Yet, like Rose, Catherine later found perspective enough to say that now 'I balance the pain of exile with the global horizons the church has given me', finding in Scotland's Iona Community 'a space where my rosebush of African mission, the Church of Scotland's burning bush and Jesus' mustard-seed tree of God's kingdom grow together'.[5]

The following two chapters together focus on a third narrative lens: the voices of missionary children in the historical record and the varying perspectives exemplified in these two narratives. The chapters converse with the previous adult narratives, paying attention to inter-narrative congruities and differences. They move to centre-stage the historical perspectives of children that do not always align with those of adults.[6] As such they

Table 4.1 Narrative thread: life was ordinary

Themes	*Indicated by details elicited on:*
Domesticity	Food, house/mission compound, relationships (family, domestic staff, mission staff), domestic tasks and responsibilities, animals, religion
Education	Home schooling, school experiences in mission contexts, school experiences in countries of origin
Recreation	Play, home/compound life, friends (expatriate and Indigenous), holidays, celebrations

pay attention to a broader commitment in childhood studies to understand 'how children have produced their own spaces outside, within and against spaces and discourses that adults constructed for them'. Their memories 'also allow us to explore how those accounts are bound together by the possibilities that one can act within available frames, such as social pressure to conform, imperatives of economic survival, or conditions given by culture, history and schooling'.[7]

This chapter teases out a commonly occurring thread through the interviews, wherein children self-narrated the idea that life was normal or ordinary (Table 4.1). Interviewees referred to such things as family life, the home, language, food, mission personnel, recreation and schooling as key elements of their childhood memories. The chapter therefore highlights representative features of these domestic lives, giving prominence to ex-children's oral memories and reflections, further augmented by other published and non-published sources. In so doing it seeks to engage further with the idea that oral history 'if sensitively used, can provide a window into how individuals understand and interpret their lives' and, in particular, its ability to provide 'a lens through which we can view remembered emotion and feeling'.[8] At the same time, notions of 'ordinary' or 'everyday life' are culturally constructed concepts that form 'highly contested terrain'.[9] The chapter argues that these experiences, while common across mission settings, differed according to things like the age of the child, family dynamics, parental disposition, cultural and political settings, decade and gender. It concludes by reflecting on the nature of memory and the role of emotional narratives in terms of their imprint on memory. Both this chapter and the next work mainly with oral and written sources that are hindsight documents which, in colonial contexts, also need to be noted for their potential to 'reinscribe or even justify imperialist or stereotypically orientalist views of empire' (see further in Chapter 6).[10]

Theme – domesticity

Religious sentiments and rationales may have shaped parents' decisions to be missionaries, but that self-understanding came later for their children. 'As a child', writes Margaret Dopirak, 'I didn't know much about how my parents met or what brought them to India – nor was I very curious about it'. It was only later, as an adult, that Margaret was more motivated to 'unravel' their stories in order to understand her own.[11] In a similar fashion, Isabel knows that her father went initially to Kenya as a missionary builder in the 1930s and met her mother already resident there, but in hindsight 'sometimes you look back on it now and wonder what was the point of it all'.[12] Instead, children's narratives tend to begin with family as the primary point of reference, focusing on people, places and activities. This is an unsurprising and natural feature of many adult reminiscences of childhood in general. British educationalist Rania Hafez neatly captures this in her own narrative by writing 'As this is about my childhood, my starting point has to be my parents.'[13] Yet perhaps there was something unique about this particular grouping of 'empire' or 'expatriate' children. In his 1947 thesis, for example, Fleming suggested that adults 'played a far greater role in the lives of this population than is true of an average American community'. In a setting like India, 'children growing up in this atmosphere [as "foreigners"] were forced to find their associates within a limited group or within the family itself'. This extended to religiously framed boarding schools, like Woodstock School, where 'relations with adults were much closer' than in America. This, along with the constant contact with many other adults transiting through missionaries' homes, meant that children could tend to be 'fairly mature in their speech, conversation, and in points of common interest'.[14]

The emphasis on family in the interviews suggests that many saw little to differentiate their younger lives in the first half of the twentieth century from their Western peers. Family rather than geography shaped early memories and identity. For Scott Gray, India in the 1920s was not at all remarkable, but simply 'where your parents were … that's all we knew and … parents are doing this and you're going with them and, and so it went on'. Veronica viewed growing up in South Africa in the 1940s in similar terms. She 'knew nothing else' and as such, 'children accept exactly what they have'. 'It's only afterwards … [that] you look at it through adult eyes and think "whoa", that was different, you know.' Janice Rowley (née Crump), growing up on the island of Nguna in the New Hebrides in the 1940s and early 1950s, mused that she did not view her childhood as different 'because I think as children, you accept what, where you are at the moment, you don't think there's anything else'. Michael repeated this same sentiment in regard to his early life in India during the 1930s.[15]

Birthplace was one point of differentiation. Rose was typical of those, like Joyce Wilkins, who very soon after birth moved overseas with their families to mission locations, which then formed the crucible for early formative memories.[16] Likewise, for others like Pat Booth, born in Shillong (Assam State, India) in 1944, mission locations fill their memories. Pat recalls 'playing with my Bengali friends, either at my place or theirs', including Shundari, daughter of the New Zealand Baptist Missionary Society's pharmacist. Family life and the compound framed her childhood, including a wider sense of family; 'I was surrounded by Kiwi missionaries who all became my honorary aunties and uncles.'[17] Often the youngest children, born in a mission context but who returned with families to their home country when very young, rely on family stories and artefacts to understand where they were born. Joan Sutherland (née Crump), aged five when the family returned to New Zealand from the New Hebrides in 1956, says that her 'knowledge … came through slides and "talks" Mum and Dad gave to various groups, and the many missionary friends who came to stay while home on furlough'.[18] Yet others moved to a mission location at a later age. Alison vividly remembers the first voyage to Africa's Gold Coast (Ghana) in late 1948, aged eight, with the uneasy mix of positive and negative emotions more commonly experienced by missionary children making the reverse journey. This family adventure included: mother and daughters crammed into unglamorous troop-ship accommodation; seasickness; performing in a Christmas pageant on board; and watching King Neptune boarding the ship at the equator 'all sea-weedy and what not'. While she remembered the voyage as an adventure, her first days in the classroom at an army school in Accra (evaluated as 'pathetic' by Alison and her siblings compared with their Glasgow schooling) accentuated a sense of being somewhere different.[19]

Family life, as anywhere, had its repetitive rhythms irrespective of location and so the details were not always easily remembered. That life was ordinary, repetitive and family-focused was underscored in a cache of letters written in 1902 by eight-year-old Willie and six-year-old Margaret Marwick in Jamaica to their grandmother and aunt in Edinburgh. Willie's diary indicated days that were demarcated repetitiously by routines and rituals – getting up, family worship and meals, going to school, personal reading and play, public attendances and family gatherings.[20] Clearly the family home in Falmouth, Jamaica, was the centre of their lives, providing emotional and physical security as well as the freedom to engage in imaginative play. For Willie, a backyard tree became a post box for posting imaginary letters or building imaginary houses, and a room in the house was reconceived as a classroom where the dollies were pupils and 'twice whipped' when a lesson was said 'wrong'. They also played at house, wherein Margaret and Willie scripted and acted out the gendered parental roles displayed daily. At night,

Willie was 'always dreaming that I am in Fairyland ... Margaret says her bed is turned into a white carriage with white horse & mine is changed into a white horse with brown on its back'.[21] Such imagination was nurtured by books, gifts from Edinburgh, and by the parents' involvement in their children's lives.

Two further observations for the Marwick children are apposite. First, home life was richly experienced and existed independently from their Jamaican locale. Willie and Margaret seldom wrote about the environment or people beyond their fence line, although they did move about quite freely and visited places like Kingston and Montego Bay. Jamaican people or elements were mentioned infrequently. Willie wrote about 'huge breadfruit trees, mango trees, Cocoanuts [sic], tamarind & a great lot of flowers'. Margaret wrote that they toasted Grannie's birthday with 'tamarind juice at dinner today'; they ate sugarcane for special treats; and sometimes mentioned their buggy driver but not by name.[22] Mostly they wrote about daily life as they experienced it. Occasionally there were hilarities, as when Margaret described Willie at the dinner table swallowing a banana whole for a joke, rendering the others helpless with laughter.[23] Otherwise, life was mundane and experienced in the moment in terms that would resonate with their Edinburgh readers. Second, family for both children primarily consisted of their immediate parents, their siblings and their close kin in Edinburgh. Returning there in 1904, the two children then lived with their paternal grandmother and aunt while going to school. Their Jamaican letters thus reveal emotionally sustaining family bonds that were maintained over a significant distance of space and time.[24] Their time living in Jamaica may have been perceived simply as an adventurous sojourn, with life in Edinburgh (before and afterwards) viewed as more important and significant in the longer term.

Both house and compound reinforced family as the primary reference point and often geographically defined or circumscribed children's daily lives. Rebecca Terry, living in Shanghai in the early to mid-1930s, recalls the 'massive missionary homes' of the American Presbyterian compound designed to emulate family houses in San Francisco or New York.

> They were three storey red brick structures with wide verandas, large enough to handle half a dozen mosquito-netted cots when summer got blistering ... The halls and staircase were simply huge. I could mount the banister upstairs and slide all the way down around the curve and land with a plop in the front hall. That center [sic] hall branched off with a smaller one along side [sic] and under the stairs – enough room to store six bicycles ... In winter the house was heated by fireplaces, four up, four down, two on each of the four chimneys.[25]

Such size also afforded Rebecca the luxury of finding her own private space. Under the eaves, in a third-floor attic storage room, she explored the contents of her parents' travel trunks and experimented with writing her first novel. All of this was remembered fondly, underscored by the poignancy of returning to the compound in 1938, after the occupying Japanese forces had burned everything down in 1937, leaving 'piles of white-burned bricks, green globs of melted window glass, and four chimneys towering over the rubble'.[26]

Rebecca was American and her context reflected domestic expectations that were shaped in a particular period and cultural milieu. Yet this same theme resounds through British world children's recollections, in the process revealing links between architectural space and imperial or colonial attitudes of the period.[27] Robin S.'s family inhabited a 'sizeable' house with a small garden in Ajmer, India.[28] He and his older brother re-joined the family in 1940 to escape wartime Britain and, as an eight-year-old, he very quickly made comparisons with the cramped English urban spaces previously inhabited. Multiple large rooms, many with specific functions, loom large in his memory along with a sense of embarrassment over the house's size, when he brought home a boarding school friend from a less well-off family. Such memories transcend geography: Joyce remembers that 'we all lived in separate, really big Edinburgh stone houses' in Mukden, Manchuria; Rose and family lived in a 'big house' with a 'big garden' in Blantyre, where 'all the mission houses were quite big'; Veronica, born in South Africa in 1948, gleefully remembers the 'huge verandas' along which they would 'fly up and down … in our pedal aeroplane'; and Janice Rowley talked about a big, sprawling wooden house in the New Hebrides that afforded space for visitors but which, on a later visit as an adult, felt much smaller.[29] The spaciousness of the house was augmented by the garden and, often, by its location within a wider domestic or institutional compound. Gardens added colour to children's lives, as well as serving more pragmatic functions like growing vegetables. One person recalled that the garden was inhabited by local fauna ('pet rabbits' or 'parakeets') and provided work for local people. This seemed 'all quite posh'. In more extreme climatic environments, like Rajasthan, gardens were less sumptuous and more precarious. Robin S.'s mother drilled into her children the need to keep the gate closed at all times, to protect her small-fenced flower garden from 'wandering goats'.[30]

Robin S.'s memory instructively indicates that the fondly remembered family home, while often congruent with Western domestic geographies, was also a place that could be very different (if only apprehended in later life). One example was the juxtaposition of the domestic missionary family with its local or Indigenous household staff. Here we note briefly that household staff often limited what domestic duties some missionary children were expected to do, which contrasted sharply with the home lives they would have lived in the West. Likewise, this served to complicate their own domestic expectations as adults. Children perceived their domestic environment as both familiar and different. Over many years Kirsten moved from an apartment block in Aden, Yemen, shared with a local family (pejoratively remembered as surrounded by sand) to a larger detached house in Mombasa, Kenya with a garden, huge baobab tree and a nearby mangrove-filled creek.[31] David, growing up in central Japan in the mid-to-late 1930s, lived in a simple house built by his father, in keeping with local architectural styles, that included straw matting and a deep fire-heated bath in which he luxuriated as a child (an experience remembered warmly).[32] Alison recognised how different her Gold Coast domestic spaces were, compared to Scotland, commenting that 'it was just such a different world somehow … when you're living in a house that's all open around the edges, more like camping in a way'.[33]

In this regard, the rhetoric that 'life was ordinary' was partly subverted by the stories told. Living in houses and compounds that were physically bounded and yet also 'open around the edges' was a variable experience for children, depending on location, gender and age. Often houses had to be shared with other missionaries or visitors and, particularly in African and Indian settings, still did not have all the amenities by the 1950s. At age ten, Alison mastered the skill of carrying 'a sizeable bucket of water on my head', emulating for fun the daily tasks of household servants. Of greater weight, in her memory, was the trip to a town where they stayed in a vacant house. All the furniture had been packed away in storage, yet the house had one outstanding feature – a luxurious 'flush toilet'. In a similar vein, arriving in Scotland in 1938 as a six-year-old, Robin S. pronounced in fluent Hindi to his grandmother on first sight of a flush toilet, 'that is a wonderful contraption'.[34]

Houses might be strongly built or positioned safely behind compound walls, but for some children, the notion of being 'open around the edges' engendered fear. Isabel (born 1938) remembers her family home at Loudon, Nyasaland, and her night-time fears about local wildlife. She recalls

> a big veranda and bedrooms and … down three steps to the kitchen at the back of the house. I can remember that vividly, because between the kitchen and the rest of the house there was a space open to the ground below and I used to be petrified when I was younger that lions, which you could hear roaring during the night, would come under the house and through that space and into the bedroom. But then I had a mosquito net and I used to think that's fine, it would keep me safe [chuckle].[35]

She revisited the house as an adult and found, to her amusement, that this space was only six inches wide. Yet other invaders were more troublesome, including mosquitoes, 'bed bugs' that would infest the wicker furniture and the parasitic putzi fly that laid eggs in clothing.[36] In the face of such threats, Murray Crozier reflects that, from a child's perspective, a bedroom mosquito net 'made such a little world to oneself', providing protection from 'all the flying insects and all the imagined ghosts of the night'.[37] Sometimes, too, what parents thought was just a child's vivid imagination turned out to be real. In Rajasthan in the late-1940s, Jim had to persuade his father that there was something under his bed and that he was not having a nightmare. He was proved right. His father found and had to get rid of a poisonous snake.[38]

Jim's childhood further exemplified the porosity of domestic boundaries. In the process, his story also provides a partial counter-narrative to parental or institutional emphases on children's safety and welfare that were so prevalent in the published historical record. He remembers around the age of seven being allowed to 'wander about the streets and roads and byways of this place. I would be the only European. I would never meet another European boy or girl. Of course I was fluent in Hindustani but nobody thought anything about this. It was not thought to be dangerous.' He went on to reflect that with 'the benefit of hindsight and thinking of my own children my blood almost freezes at this and yet I came to absolutely no harm'.[39] Such parental licence occurred often for those growing up in India or southern Africa, but less so for places like Manchuria where political turmoil and warfare created complications. The Church of Scotland compound in which Dawn lived in Mukden had secure gates and guards on patrol.[40] Gender was also a factor. Young boys seemed to gain such freedom more often, although dictated by context. In the New Hebrides, brother and sister Donald and Janice each recount stories of regularly playing with Melanesian friends in a local village. For Janice, this was not surveilled during the day. Yet Janice was censured for her actions: 'I was not allowed to go to the village after dark and on the one occasion that I did, received a smart tap on the bottom with a rolled-up *Outlook*. My feelings were hurt more than anything else.' In the interview Janice revealed further that it was her father who dispensed the discipline, that it was a 'whack' rather than a 'tap', but she offered no reason for the night-time curfew and whether or not it applied just to her as a girl.[41]

Age, parental dispositions and historical period were further factors in the extent to which the world beyond house or compound was accessible. Both Ian and Scott Gray recounted bicycle trips as younger boys to the local bazaar in Jagadhri, northern India, to buy butter, but always in the company of household staff. Another India resident suggested that busy parents often left younger children to their own devices or in the care of staff. The increasingly common experience of missionary families or compounds having a motor car also made a difference in where and how far children ventured.[42] After 1945 missionary lifestyles began to afford new opportunities. For a girl like Alison, coming from the strictures and dangers of war-torn Glasgow, African life felt much freer; 'I loved all of the Gold Coast freedoms.'[43] Life in tropical Africa was in her view much better and far less dangerous.

Finally, here, some comment on the place and perception of religion. Fleming argued – for his India study participants – that because religion was a key factor in their geographical location, then 'the emphasis on religion in the homes of this population was rather central', and tended to mirror patterns of their middle-class American peers.[44] Yet, children did not always say a lot about this, at least not in regard to their family environment. Because religion was 'central' to family identity then perhaps it was seen as just another element of 'life as ordinary', part of the warp and weft of daily life, the details of which were either easily lost or glossed over. Typically Willie Marwick, in Jamaica, almost nonchalantly mentioned attending 'worship', reading the Bible or going to 'open air meetings' in his letters to Edinburgh without further commentary.[45] Likewise, Fleming's American ex-children – Baptist, Methodist and Presbyterian – recalled mundane details without elaboration: family and household routines (prayers, devotions and mealtime grace), church services in either English or local dialects and sabbath restrictions on games or travel.[46] More reflectively Dawn attributed always having a 'strong belief in God' to her childhood years and the missionary context.[47] In a similar vein Scottish theologian Thomas F. Torrance, growing up in China between 1913 and 1927, wrote that 'through my missionary parents I was imbued from my earliest days with a vivid belief in God'. This inherent belief was bolstered and sustained through his father's modelling of scripture memorisation, family prayers and hymn singing. These 'nourished our spiritual understanding and growth in faith' as children and cemented in him a deeper understanding of his parents' missionary motivation and task.[48]

Occasionally other colourful images emerge. One of Robin S.'s brothers recalls Anglican Christmas services in Ajmer and being entranced by the carol 'O Come, O Come Immanuel', to the extent that he was routinely transported back to boyhood Ajmer whenever he heard it as an adult. Younger brother Alan's recollection was less charitable: 'I didn't like the Anglican Church because they put the lights out during the sermon & I couldn't see to draw!'[49] Catherine Hepburn (Nyasaland) vividly and positively remembers, in the late 1950s, 'open-doored and full churches with people free to come or go … breastfed babies and lively children everywhere and welcome … the rhythm of the music and dance, the colours of difference – black, white and brown – in the one congregation'. There were also 'times of pain, anxiety and grief; but even my first funeral at the age of six was an experience of deep sorrow set in the perspective of Easter joy as the whole congregation moved to the graveside singing resurrection hymns'.[50] Pat Booth, a decade earlier, also valued the imprint of the local or Indigenous on her early religious formation. She attended morning prayers in the New Zealand Baptist compound with her father, where she 'learnt to recite the Lord's Prayer in Bengali before I learnt it in English (*Ahmahdher Shawgoshtaw Peetha*)'. At Christmas, everyone decorated their homes with oil lights or candles, 'copying the local tradition of Divali, the Hindu Festival of light', and the whole compound community sat down together 'to eat a *Bohraw Bhoj* (big feast) of goat curry and rice, served on bamboo leaves' (later supplemented by a 'Kiwi meal, put together from food parcels from New Zealand').[51]

At the same time, children gave voice to other twists on this theme. Isabel mused that her childhood religious observance was more a matter of obligation than conviction: 'I suppose my parents being missionaries you sometimes felt that you attended church merely not to let them down in any way without necessarily enjoying it.'[52] Children could also be resistant. Thirteen-year-old Albert Barnes, from an American Christian & Missionary Alliance family in Argentina, recalls how he and his brother were put on the spot to publicly pray in a service while visiting a local Baptist church in 1939. While all eyes were closed his brother quietly walked out and Albert in a moment of panic 'got up, and also left the church'. They did not tell their parents at the time, but many years later this tale evoked a good deal of laughter among the family.[53] While some parents were perceived as being religiously prescriptive, others were remembered in more appreciative terms. Kirsten's reflection stands out in this respect. While she is now a person of faith, at the time

> my mum and dad did us proud 'cos a lot of people that I know who are born and brought up in Christian homes have been put off Christianity because of certain things. My mum and dad never forced us to have a faith but they gently went about it and encouraged us and have been very supportive of everything we [have] done.[54]

Therefore, children's experiences of and reactions to religion realistically fell along a spectrum, from that of Kirsten to the much more pejorative stance taken by Ida Pruitt in China who, as a child, was already unimpressed by the Christianisation of Chinese practices and religious spaces.[55] Furthermore, hindsight and memory focused such experiences through the lens of feelings, resulting in emotionally configured narratives about missionary children's religion that could be complex and highly individualised.

Theme – education

Missionary children's education, as noted already, was always a major concern for parents and supporting denominations or organisations. It was also a central feature of how ex-missionary children subsequently narrated and reflected on their lives. For those children from the 1870s onwards, this expectation and feature were further amplified by the concerted push in most Western societies for national systems of free, comprehensive and compulsory primary and later secondary schooling. As a result '[s]ince the nineteenth century, childhood has been significantly constructed around notions of the schooled child'.[56] In this respect school and education played as central a role for missionary children as they did for their Western peers, but in a variegated fashion. Within one educational lifetime, missionary children could experience schooling in a complex range of local, regional, national and international settings. Here the focus is on children's local experiences of and reactions to primary education, which to date is less emphasised in scholarship compared with the high school experiences that tend to dominate fictional and non-fictional literature.[57]

Schooling experiences are threaded through missionary children's accounts as normative. Willie and Margaret Marwick's 1902 letters accentuated this theme, as well as the ordinariness of it, by simply describing without further commentary lessons taught, books read and occasionally teachers by name. Typically, Willie regularly did 'sums for 1 hour then read in the bible, do writing, learn spelling, say bible, & learn to say history & geography'. In the afternoons it was 'spelling for the next day, & read in the green book I told you about'. On certain days these were interspersed with lessons on 'history & grammar', 'learning tables' and 'written dictation'.[58] Both children were matter-of-fact and implicitly positive about their experience. Education was a foundational cultural value in the Marwick family.[59] Their letters, for example, suggest that their mother carried on school-like activities at home during summer holidays, requisitioning the missionary manse's study as a substitute schoolroom.[60]

This normative experience tended to occur in one or more of four modes for primary-aged children: local schooling, home-based schooling, weekly boarding or seasonal schooling in hill stations or holiday locations. One further mode, attending school while with their families on missionary furlough, will be considered in Chapter 5 because of the disruptions such experiences often engendered for children. As a foundational experience, schooling even endured through the exigencies of war. Joyce and Dawn, forced to leave Manchuria in 1941, sojourned with their families for three years in Vancouver where, for the most part, they each remember positively attending a Canadian day school. For others, that experience was less happy. Children interned with their families by Japanese occupying forces in China carried on a semblance of schooling within the camps. Others, like Faith and Christopher Cook, were removed far from harm's way in China and spent the war years unhappily at the St Andrew boarding school in Kalimpong, India.[61]

Only very rarely did children in this period attend school alongside local children. This separation is noted by Stephanie Vandrick, for example, in analysing North American memoirs, especially in the Indian context.[62] Racial mixing in educational settings was possibly more acceptable for pre-school-aged children and was more commonly referred to by children attending school after 1945, in a rapidly decolonising empire. As a pre-schooler, Pat Booth joined in afternoon sessions at the local mission school with her Bengali friends, but only because 'I must have been driving my mother crazy'. A photograph shows her as the only white face in her Sunday school class of 1947. Later boarding at Mt Hermon School in Darjeeling, from 1949, she was among predominantly non-European children. Kirsten, attending St Augustine's School in Mombasa aged ten, recalls being the only 'white girl in the whole school complex' and named both Kenyan and European girls as her friends.[63] In the Belgian Congo (Democratic Republic of the Congo), late 1930s, Robin W. thinks that his older brother attended 'nursery school along with other African kids' and that this open attitude reflected their parents' determination to open their home to any and everybody.[64] Therefore mixing, or lack of it, was variously a factor of context or politics (see further).

The decision to attend a local school, to home school or to board reflected a mixture of parents' Western attitudes towards or expectations of education as well as issues of geography, access and sustainability. The experience of the Allan family in Bolivia – wherein Mary with children Margarita and Joe spent seven years in La Paz for their schooling while her husband George lived apart several days' horse-ride away – was typical of the compromises made.[65] For some children the decision was easy. Rose attended a school for European children attached to the Blantyre mission; in her case, this was a school complex built by her father. She vaguely remembers a sole teacher who was 'very good' and a dictionary won as a prize for a gardening competition. In hindsight, she remembers more about her high school years.[66] Other children sometimes had no choice. Ron Malcolm attended school at Chefoo in eastern China as a day pupil from about 1916 to 1923, simply because both of his parents (CIM missionaries) taught in the two high schools along with a maternal aunt.[67] For many children, however, home schooling for their primary years was the preferred option, as parents perhaps put off the inevitable separation looming for high school education.

In this respect, the domestic spaces of the home were important sites of early education. Many mothers were qualified and experienced teachers, reflecting middle-class gendered vocational patterns of the period, and actively taught their children. Louisa, initially home schooled at Livingstonia, Malawi, in the early 1940s, referred to her mother as 'a primary school teacher, actually a very good school teacher', who later was the 'temporary head mistress' at the Blantyre school before the end of the war.[68] There were exceptions to this gendered pattern; in Mukden, Joyce's father taught her siblings science subjects.[69] However, parents as teachers were both a bane and a blessing for their children, and in hindsight, this was remembered with feeling. One New Zealand girl in northern India remembers her mother's relatively relaxed approach to their home schooling. She had to knuckle down and work through the correspondence school materials but recalled that 'my mother used to let us go and play after we finished our lessons'. This contrasted with a neighbouring family whose children 'had to sit, have lessons from 9.00 to 3.00', replicating a Western primary school day of the 1930s.[70] Marie's experiences were remembered differently. She was home schooled in Pakistan in the late 1940s. Her teacher mother came from Skye and was keen for the children to learn Gaelic. The outcome, however, was that 'I remember us all three [children] bursting into tears because we were also learning Urdu, which is the formal and written language of Pakistan [but] we were largely speaking Punjabi which is the oral communication of all the people … [and] we just couldn't cope with it'.[71] The emotional imprint on memory is also clear for Ian Gray. Later a teacher himself, he remembers as a six-year-old that his teacher mother administered at home 'lessons sent by the Correspondence School in New Zealand'. For her, education was 'the next virtue to Godliness'. But it was not all easy:

> Mum and I were sitting in an old double school desk on the verandah and I was having trouble memorizing my multiplication tables. Both of us were in tears of frustration. Schooling in Jagadhri was an intense exercise and I am sure influenced my approach to learning and classroom teaching in later years.[72]

Ian's reference to 'correspondence school' is significant. While the details are lacking, it is clear that home schooling could only be sustained by parents for a limited time and that they required further support. From about age seven, Louisa clearly remembers a transition whereby her mother 'realised she needed … a more structured format for me', to better prepare her for higher education, and that 'she got that from a correspondence course'.[73] This concern for children's further education was uppermost in many parents' minds and propelled them towards other means of support. Scottish children like Marie, Dawn and Joyce referred specifically to materials from the 'PNEU', but with little further understanding of what this meant.[74] Others, like Ian Gray and Michael (Scotland), mentioned 'correspondence school' materials or 'some kind of publication which was for home education'. Dorothy Kirk (New Zealand) specifically remembered that in China her early schooling 'was done by my mother, under an overseas system developed by the P.N.E.U. ... & I was soon able to read, write & do sums'.[75] Each reflected particular national differences.

The PNEU was the Parents' National Educational Union, which began in Northern England in 1892 and owed its existence and philosophy to English educationalist Charlotte Mason.[76] In part it was both a response and complementary to the comprehensive, compulsory schooling expectations of late-nineteenth-century England, providing families with systematic materials shaped by modern educational thinking to prepare children at home for secondary and higher education. In hindsight, Dawn thinks that both she and her teacher mother struggled with the new ideas and methods expressed through these materials. For example, 'we weren't supposed to learn the tables, the multiplication tables off by heart', which she thinks has hindered her throughout life.[77] Christina de Bellaigue argues further that the PNEU specifically attracted the attention of clergy and missionary families in the 1900s because of its 'inter-denominational' and 'inter-faith appeal' and therefore gained support in such imperial settings as Australia and Ceylon. She notes that the PNEU had 'particular appeal for families who wanted to keep their children with them'.[78]

Elsewhere similar initiatives were adopted but for different reasons. The New Zealand Correspondence School was established in 1922 to support children located in remote, rural parts of the country unable to attend primary school. In 1914 Victoria was the first Australian state to institute similar correspondence schooling for remote pupils. By the 1930s these institutions also supported expatriate children overseas. In 1938, for example, the 2,300 children catered for by the Victorian correspondence school included 'missionaries' children in China, India [and] the South Seas'.[79] These initiatives provided the children with partially remembered educational materials. At the same time, they also reinforced public perceptions, in the media, of missionary children as geographically and metaphorically 'marginalised'. Yet this was not children's self-perception of who or where they were. Going to school or learning was deemed by them to be 'normal', irrespective of location.

Children and parents also shared one other educational space – that of the hill stations and other 'hot season' locations where children attended a range of expatriate schools, especially in India. Typically, as recounted by one ten-year-old New Zealand girl at Woodstock School, 'I went up and boarded for the first part of the year and then when mum came up to the hills I was with her and then I boarded again at the end of the year.' She proudly recounted that she 'received a certificate for being at school every day of the year'.[80] Mothers often moved semi-permanently, maintaining a second household in these localities where some children boarded at a school and the others lived at home. This was the experience, for example, of Robin S., Alan and another brother who attended the Lawrence School at Mt Abu, Rajasthan. They were day pupils, living with their mother who rented a house from the Irish Presbyterian Mission. Their father, as did many others, joined them for the summer holiday months, temporarily bringing the family together.[81] Jim's mother, a teacher, taught at Woodstock, allowing the family reduced school fees. She kept a house and Jim's brother, younger by three years, lived with her as a day pupil. Jim boarded, remembering initial but very brief bouts of being 'exceedingly homesick' prior to his mother's relocation to Landour. More important was a 'Primary Two' teacher who helped him to develop memorisation techniques and effectively introduced him to codes and ciphers (significant in that he later had a long career as a computer programmer). Overall, Jim recalls Woodstock fondly as 'wonderful' – a 'boy's paradise'. But his younger brother's memories of these years, he thinks, were 'not particularly great'.[82]

Missionary children's primary schooling, especially *in situ*, remains understudied. Two further observations are apposite for this present discussion. One is the impact of politics on children's early educational experiences. Felicity Jensz and Hanna Acke helpfully distinguish five levels or modes wherein missionaries might function as 'political actors' – 'as individuals; as congregations or local nodes of supra-regional religious groups; as missionary organisations; as denominations; and as nations'[83] – which in turn, by implication could also have an impact on children's experiences. Three examples illustrate the complexities for children. First, a mix of family cultural values and nationalism could both define and circumscribe children's schooling. William Marwick's insistence on the children being largely educated in Scotland, in the early 1900s, was more generally the norm for British missionary parents. At the same time, it also reflected family-specific factors, namely a high view of the Scottish educational system and a love of Scottish literature. It can be seen, for example, in William's lauding of George Macdonald's poetry and of the 'Scotch' language to son James and his oft-expressed hopes that George would live up to older brother Willie 'to follow in his footsteps' and to 'do well'.[84] There ran a longitudinal seam through the wider Marwick family's history, focused specifically on attendance at the George Watson merchant colleges in Edinburgh and represented through the schools' prize lists and wartime memorial boards.

A simple encounter for Dawn, in 1930s Manchuria, provides a second example, illustrating how children were unwittingly caught up in wider political tensions. Her mother home schooled the children in the mornings and taught English in the adjoining mission school (where Dawn's father and a Chinese teacher, 'Uncle Charlie', were joint headmasters), leaving the children free. One afternoon, over the fence between their home and the school, Dawn cheerfully read English-language stories on request to some of the Chinese boys. They were caught: 'Uncle Charlie was not pleased, like Charlie was a joint headmaster and no, no this wasn't done.'[85] Dawn referred to this incident while outlining her rare contact with any Chinese people apart from their cook's daughter. Here, however, there were possible layers of complication for a young girl in 'Uncle Charlie's' actions that she barely perceived at the time. Was he embarrassed that Chinese boys were being taught by a white girl? Had she transgressed unspoken gender boundaries? Was he fearful that the real arbiters of power, the Japanese military, would find an excuse to shut down or take over the school? A simple moment of joy thus became highly problematic for a missionary daughter, one which perhaps reinforced in her mind enduring notions of national or cultural difference. Dawn emphasised, at a number of points, that being 'British' has been the abiding imprint of her missionary childhood years.

Complex political settings could also frame children's actual educational experiences, as in the third example. Veronica grew up in a Church of Scotland family working among the Venda People of northern South Africa in the 1950s, until her return to Scotland at age nine. Circumstances dictated that she must attend primary school thirty miles away, at an Afrikaans medium school, as a weekly boarder with a German Lutheran family. Under apartheid, she thinks that her parents may have been imprisoned if she attended the local mission school. Neither could Veronica be home schooled, as her parents wanted, because her mother 'didn't speak Afrikaans and so she couldn't teach us Afrikaans', which was a compulsory subject. All of this she accepted, along with the multi-cultural and multilingual competencies developed: 'Talk about cross cultures, you know. Sort of Scottish one at home and playing with African kids, Afrikaans for school and German for home time with the German missionaries. You know you just learnt to cope with it all.'[86] As the next section elaborates, her play was also framed by geographical and political context.

The second observation draws attention to modes of informal education that were constitutive for children's lives. Olsen rightly argues for a wider history of informal education, particularly for this period in which state-sponsored compulsory, formal and increasingly prescriptive education fast became the Western norm. Such a history could include, among other things, a focus on 'everyday interactions of children with each other' as well as 'with their parents and other authority figures'. In particular, she notes the 'power' of informal education to 'fill the gaps left by the formal educational curriculum' while at the same time 'appealing to wholesome pleasures and "positive" emotions like joy'. This more 'holistic' approach, she suggests, 'connects informal education to enculturation and the acquisition of the "correct" emotional toolbox' for children and young people.[87] While Olsen's focus is on 'emotional training' in relation to citizenship and nation-making, in the context of this present chapter the concept helps us to consider how else missionary children were or were not educated in the broader sense of the word.

Two brief examples are at least suggestive of this line of enquiry. One is the poignant retelling of an early childhood experience by Joyce Wilkins in India in the early 1900s that indicates the power of such informal learning to shape and entrench childhood (mis)understandings of God and self. On Sunday evenings she and her sisters remained at home with their ayah Emily, while their parents attended a regular church service. Joyce and Emily shared a secret. Emily could speak English, unbeknown to their mother, and on Sunday evenings she and Joyce would converse together in English. Emily taught Joyce orally all the verses of Augustus Toplady's hymn 'Rock of Ages'. In the process Joyce misheard various words, and thus erroneously committed to heart such phrases as 'cleanse me from its *guilty power* (guilt and power)', '*knot* the labour of my hands (tie a knot in all I try to do) / Can fulfil *MY Lord's* demands (Thy laws demands)', and 'when *mine eyelids burst in death* (now, "my eyelids close in death") / when I *saw the* realms unknown (soar to)'. Those misconstrued words remained with her into adulthood, but as a child, the hymn held a 'horrid fascination for me, with feelings of terror conveyed by the imagery and an awful sense of guilt for my own wickedness and for the fact that I was deceiving Mother by speaking to Ayah in English'.[88] The fact that this instance of informal education was also interracial was not commented on further by the adult Joyce, although her stated childhood sense of guilt suggested an implicit awareness of hierarchical transgressions.

The other example of informal education comes from Fleming's study of ex-students from Woodstock, recounting their perspectives on sex education gained as children and adolescents in the 1920s and 1930s. By this period approaches to formal sex education globally were shifting towards more 'age-stratified lines' in which adolescence was identified as the prime time both of 'physical and emotional upheaval, and also the time for an education on sexual desire'.[89] By the time Fleming's participants were at school in India, American schools and curricula were becoming the usual channels for such education. However, sixty-four of the eighty-eight participants considered that they had received inadequate 'sex knowledge' at the point of return to America and indicated that what they did know came just as much from other sources as from their formal schooling.[90] Woodstock school was adjudged to be lacking in this respect. In one person's view, 'My parents and the whole set-up there (Woodstock) were no help. I was a babe in the woods on that subject when I first came to U.S.A.' Another assertively claimed that 'Woodstock falls down badly on this point' and that this was 'one of the most reprehensible lacks at Woodstock'. This was not isolated. Other memoirs pick up this same theme of under-preparedness for life from other mission school contexts.[91] Fleming's participants' responses suggest that they learnt informally from books, talking with one another and from subsequent first-hand experiences in America. This was probably no different from many of their Western peers, in that co-existing formal and informal modes of sexual learning were the norm. Fleming notes this but adds that the lives of youngsters growing up in the complex overlapping cultural contexts of evangelical Christianity, controlled boarding school and conservative Hindu India could be much 'more complicated'. They represented a group of young people who were 'sheltered to some degree from sex conversation of the street and that heterosexual development was hedged about with certain restrictions at home and at school. The chief difference seems to be the rather sharp change which this population experienced upon returning to America.'[92]

Theme – recreation

Going to school and time spent learning were important, but not always uppermost either as a childhood priority or in adults' recollections of what they did as children. With some hilarity Janice Rowley recalled that while she regularly had school in the mornings with her mother, on the island of Nguna, other activities proved more enduringly attractive: 'I used to say to mum oh if you had a bell like they have in New Zealand, I'd come to school, I don't think that really worked either [laughter], I'd be off to the village like a shot [laughter].' Siblings Donald and Joan were her home playmates, as were the daughters of a French family 'down the road'. But most of her time, she thinks, was spent with her New Hebridean friends, either around the house or in the nearby village. Their time together was spent 'catching birds [laughter], swimming, I don't know, just what kids do I s'pose … yeah, um … climbing trees'. She still remembers her friends' names – Emma, Mercy and Dosunday – and remains in touch with one of them over sixty years later.[93] Similarly, thinking about her younger years in Pakistan in the late 1940s, Marie's enduring impression of her earlier years is of 'a lot of play because I think that's what we did most of the day'.[94] This emphasis on leisure time emerges particularly from the interviews, although not absent in written memoirs, and reflects the potential of oral history to elicit mundane features of everyday life, such as recreation, that often leave a 'minimal trace in the archives'.[95] Elements of this have been commented on throughout the chapter. Here a brief focus on recreation helps to differentiate children's daily lives further and to accentuate again the impact of context and politics.

What constituted recreational time, places and pursuits for missionary children was highly variegated. It ranged the complete spectrum from the Crump family sitting on the veranda after the evening meal, singing together 'Waltzing Matilda' and watching the flying foxes overhead, to Michael attending birthday parties in Rajasthan, complete with elephant rides.[96] For children in India, an elephant hired for a birthday party was not unusual, with children encountering them in a range of settings. Margaret Dopirak and family went to a nearby Hindu temple for her third birthday, where her sisters merrily rode the resident elephant while she cowered in fear in the car and refused to join in.[97] Birthdays were otherwise remembered variously occurring while families were on summer holidays or on furlough. They were occasions 'for a bit of a fuss and bother' which helped to maintain wider kinship ties through gifts received.[98] Occasionally there were other more lavish affairs. Joyce recalls that the 'big social event' for British families in Mukden was the consulate Christmas party. All the resident British children attended, riding in horse-drawn droshkies over snow-covered streets driven by members of the resident White Russian refugee community.[99]

More commonly leisure time was remembered in simple, everyday terms as something done with family, other missionary or expatriate children and sometimes with local or Indigenous children. For some, like Jim in Rajasthan, this was often time spent alone. As the oldest child, he ranged beyond the house, including regular bicycle rides out to Kota Airport.[100] In this respect Vandrick makes a fair point, observing that in published memoirs leisure was often gendered – whereby 'boys tended to have more vigorous adventures' or had 'more freedom to play outside with local boys'.[101] This is a less sustainable conclusion when the wider oral evidence is considered and again was partially dictated by geography or culture. For most children holidays encompassed sojourns in other places – often on working trips with parents and over the summer in cooler locations – and intermittently in other countries while on furlough. Quintessential British summer experiences like travelling on a steamer on the Clyde River and riding donkeys on a Firth of Forth beach were well-remembered by Ian and Scott Gray, while the family was on furlough in 1934.[102] Some did not travel far. Dorothy Kirk, living in Canton from 1914 to 1928, spent the summer months on Cheng Chau Island (Cheung Chau) in nearby Hong Kong.[103] By the 1950s local holidays might be by car as well as by bus or train. Alan and Robin S. both fondly remembered an old French car restored and used by their father, and a final sight-seeing trip before leaving India on a private train coach belonging to a railway official who was a family friend.[104] At least two interviewees remember flying by the early 1950s.[105]

Play or playing was the most remembered element across all interviews, especially as the first thing that came to mind about childhood. In many instances, it threatened to be the only point of conversation until other themes and topics were prompted. Its ubiquity in the oral record also tends to be mostly unreflective, suggesting something taken for granted as normative for everyone irrespective of geographical or cultural context. However, the imaginative activities engaging Willie and Margaret Marwick in their Jamaican home and garden, noted earlier, suggest something more complex. Recent surveys of scholarship on children's play note, among other things, difficulties of definition; the influence of different social conditions; the relationship of play, space and place; the meaning and use of objects; children's agency and parents' influence; and the intersection of class, gender, race, disability and religion among other categories.[106] Within the history of childhood and childhood studies more broadly, play is understood to be an important indicator of identity and experience. Therefore, recent research 'has offered a significant contribution in that it genuinely engages with children's own culture rather than simply adult views of children's lives'.[107]

When the focus turns to imperial or missionary settings, play becomes even more complex. Mary Clare Martin and David Pomfret, for example, separately excavate both homogeneous white and cross-cultural play encounters from the early to mid-nineteenth century onwards – in settings as diverse as Hong Kong, tropical Africa, the Caribbean, India and New Zealand – in a way that provides a more nuanced and sober view of play and its cultural meaning.[108] Missionaries' children played with Indigenous children, often encouraged by parents, thus taking part in the wider 'evangelizing process' usually thought of as an adult domain. Furthermore, what materials they played with – both homemade and manufactured – implicated them in 'the relationships between colony and metropole' and 'globalization and indigeneity'.[109] Oral evidence adds further complexity. Parents' disposition, geographical or cultural settings, and political contexts differentiated how and where play occurred. For example, it appears from the interviews that children who grew up in southern African contexts were more likely to have played with local children than in other settings. However, there were complexities within this. Louisa, for example, realised at a particular age that her African playmates began to disappear: 'they were not free to come and play as it were with me because they had household jobs to do', like making the fire, cooking food and looking after babies.[110] In a different context, but again occurring in recreational time, Isabel's recollections of family holiday trips from Nyasaland to East London in South Africa include frightening and confusing moments of cultural and political displacement: once when her brother was violently attacked by a local gang, and the other when she and a sister 'caused a bit of trouble because on buses, for instance, we liked to sit on the upper deck unaware that this was only specifically for blacks'.[111] With these complexities in mind, the discussion returns to the contexts of two particular children.

In 1930s Manchuria, play for Dawn was both physically and mentally circumscribed by the political circumstances of the Japanese occupation, but also hedged about by parental cultural expectations or fears.[112] The Mukden compound marked the key edges of her daily world as she remembers it, but occasional expeditions beyond might result in the purchase of toys or play-things. Wider play, with other missionary children, was restricted largely to the summer periods spent on the coast. Age also marked key transitions. As a pre-schooler, she played daily in the compound garden with the Chinese cook's daughter (unnamed), who lived with her family on site (off limits for Dawn). This stopped once Dawn was of school age and began to be home schooled by her mother. She remembers the odd foray into the kitchen to watch the cook at work, occasionally trying out chopsticks for fun but never for regular use. In hindsight, her recreational kitchen visits underscored the essentially British ambit of her childhood, which further reinforced a sense of being British throughout her life. On one visit she was surprised to find the cook's helper studying from an atlas that showed China 'in the middle with the British Isles away on the outskirt'. She acknowledged the validity of this redrawing of geography, but it was a shock at the time because 'I had been so used to thinking of the world as being Great Britain in the middle'. Food more broadly defined her world: 'we were kept more or less to British things' – like eating chicken and potatoes – 'kept to a British sort of style of eating'. Dawn thinks that as a child she never visited another Chinese house or had a meal with a Chinese family. She mused that her parents 'thought it was the obvious thing to do' in that the family would 'be coming home to this country eventually and we were British so that was just the way it was and probably it was the food they preferred'. This has lasted throughout her lifetime, in terms of food preferences ('I have no idea what actual Chinese food as such tastes like') and a sense of being primarily British.

For Veronica in 1950s South Africa, play was much more varied and nuanced, both conforming to and militating against the newly emerging politics of apartheid.[113] Like Dawn, the family home was a primary site of play, utilising a wide smooth-concrete veranda, a range of toys includ-ing a pedal aeroplane, the garden with trees to climb and a termite mound turned into a mudslide, and in later years a tennis-quoit court built by their father. These engaged Veronica and her siblings in imaginative, inventive and object-centred play which to a certain extent was gendered. Later, while boarding weekly with the Schulz family for school, all the children engaged in a lot of outdoor play, some in her opinion bordering on 'dangerous' – much like, she thinks, what her British peers would have engaged in at the time – about which 'Health and Safety would have a fit nowadays but we never got hurt. It was brilliant fun.' At the same time, particularly as a younger child, she remembers a dearth of same-age other missionary children to play with. Her main memory was playing often with local African children, but within certain restrictions. These children never entered her home nor did she theirs. Instead, they all played together on nearby sports grounds that acted as neutral territory. Veronica also remembers watching the children from the mission school parading as Brownies (called 'Sunbeams' in the South African context). Again, in hindsight, Veronica views these interactions through a wider lens, particularly her parents' disposition. African children might not have entered their home, but adults did: 'my father did do certain things like, you weren't supposed to entertain black Africans in your house and he would, particularly black ministers'. Their cook would stand watch and warn him if anyone suspicious appeared. More broadly she thinks that her father 'was concerned that we would pick up anti-black sentiments because we didn't have any at that point'. To this end 'one thing that we knew from the very beginning was that everybody is the same whatever colour their skin is, whatever language they speak'. Play and interactions across racial lines, among everything else experienced as a missionary child, helped her as an adult to be 'very tolerant' and in other ways 'intolerant of ignorance' both as a parent and an educator. Thus, missionary children's play needs to be seen, read and understood within complex systems of thought and action, as well as reflecting the mundane and normative actions of everyday childhood.

Conclusion: memory and emotional narratives

This chapter has outlined some representative ways in which missionary children lived over the transitional decades from the late nineteenth to the mid-twentieth centuries, focusing on a dominant narrative strand that 'life was ordinary', with a particular focus on domesticity, schooling and recreation. While some archival or published memoir material has been drawn on, in the main this narrative thread emerges from interviews conducted with adults who were missionary children from the 1920s to the 1950s. By way of conclusion, but also connected to the next chapter's focus – and in the process blurring the boundaries between 'ordinary' and 'complicated' – the relationship between memory and emotions is tentatively explored by asking: how was memory constructed, and to what end?

Memories represent difficult terrain to traverse. In talking about her early years in Manchuria, Joyce candidly admitted that 'I don't know how much of this I remember and how much is family mythology but ...'.[114] Joyce Wilkins, in her memoir, also identifies the problematic nature of childhood memories, recalled by 'looking back through a long tunnel of recollection' that was decades old. More importantly, in her mind the details that she recalled 'reveal something of my feelings at the time of which I write'.[115] This, perhaps, is to be expected. Historians of experience helpfully argue that historical experiences, while often recounted in individual terms, are 'a strongly cultural, social, and *societal* [original emphasis] phenomenon, bound to power relations, institutions, and systems of meaning'. Such experiences can 'blend into memories', further 'shaped by the person's or social group's earlier experiences and memories'.[116] Here the interviews and memoirs further reveal a complex of information and emotions. These complexities are more reflectively captured in Vandrick's reflection on her own missionary childhood in 1950s India, wherein she wrestles with a 'mismatch between ... my negative view of colonialism and ... my strong instinctive emotional attraction to some aspects of colonial days'. These feelings 'surged back with a new force' as she wrote her book *Growing Up with God and Empire*. She simultaneously found herself 'savouring' books and films of the time and acknowledging the 'nostalgic feelings' around the 'ritual of English afternoon tea'. At the same time 'my feelings are ambivalent; these ... have the scent of guilty pleasures. I sometimes feel that I belong to a club that I object to but long for, and can't stop remembering and dreaming about.' Margaret Beetham, daughter of Church of Scotland missionaries Lesslie and Helen Newbigin in southern India, articulates a similar tension between the feelings and the ethical dilemma evoked by remembering her childhood experiences – especially in the light of her own position as a feminist scholar and wider postcolonial critiques of the imperial and colonial past.[117] With these complexities in mind, American psychologist Elliot Mishler helpfully draws attention to the 'psychological, cultural, and social functions of how a story is told' as well as a story's 'particular contexts'. In so doing he emphasises the non-linear ways in which life stories unfold, in their telling, as a collaborative process between storyteller and listener, and he accentuates the experiential nature of memory recall.[118] Here, then, the focus is on emotional narratives, adult hindsight and how oral and written sources might speak to one another. Together they suggest that meaning-making, by adults recalling their childhoods, is a life-long process wherein events only make wider sense through processes of contextualisation or introspection.[119] Thus oral history, as a form of 'autobiographical narration' of childhood, is significant for its role in the longer-term 'constitution of biographical meaning'.[120]

First, one interview casts light on memory construction through a mixture of feelings, the interview process and hindsight. Kirsten's interview exemplified the extent to which historians of childhood need to pay attention to identity formation as 'an ongoing, lifelong process "by way of which the person in question seeks to ensure the continuity and coherence of his or her life practice"'. The way in which it developed also echoes other oral historians' experiences of interviewing adults about their childhoods.[121] Kirsten's memories of living in Yemen as a young girl in the 1950s, and then in Kenya, were shaped initially in vague and relatively unelaborated terms early on in the interview, explained partly by her age at the time: early on 'my memories are of sand and sand and sand and sand'.[122] Every Monday, after school, this tedium was broken by trips to the beach, swimming and savouring free fizzy drinks from a nearby 'Canada Dry factory'. Kirsten concluded these observations by saying 'that was Monday. The rest of the week was just boring really.' Yet over the duration of the interview, Kirsten proceeded to add layers of detail about her home life that undid her sense that life was mostly 'boring' or that she could not remember much, with one memory prompting another and not always in a chronological fashion. She noted how the sounds of chickens often take her back to a brief sojourn in Jerusalem while her father completed a locum there. The negative image of never-ending sand then reminded her of the camels that invaded their Aden property to eat apples off a tree, and of sandstorms during which they would eat their meals under the kitchen table. This then prompted her to remember her mother giving them different kitchen duties – one grinding coffee, one creaming butter and sugar for cake baking and one peeling potatoes. From this she mused further about her mother's guilt – expressed in the kitchen but not understood at the time – over having her children at home while neighbouring military mothers sent their children to Britain for school. Reflection on her parents, particularly how they must have felt at the time and her appreciation of their attitudes towards such things as the children's faith development, emerged as an important element of her memory-making through the interview process.

Alongside these remembered details, emotional recall was also important for Kirsten – especially the residual emotional imprint of her memories as she began to articulate them in a quasi-extempore manner that allowed both details and feelings to take shape through the interview. The dominant emotional tone of her narrative was positive and warm, with 'enjoyment' the word most often used to indicate how she thought longitudinally about her childhood and youth. At the same time, she used particular words at various points to describe her estimation of places or events. These variously included incidents or life as 'nice' or 'boring', 'fun' and 'good', alongside being 'upset', experiencing 'bad dreams' and being 'scared'. These, allied with clear changes in tone, served to demarcate an emotionally shaped narrative with its progressive phases from childhood to adolescence. Read through this emotional lens, coloured further by a complex mixture of age, stage and adult understanding, Kirsten constructed a narrative during the interview that moved from a less positive view of her earlier years in Aden; to a more positive take on life in Kenya; to the less comfortable transitional phase of adjusting to school and life in Edinburgh on the family's definitive return. The legacy of this childhood was also articulated in emotional terms: becoming a 'more tolerant person', having 'a warmth for people that are in the minority' and having a religious faith that was both experiential and cerebral.

Kirsten's process of recall, and the constitutive role of emotions, are not unique. Introducing the sources for her book on British children growing up in imperial India, Brendon somewhat unreflectively observes that 'More vivid than anything else, perhaps, is oral testimony … For I found that feelings were readily unlocked in the course of conversation.'[123] The link between children's historical memory and feelings is a current focus of new, hot-off-the-press scholarship.[124] From wider literature, the following points emerge. The relationship between emotions and oral testimony with respect to memory recall or construction is clearly contested and debated, particularly in instances where there is a long time lag between the interview and the period of recall. Jenny Harding notes that in recent scholarship, 'things have turned increasingly personal. And, memory, emotion and experience are entangled in processes of personalisation.'[125] These complexities include *inter alia* the performative and embodied nature of interviews, the extent to which narrative development is controlled by interviewer or interviewee, intersubjectivity with respect to interviewees' or interviewers' world view or life experience, the particular emotional communities developed between interviewer and interviewee and the relationship between emotions expressed in the interview and those experienced in past time.[126] In a focused discussion on instances when emotions spill out into the interview, historian Katie Holmes draws a useful distinction between ideas derived from psychological literature (where often in the interviews conducted there is 'little time between emotional events and their recall' and 'scant attention' to the setting or circumstances of the recall) and oral history's greater allowance for time lag and its impact on memory. From a historian's perspective, she wonders if 'we might ask if it is possible to find recognizable traces of original or "historical" emotion and, if so, what this can tell us about our interviewing practice and the significance of emotions expressed within'. Holmes goes on to argue that 'it is possible to recognize historical emotion, but it will always be influenced by past and present events and be mediated by the nature of the interview relationship'.[127]

What stands out from the narratives created here is the way in which the past left an emotional imprint on how they remembered their childhoods, rather than moments of emotional overspill or even attempts to identify original emotions in historical time. This was clear from Kirsten's narrative but also in others, with a generally positive tone to most (but not all) interviews. That latter point is important to bear in mind, as noted in the Introduction, as it is primarily a function of who responded willingly to the call for interviewees in the first place. A few instances from interviews canvassed in this chapter are apposite, highlighting among other things the power of relationships at the time with respect to emotional imprint on memories.[128] Life details, emotions and memory are interwoven in a way that delineates individual storytelling but that also constitutes shared communities of experience, across varying geographical or cultural settings. While individual stories differ across time and space, there also emerges shared experiences of struggle, adjustment and emotional navigation.

Very generally descriptions of play, previously noted as ubiquitous across many of the interviews, were couched in emotionally warm and positive terms as key features of childhood memories. More particularly, in talking about his early years in Japan in the 1930s, David remarked that he has 'very positive memories of that experience', particularly playing with Japanese children, 'of just being welcomed into a very warm missionary community' and of 'having a very positive relationship with the woman who cared for us'. Veronica's story of growing up in South Africa has been referred to earlier, with a particular focus on play, education and the impact of political context. As such, it is a story characterised by a marked depth of reflection and a carefully considered sense of what it all meant in hindsight. At the same time, it is a story suffused with feelings of enjoyment, fun and mirth. Indeed, 'fun' was a word used often by Veronica as she recalled her early years up to about the age of nine (when the family returned to Scotland), and there were many moments of laughter throughout the interview. Isabel narrated her story growing up in Nyasaland using a rich set of detailed memories framed by a range of emotional nuances: an overall sense of 'enjoyment' and that her life was 'normal'; a mixture of remembered anxieties (the nightmares about lions) and amusement as she put this into later perspective; and remembering boarding school as something to be endured and the great sense of 'relief' when she could go home for the holidays. Finally, for Joyce, while her detailed early memories are a mixture of what she remembers and what she has since been told, there were clear emotional resonances as she recounted living in 1930s Manchuria. Prime among these were: an abiding deep love and respect for her parents, especially in terms of the ways in which they valued Chinese people, culture and history (which later resonated in her own life and political engagement); and the memory of the warmth of community experienced within the wider missionary extended family. This latter imprint endured. Joyce felt acutely the absence of these people on returning to Scotland after the war, to family who were blood kin but not known and who she 'didn't trust in the same kind of way as a child'.

Second and finally, then, these latter examples indicate that emotional narratives can be positive, negative or perhaps more realistically a combination of both. Kirsten's narrative indicates that different life phases might elicit differently hued emotional responses in the recall of childhood. This temporal change came most often when children relocated over varying geographic scales for education, and this could be complex. For instance, one man narrated his childhood in terms of distinct phases that incorporated living with his parents in a mission setting and two stints in a missionary children's home to attend school while his parents remained abroad. Between the two periods of institutional residence, his mother returned to Scotland for three years and he lived with her. He described this period as 'probably the happiest part of my childhood', narrating the other phases in both positive and negative tones or sometimes at best with ambivalence.[129] This could be further complicated by gender. Against the grain of what was a carefully detailed, reflectively sophisticated and generally positive account of her childhood in Nyasaland, Louisa recounted how she effectively became a mother to her two younger brothers, while they were all together at a primary boarding school in Blantyre. This was 'a heavy duty' and an 'unhappy' experience personally, but also for her brothers who were just as unhappy without their mother.[130]

The inherent complexity of emotional narratives is further borne out in one final example. Ian Gray's childhood in India has featured already in this chapter and his story also forms an introductory backdrop to the next chapter. Ian's emotional narrative differs significantly from his slightly older brother Scott and is neatly foregrounded here with reference to a particular incident narrated doubly through the printed word and interview.[131] That incident underscores the differentiated nature of missionary children's religious experience canvassed earlier in the chapter. Ian's memoir (published in 2014 and unknown to me prior to the interview) was framed primarily as a family biography. The subsequent interview was more personal and provided Ian with an unplanned opportunity to reflect further. In the process, it proceeded to reveal the 'ruptures' or 'changes' that may come to light when written (published) autobiographies are complemented or interrogated by parallel oral histories.[132]

In the midst of describing his Indian life, Ian recounted hunting sparrowlike birds with his airgun. He writes:

One day I managed to shoot one but must have felt remorse as I held the tiny quivering body in my hand. I clearly remember digging a hole in very hard ground and comforting the corpse, assuring it it would soon be in heaven. My childish faith was strengthened, a day or so later, when I found, no dead bird, but only an empty depression in the ground.

In this written account Ian revealed, perhaps, a wider childhood education about other religions. His father asked him to desist from shooting these birds, as 'the local folk were not happy ... [because] they believed [that these birds] carried the spirits of people gone before'. Instead, he suggested that Ian hunt rats or snakes.

Ian repeated this story in the interview, with much of the same detail, but what he added is interesting (additional comment indicated by italics). Here he said:

that I finally killed one and I held that little quivering body in my hand and immediately *my basic Christian upbringing said*, you poor wee thing I've really killed you. Well I had to get to heaven quickly, I'll bury you, so I dug a little grave and buried that little bird. I probably would have been seven or eight or something like that. Well my faith was significantly strengthened when I came back, the ground was very hard, I dug a little hole and put it in. *Whether I expressed a prayer or not but came back the next day and there was nothing there. It had gone to heaven. If I had probably looked behind me the cat was probably licking his lips but that was my childish recollections and that was the sort of brainwashing that I'd had.*

This incident was recounted in the first half of the interview, with a focus on details and stories. Yet its self-reflective tone previewed an increasingly negative discourse later in the interview, focused on the exigencies of boarding school in India and then New Zealand (see next chapter). And while Ian communicated a deep regard for his parents' character (especially that of his mother), there was a good measure of equivocation about their religious motivations and dispositions, from which he had progressively distanced himself over his adult life. The interview, as commentary on the written text, thus provided the opportunity to articulate in a less publicly defined space a further degree of self-understanding. In this respect, echoing Holme's emphasis on the co-constructed nature of memory recall, these two sources together flesh out Mary Jo Maynes's contention that central to life stories are 'accounts of what people have done during their lives set in the context of their evolving understandings of why they have done so, and with what consequences'. In this way 'narratives of childhood can be very telling indeed ... as sources of insights into the impact and meanings of childhood', which also signify ways in which childhood is a 'phase of the construction of agency and subjectivity'.[133] Focusing on using oral sources to excavate children's historical religious lives, Grace Bateman similarly argues that we need to 'remain aware of the freedom of choice that people express from childhood onwards, to make personal meanings of religious experiences'.[134] Here we note also the important emotional packaging that is an important part of that reflective process. In Ian's case that became the dominant frame within which he both talked and reflected, indicating that there was an important other dimension of missionary children's lives that cohered around the experience and memories of separation. This casts a long shadow over many ex-children's perceptions of their own childhoods and over how those lives have been interpreted through historical scholarship. Life was ordinary but it was, simultaneously, complicated.

Notes

1 The following narrative is reconstructed from an interview with Rose, Scotland, 8 January 2015 and private communication by email, October 2014. 'Rose' is a pseudonym as this person did not want to be identified.
2 Hepburn, 'The Burning Rosebush', p. 123.
3 *Ibid.*, p. 126.
4 *Ibid.*, pp. 126–27.
5 *Ibid.*, pp. 127, 132.
6 See again Dodd, 'It's Not What I Saw'.
7 Millei, Silova and Gannon, 'Thinking through Memories', 328.
8 Kennedy, 'Telling Tales', p. 351; Kenny, 'Basically You Were Either', p. 235.
9 Kenny, 'Basically You Were Either', p. 235; in turn quoting from Bennett, *Culture*, p. 4.
10 Pomfret, *Youth*, p. 66; in turn interacting with Baena, 'Of Missess'.
11 Dopirak, *Missionary Kid*, p. 6.
12 Isabel, interview, Scotland, 21 January 2015.
13 Hafez, 'Playing', 119.
14 Fleming, 'Adjustment', pp. 25, 26.
15 Scott Gray, interview, New Zealand, 15 June 2014; Veronica, interview, Scotland, 10 January 2015; Janice Rowley and Joan Sutherland (sisters), interview, New Zealand 19 March 2015; Michael, interview, Scotland, 20 January 2015.
16 Wilkins, *A Child's Eye View*, p. 28.
17 Booth, *Pat's India*, p. 22.
18 Crump and McKenzie, *Christina's Story*, p. 102.
19 Alison, interview, Scotland, 13 January 2015.
20 NLS, Marwick Papers, Acc. 4886/2, Letters of Children of Rev. W. Marwick from Jamaica to Relatives at Home, 1902, Willie to Grannie and Auntie, 6 December 1902.

21 *Ibid.*, Willie to Grannie and Auntie, 10 May 1902, 25 July 1902, 8 November 1902 and 6 December 1902; and Margaret to Grannie, no date.

22 *Ibid.*, Margaret to Grannie, 19 April 1902; Margaret to Grannie and Auntie, no date; [No name] to Grannie and Auntie, 12 April 1902; Willie to Grannie and Auntie, 4 July 1902.

23 *Ibid.*, Margaret to Grannie, 15 April 1902.

24 See again Faith Cook's comments on maintaining a 'postal relationship' with her CIM parents in 1950s Malaya (chapter 2) in *Troubled Journey*, pp. 100–101; as well as Pedersen, 'Anxious Lives', 7–19; and Duff, *Changing Childhoods*, pp. 50–51, 54–56.

25 Terry, *Help Me*, pp. 9–10.

26 *Ibid.*, p. 10.

27 Picked up in Chapter 6. Esme Cleall argues that in some Southern African contexts local architectural styles were juxtaposed in missionary writing with Western styles, in order to accentuate the virtues of the latter over the former. In the process: '[t]he tendency to see "civilisation" (or lack of it) inscribed on both people and place is typical of the slippage between 'race' and 'culture' in missionary writing'. Cleall, *Missionary Discourses*, p. 39.

28 Robin S., interview, Scotland, 14 January 2015.

29 Joyce, interview, Scotland, 19 January 2015; Rose interview; Veronica interview; Janice Rowley and Joan Sutherland interview.

30 Unnamed, interview, Scotland, January 2015; Robin S. interview.

31 Kirsten, interview, England, 3 January 2015.

32 David, interview, New Zealand, 27 March 2015.

33 Alison interview.

34 Alison interview; Robin S. interview.

35 Isabel interview.

36 *Ibid.*

37 'Murray Recalls His India Days', in Crozier, *Will the Rajah?*, p. 177.

38 Jim, interview, Scotland, 12 January 2015.

39 *Ibid.*

40 Dawn, interview, Scotland, 15 January 2015.

41 Crump and McKenzie, *Christina's Story*, pp. 71, 78; and Janice Rowley and Joan Sutherland interview.

42 Scott Gray interview; Ian Gray interview; Gray, *We Travel Together*, pp. 14–15; Unnamed interview, Scotland; Unnamed, interview, New Zealand, 7 March 2015.

43 Alison interview.

44 Fleming, 'Adjustment', pp. 44, 45.

45 See note 20.

46 Fleming, 'Adjustment', pp. 44, 45. Sabbath proscriptions on play and dress were also a feature of Joyce Wilkins's childhood in India in the early 1900s, as a daughter of English Baptist missionaries. Wilkins, *A Child's Eye View*, pp. 12–13.

47 Dawn interview.

48 Thomas was the second of six children born to Thomas and Annie Torrance, missionaries in China with the CIM and later American Bible Society. He attended a Canadian missionary school in Chengdu until 1927, when political instability forced the family's eventual return to Scotland. Torrance was fourteen years old at that point. McGrath, *T.F. Torrance*, pp. 3–18, particularly p. 13. Here McGrath quoted from an unpublished autobiographical manuscript penned by Torrance titled 'Itinerarium in Mentis Deum'.

49 Robin S., private communication, August 2015; Alan, private communication, October 2014.

50 Hepburn, 'The Burning Rosebush', p. 125.

51 Booth, *Pat's India*, pp. 25–26.

52 Isabel interview.

53 Barnes, *The Life Journey*, pp. 9–10.

54 Kirsten interview.

55 Pruitt, *A China Childhood*, discussed in Chapter 6.

56 This observation is made specifically with reference to colonial New Zealand but applies equally to a broader collective of emerging Western nation states. May, 'Recollecting Childhood', p. 96. Two helpful surveys of the development of education in relation to the histories of modern childhood are found in: Sandin, 'Education', pp. 91–110; and Reese, 'Education', pp. 99–116.

57 For context, see general observations on scholarship of missionary children's education in Vandrick, *Growing Up*, pp. 64–67. The focus on children's more general experiences of or reactions to schooling, in the history of education, reflects *inter alia* the influences of 'history from below', subaltern histories, gender history and, more recently, the emotional turn. Education is also considered in Chapter 5.

58 NLS, Marwick Papers, Acc. 4886/2, Letters of Children, Willie to Auntie, 5 April 1902. In this context one or more of the teachers at least temporarily boarded with the Marwick family, affording closer proximity between teacher and pupils. Margaret's reference to beginning music at school and playing on a 'digitorium' (a device to help students develop their piano playing skills) also indicates artistic elements to their curriculum (Margaret to Grannie and Auntie, 17 November 1902).

59 Morrison, 'It's Really Where', 431.

60 NLS, Marwick Papers, Acc. 4886/2, Letters of Children, Willie to Auntie, 25 July 1902.

61 Joyce interview; Dawn interview; Miller, *Pigtails*, pp. 137–59; Cook, *Troubled Journey*, pp. 30–50. For further context on the complex and concept of St Andrew's children's home and school at Kalimpong, see McCabe, *Race*, pp. 44–67.

62 Vandrick, *Growing Up*, pp. 67–68.

63 Booth, *Pat's India*, pp. 24, 59–65; Kirsten interview.

64 Robin W., interview, Scotland, 9 January 2015. His parents were Scottish missionaries with the Regions Beyond Missionary Union.

65 Hudspith, *Ripening Fruit*, pp. 19–20, 58.

66 Rose interview.
67 Hocken Library, Dunedin (hereafter Hocken), Ron Malcolm Papers, AG-775–006/001, Personal Papers, c. 1910–1939, School Reports and Results; Morrison, 'Reimagining', 473, 476–77.
68 Louisa, interview, Scotland, 12 January 2015. 'Louisa' is a pseudonym as this person did not want to be identified.
69 Joyce interview.
70 Unnamed interview, New Zealand.
71 Marie interview, Scotland, 7 January 2015.
72 Gray, *We Travel Together*, pp. 13–14.
73 Louisa interview.
74 Marie interview; Dawn interview; Joyce interview.
75 Ian Gray interview; Michael interview; Dorothy Kirk, '80 Years of "Living"', Dorothy Kirk Papers [hereafter Kirk Papers], Private Collection, Ian Waldram, Scotland.
76 de Bellaigue, 'Charlotte Mason', 501–17; further referencing Behlmer, *Friends*.
77 Dawn interview.
78 de Bellaigue, 'Charlotte Mason', 505, 508, 515, in turn referencing broadly Pietsch, *Empire of Scholars*.
79 'Our History'; Preston and Campbell, 'Correspondence School'; Stacey, 'The History of Distance Education', 254–55; *News* [South Australia] (31 May 1933), p. 8; *Newcastle Sun* (20 July 1938), p. 5.
80 Unnamed interview, New Zealand.
81 Robin S. interview; Alan interview, Scotland, 17 January 2015.
82 Jim interview.
83 Jensz and Acke, 'Introduction', p. 10.
84 NLS, Marwick Papers, Acc. 4886/39, 'Letterbook 1906–1908', William Marwick to Master J.D. Marwick, [undated] 1908; William Marwick to George, 12 August 1908.
85 Dawn interview.
86 Veronica interview.
87 Olsen, *Juvenile Nation*, pp. 7–8.
88 Wilkins, *A Child's Eye View*, pp. 27–28.
89 Pande, 'Feeling', p. 46. Further context is given in: Romesburg, 'Making Adolescence', pp. 239–40; and Moran, 'Sex Education', pp. 740–41.
90 The following details come from Fleming, 'Adjustment', pp. 17–19.
91 For example, Dopirak, *Missionary Kid*, p. 233.
92 *Ibid.*, pp. 18–19.
93 Janice Rowley and Joan Sutherland interview; Crump and McKenzie, *Christina's Story*, pp. 78–79.
94 Marie interview.
95 Kenny, 'Basically You Were Either', p. 235. Note, however, that missionary archives (published and unpublished) hold great potential for excavating such details, as argued for by Martin, 'Play', pp. 62–63, and Martin, 'The State of Play', 335.

96 Crump and McKenzie, *Christina's Story*, p. 79; Michael interview.
97 Unnamed interview, New Zealand; Dopirak, *Missionary Kid*, p. 24.
98 Marie interview; Jim interview; Alan interview; Unnamed interview, New Zealand.
99 Joyce interview.
100 Jim interview.
101 Vandrick, *Growing Up*, pp. 96–97. Leisure time and play is one theme given scant attention in Vandrick's overall analysis of missionary children's published memoirs.
102 Ian Gray interview; Scott Gray interview; Gray, *We Travel Together*, p. 21. Holidays in the Clyde area were also recalled by Michael in his interview.
103 Dorothy Kirk, '80 Years of "Living"'; Ian Waldram, 'Hong Kong', Dorothy Kirk Papers.
104 Alan interview; Robin S. interview.
105 Kirsten interview; Marie interview.
106 Martin, 'The State of Play', 329–35; Martin, 'Play'.
107 Davey, Darian-Smith and Pascoe, 'Playlore', p. 41. More generally see Cross, 'Play', pp. 267–82.
108 Pomfret, *Youth*, pp. 86–94; Martin, 'The State of Play', 335.
109 Martin, 'Play', p. 61.
110 Louisa interview.
111 Isabel interview.
112 This section is based on Dawn's interview.
113 This section is based on Veronica's interview.
114 Joyce interview.
115 Wilkins, *A Child's Eye View*, p. 135.
116 Kivimäki et al., 'Lived Nation', p. 12.
117 Vandrick, *Growing Up*, p. 121; Beetham, 'Dust and Mangoes', pp. 148–49.
118 Mishler, 'Narrative', pp. 37, 38.
119 Insights derived from the psychology of childhood traumas, applied to particular historical contexts, as in Kaarninen, 'Red Orphans', pp. 169–70.
120 Kleinau, 'Autobiographical Writing', 379.
121 *Ibid.*, 380 (in turn quoting from Koller, *Bildung anders denken*', p. 35), and 385.
122 This section is based on Kirsten's interview.
123 Brendon, *Children*, p. 6.
124 Advance notice of a significant new publication by Lindsey Dodd came out just as I completed final revisions for this book. Its focus is on the relationship between emotions and memory, in the oral history narratives of French adults remembering their childhoods during World War II. It is simply referenced here as I have not yet been able to consult it. Dodd, *Feeling Memory*.
125 Harding, 'Looking', 97.
126 Bornat, 'Remembering', 43–52; Boschmann, 'Speaking', 1–23; and Holmes, 'Does It Matter?', 56–76.
127 Holmes, 'Does It Matter?', 58–59.

128 The following examples are drawn on: David interview (Japan); Veronica interview (South Africa); Isabel interview (Malawi); and Joyce interview (Manchuria, China).
129 Unnamed interview, Scotland.
130 Louisa interview.
131 This section is based on Gray, *We Travel Together*, p. 14, and on Ian Gray's interview.
132 See again Kleinau, 'Autobiographical Writing', 380–81, 389.
133 Maynes, 'Age', 119.
134 Bateman, 'Signs and Graces', p. 218.

5

Children's and young people's narratives: life as complicated

The fuzzy boundaries between life as 'ordinary' or 'complicated' are fore-grounded in the narratives of Ian and Scott Gray, two Scottish-New Zealand Presbyterian boys already encountered, who lived in northern India in the 1920s and early 1930s. Their daily lives rotated mainly around family routines, school timetables and shared recreational pursuits that were circumscribed geographically by mission compound walls. Yet, they did venture beyond those walls in ways that pushed out their physical boundaries and that challenged the parameters of what might constitute 'ordinary'. Two memories illustrate this and begin to open up this second aspect of children's missionary lives. At home near Jagadhri, Ian writes in his memoir that:

> We had bicycles and a special reward for good behaviour was for us to be allowed to ride with the servant to the railway station at Abdullapore about four miles away along a very dusty rutted road to collect the butter which came from, I don't know where. It was quite a challenging, almost hazardous journey. There were no traffic rules. Plodding bullock-carts, with their cruise-control set at 2 miles an hour, held a constant course in relation to the side of the road. Coolies, with huge bundles of forage on their back, lurched forward, their load suspended from a broad strap across the forehead, unable to see beyond a few metres in front. A camel train would pick its way smoothly past the bullock carts and occasionally, very occasionally, a Tin Lizzy, Model T ford, would try to bulldoze its way, the driver or passenger squeezing the rubber ball on the horn peremptorily demanding right-of-way, and usually to no avail. Those rides were exciting and made even more so when the servant, pointing to a sack-draped hovel, said there was a Mad Man in there and look out, because he chases little boys.[1]

Ian's other strong memory is of family trips with their father on a series of 'camping trails', undertaking itinerant preaching and other work around regional villages over winter months:

> We would be camped near a village. Every morning my father would have a medical session and I can remember hovering as close as I would be allowed,

watching with fascination as my father ... treated some gory, badly infected wounds, pulled out a tooth or dispensed pills, mainly for malaria. During the day my father, with his team of preachers would seek to persuade the villagers, mainly Hindu, that the Christian Way would offer them more hope in Life, and Death. In the evenings there would be a lantern-slide show about the Christian Story. But Scott and I still had our lessons, my mother saw to that. After a day or so at that site the tents would be folded and with all the rest of the paraphernalia loaded onto bullock carts to trundle away to the next site perhaps five or ten kilometres further on in the circuit.[2]

Scott also referred to these trips, fascinated as he watched as his father 'went along a line of men or women sitting there, on their haunches' pulling out 'the troublesome tooth at their request'. He went on to be a dentist and lecturer in dentistry at the University of Otago.[3]

However, 'life as complicated' extended further than these immediate childhood experiences. Scott and Ian were the eldest of five children born between 1923 and 1934, with Ian younger by eighteen months. Around the compound and in earlier years they were close companions and playmates. To some extent this changed, with the move to semi-boarding at Woodstock School at Landour and then a more definitive separation from their family while at high school in Christchurch, New Zealand. These experiences were shared simultaneously by both boys. Their relatively small age difference was enough to render the ongoing experience of missionary childhood different for each, at least in perception. Scott indicated that the regime of the boys' school experience in New Zealand was at first an emotional shock, compared with the co-educational and Christian nature of Woodstock School. He remembers being confounded by 'the control, the regulations' and the 'strict' discipline. For the first few nights, 'we would cry ourselves to sleep and then I suppose we, we got used to things'. No one asked 'how are you feeling? How are you getting on?'[4] Longer term, he thrived. Yet his interview responses were relatively unreflective, compared with brother Ian, with little recognition that Ian's experience was much different.

In his memoir, Ian thinks that earlier primary school years at Woodstock engendered a 'deeply engrained fear and detestation of life in a boarding school, an attitude later school experiences would only strengthen'. In New Zealand such difficulties were accentuated by being perceived as different, often enduring the stigma of being called 'N_____' because 'I spoke differently and I had come from India'. A perceptive school principal suggested that Ian join the boxing class, whereby Ian learnt both pragmatically valuable skills and gained a greater sense of confidence. Still, he thinks that his schoolwork suffered. When both boys re-joined the family in Auckland in 1939, relocated because of war, he had to repeat a year of high school as a result. In retrospect, he writes, 'I am quite happy to let those four years sink into the limbo of the past'.[5] His memoir hints at the significance of sibling differences and this was reflected on further in the interview. He candidly opined that

> Scott had a different personality from me. I was a secondary element in the Scott Gray team and I probably just didn't develop the confidence that Scott had and has shown throughout his life. In my case I think the same reason I probably have had occasions where I really wasn't sure that I had the ability to cope and so I think right back to that stage influences of missionary practice were beginning to have their effects on my personality and my total attitude to life and philosophy.[6]

These experiences served to form his own approach to both parenting and education, particularly as a teacher and school principal. While these were formative experiences, they did not necessarily constrain his own career. Ian and wife Lesley, with their three children, lived in Vanuatu between 1953 and 1960, where he was the founding principal of Onesua School, a joint educational venture of both the Vanuatu and New Zealand Presbyterian Churches. This was a significant life experience and remains so still.[7]

Separation of missionary children from their parents – whether repetitive or definitive, short or long term, short distance or further afield – is a dominant trope that, in turn, has been discursive in terms of its influence on historical research and writing. However, wider academic and professional scholarship on both missionary children and third culture kids increasingly strikes a balance, in that separation is viewed as one among a number of other issues to be considered equally, including identity and belonging, the ages at which different life transitions occurred, varying experiences of schooling and reintegration to countries of origin.[8] Ian Gray's story exemplifies this while adding credence to Vandrick's contention that many ex-missionary children 'seem to be trying to work out their childhood feelings through the very act of writing their memoirs'.[9] Together Scott and Ian's stories broaden the scope of what it meant to live a complicated life, drawing attention to a wider theme of disruption that was often framed ambiguously by adults in hindsight. Negative and positive elements sit cheek by jowl in the storytelling, often uncomfortably or unreflectively, complicating any attempt to conduct a wholly 'negative' reading of missionary children's lives. Separation was certainly an important part of this narrative, but not all of it.

This chapter therefore extends the conversation begun in Chapter 4, by teasing out a second narrative thread of life as complicated (Table 5.1). Those complications occurred often in their daily domestic spaces but were amplified through complexities of travel, relocation and family separation which, for the most part, related to or were compelled by the perceived

Table 5.1 Narrative thread: life was complicated

Themes	Indicated by details elicited on:
Identity	Friends (expatriate and Indigenous), language acquisition, family connections, sense of own identity, transitions, life trajectories
Mobility	Transportation modes, schooling, travel, holidays, furlough, seasonal transitions, life phase transitions
Separation	Episodic or longer term, schooling and boarding, travel, transitions, furlough, impact of war or family fortunes, missionary homes, wider family, split family, emotional and life-trajectory impact, sense of alienation from parent(s)

educational needs of the children or the changed circumstances of their families. Interviews and memoirs reveal that these complications varied with respect to things like family dynamics, personality, place in the family, gender, geographical or cultural location, decade and politics but were also further complicated by exigencies of war, ill health and death. These are explored broadly by way of three emphases that cut across the themes: complex experiences; emotional navigations; and identity formation. Missionary children's immersion in multi- or cross-cultural contexts will be a focus of the following chapter.

Complex experiences

In the first instance, 'life as complicated' is elaborated through a focus on the complex experiences of language, mobility and education – complexities often perceived at the point of a major transition or through adult hindsight. Using a recently proffered procedural model, 'experience' is understood in this discussion as a broadly conceived mix of everyday 'lived experience' ('part of social reality, what happens to people and how they understand it') and as a 'social process' (which pays attention to 'the social relationships and interdependencies in which experience is produced').[10] The details of this are aptly foregrounded in the adjustment experiences of the young Americans who previously attended Woodstock School in India in the 1920s and 1930s, recorded in Fleming's research.[11] Simple things like speech and clothing marked them out as different or less acceptable. One remembered having a 'different accent which made me different' and another noted that 'I used to speak too [emphasis original] well (enunciation and grammar)' to the extent that 'it was noticeable'. Girls realised that how they had dressed or been dressed had been hitherto given little thought. Recreational opportunities were constrained by context, often throwing children and adults into each other's company to a greater degree than their American peers. Their homes brought children into direct contact with other cultures and perhaps even a more diverse socio-economic range of visitors.

At school age, children and teenagers lived in multiple homes and places dictated by seasons, the school year and family priorities and, in Fleming's estimation, this experience was met by 'mixed feelings' at best.[12] Younger children might anticipate school boarding with sadness and trepidation, but as they grew older the return to school was an adventure made more palatable because of reunification with friends. Yet even that experience was not necessarily straightforward in that, for many, time at Woodstock might be split between school boarding and residing with parents who came up to Landour for the hot summer months. Some were happy with this, but others, mostly teenagers, were irritated by their parents' proximity. Like Ian Gray, there were also individuals who hated boarding due to disposition or who did not fit into prevailing elements of school culture. One recounted that as a junior student, 'I didn't mix too well with the kids as I was nervous, I did not like to fight and I was not athletic'. School culture and boarding structures also separated girls and boys, and this in students' opinion contributed to later social adjustment difficulties in America. Religion was also a complicating factor. What was taken for granted as natural to family or school life in India did not necessarily translate well to the American context, which was much more diverse with respect to religious polities and attitudes. Thus the status quo was challenged. For some, church attendance declined or stopped while for others, seeking religious integrity, there ensued significant personal struggles. In sum, the context-specific complexities of these American students were the complexities of other missionary children writ large.

Language

Missionary children's lives were inherently complicated due to the multi-cultural or non-European spaces in which they were born or entered from very early ages. Vallgårda's observation, regarding Danish children in southern India, applies equally to children of other nationalities in this same period: they 'regularly crossed the boundaries between Indian and Danish, heathen and Christian, placing them in a liminal space where they had to navigate different linguistic systems as well as conflicting cultural codes and moral orders'.[13] Daily life was made up of many such navigations which were not always obvious to children. Play was one very good example of this, as discussed previously, but so too was language acquisition and use, particularly for those born *in situ* or in contexts that allowed greater mixing of children and other cultures.[14] Margaret Dopirak recalled fondly her Indian ayah Hannah – who 'gave us our baths', 'put us down for our naps' and 'taught us catchy little songs in Hindi' – and remembered that 'my first words were in Hindi'. Ian Gray reckons that due to their unnamed ayah, 'Scott's and my mother tongue was Urdu'. Likewise Kamala Jackson, in southern India, learnt Telugu as an infant before she could speak English, and later English acquisition was influenced by Telugu word order.[15] Missionary children, as with other Empire children, potentially became comfortable with and adept in local cultures through the intimacies of informal language learning. In the process, 'the home became a shared space of trans-cultural connection and multilingual competence'.[16]

Early acquisition of local languages or dialects was a commonly shared experience across most of the interviews and memoirs for the period 1920– 50, as was the need to learn other languages specific to schooling, mission- ary contexts or family background. Most remembered that at a young age, they were relatively fluent in a local language. Not untypically perhaps, Faith Cook writes that because she and brother Christopher were the only children in their parents' CIM station in the early 1940s, they 'had none but each other and our Chinese friends as companions. Soon we became totally bilingual, our command of Chinese more accurate than that of our par- ents who often struggled with the confusing inflexions of the Mandarin dia- lect.'[17] Some retained partial language capacity as adults, especially selected words or phrases, but many others soon lost this. Kirsten's schooling and living contexts of first Yemen and then Kenya required her to be able to use Arabic, then Swahili alongside English and Danish (her mother's national- ity) in the home. She thinks as a child and teenager that she could speak better than she could write in these languages, but that this ability has long passed. David conversed in Japanese with his local playmates in the 1930s and later, in New Zealand during the war, remembers as a family tuning in to listen to shortwave radio Japanese language news broadcasts. He lost that fluency but, at a much later date speaking at a memorial service for the Featherston (Japanese prisoner of war camp) tragedy of 1943, he was still 'able to get a little bit of Japanese' and could 'actually pronounce it well satisfactorily [laughter], and I felt comfortable doing it'.[18] This was more complicated for others. Marie and her siblings in newly created Pakistan learnt both Urdu and 'Punjabi', as well as enduring their mother's pressure to keep their traditional Gaelic language alive. Rose's youthful peregrina- tions between Nyasaland and South Africa for high school meant that she imbibed something of the local dialect as well as having to learn Afrikaans (a compulsory language), plus French and Latin as part of the traditional school curriculum. Veronica navigated her way between the local Venda language, Afrikaans at her South African school and the German of her Lutheran host family while weekly boarding.[19]

While such language acquisition could be taken for granted, children did not always understand the politics of language. This was apparent, for example, in Joyce Wilkin's semi-realised guilt about secretly sharing English conversations with her Indian ayah Emily, hidden from her mother.[20] As such she dimly perceived, perhaps, long-held parental fears in India and parts of Southeast Asia that children's capacity in the vernacular might upset the racial status quo and so should not be encouraged longer term. However, in other settings like that of the South Pacific, 'not only did many missionary children speak Indigenous languages, but this was perceived as an advantage in equipping them for future missionary work'.[21] From a Western angle, adult parodying of children's 'pidgin' vernacular abilities – as 'benign' or 'as a sort of amusement' – contributed to a wider infantilisation of local or Indigenous people.[22] From a non-Western angle, language was equally political. This was most apparent in an incident retold by Jim, from his boyhood in 1940s northern India. Like so many, Jim's early years spent with his ayah enculturated him in idiomatic Hindi. He easily conversed with compound personnel and local shopkeepers and amused his father as 'I would use words and phrases and expressions and idioms which he would never think of'. However, this ease with Hindi also undid him:

> There was one occasion I remember where the Chief of Police arrived to visit my father and he got out of his car and asked me in English where my father was and I responded to him in Hindi and told him where my father was but oh dear the man. His name was Gopal Singh. He was very offended and my father told me this afterwards. He was very offended because of course by responding to his English in Hindi I was demonstrating as a child that I understood that English was for white faces and Hindi was for brown faces and he was greatly offended.

Jim's boyish assumptions about language as just a natural element of everyday life did not translate well, in this case, to understanding the complexities of class, race and colonialism. While language could be a rich and troubling playing field on which some missionary children might mimic racial or cultural paternalism,[23] in Jim's case language was a positive memory of childhood which, at the time, also represented a hidden and potentially dangerous juvenile minefield.

Mobility

Missionary children's lives were geographically mobile lives, and this element deserves much more attention than has hitherto been given. Scott Gray spoke for many when he summed up his childhood as 'nomadic'.[24] This peripatetic lifestyle was often compelled by schooling decisions or contexts and was a feature of what it meant to be an Empire citizen. Here we note the ways in which mobility was a constant and sometimes disruptive experience of juvenile life and how that was remembered or perceived. This was an era that witnessed large volumes of migrants making significantly big global transitions. However, apart from British children caught up in Empire-wide child relocation schemes, children as migrants do not have a high profile in historical scholarship.[25] Richard Jobs and David Pomfret point out, for instance, that 'in spite of the recognized importance of youthfulness to twentieth-century international migrations ... "it is rare to find this key factor the focus of debate"'.[26] Nineteenth- and early twentieth-century missionary children's mobility is canvassed in limited literature to date, but mostly elucidated within the context of family or from parental perspectives and, for British children, more specifically in relation to imperial India.[27] Missionary children endured the same exigencies of long-distance travel as many other juvenile Western migrants, but amplified in that their journeyings were frequent, repetitive and over varying distances. Furthermore, the frequency and mode of travel changed over time. For early twentieth-century children, there were increasing 'opportunities to both move more swiftly and more frequently across borders and over much larger distances', which 'inspired a sense that the world was both becoming a smaller place and that it was spinning faster on its axis'.[28] Here we consider cycles of movement over varying scales of distance in response to climatic seasons, school terms and as a part of parents' regularly spaced furloughs.

Nineteenth-century migration experiences were long and variable for children and tended to shape the longer-term public imaginary in imperial metropoles, emphasising perceived dangers. Illness and death were frequent travelling companions with tragically high mortality rates, for example, on migrant ships between England and New Zealand and as noted in migrants' diaries.[29] For missionary families, long sea voyages were also mixed experiences. This was typified in the bittersweet experience of the Moffat family (LMS) in transit between southern Africa and England in 1838, losing six-year-old son Jim to shipboard illness (one of three Moffat children who died longer term), while at the same time, Mary gave birth to a daughter.[30] Illness rather than death, however, was a more constant reality that rendered sea travel a wretched experience in children's memories. Six-year-old Joyce Wilkins travelled from India to England with her family on the *SS Syria* in 1908, marking an end to her Indian childhood. Initial excitement soon gave way to the unenjoyable sensations of sea sickness, made worse by hearing about another child severely injured while on board. After a brief stop at Colombo, Joyce 'developed high fever and spent the rest of the voyage seriously ill and confined to the cabin'. She was 'nursed night and day by mother' assisted by others, including a trained nurse, and remembered the ice packs and tightly wrapped water-soaked sheets. More than anything, however, it 'was all done with a sternness and no-nonsense attitude … and I lay there, shivering and whimpering in those wet sheets, and felt that I was being punished for all my wickedness'. Landfall in Liverpool and a long-awaited reunification with older sister Dorothy marked a welcome end to her journey.[31]

Decades later the journey could still be an ordeal. In 1948, Alison remembers incarceration in the lower decks of the yet-unconverted troopship *Empire Bure* en route to Africa's Gold Coast:

> twelve people in a cabin meant for eight, that's to say there were four mothers and eight children all eight years or under and it was bad enough for us but what it must have been like for the mothers I do not know, we were all absolutely sick in the Bay of Biscay … it was just dire.

For Joyce, an abiding memory of stormy travel across the northern Pacific from Japan to Canada in early 1941 was of goldfish in open tubs being swept out to die on the deck; she remembers that this 'broke my heart'.[32] And significant experiences of illness were not necessarily confined to ocean travel. In 1918 Lucy and Winsome Burt caught the Spanish flu on the train crossing Canada, finally *en route* from China to England at the end of World War I, and with their mother had to be hospitalised in Toronto.[33]

Yet as the new century developed, long-distance travel became safer and faster and was remembered as more of an adventure. English BMS children in northern China, for example, often sojourned overland by rail. Twelve-year-old Harold Burt accompanied his father on furlough through Siberia and Russia in 1909, visiting the Kremlin in Moscow and staying in Berlin.[34] For many, however, those journeys involved long stints of ship-board life. The daily monotony perhaps explains why many cannot remember the details (the sense of boredom itself being another residual emotional imprint on memory). Scott and Ian Gray travelled with their family on furlough in 1934 first from India to Scotland and then eventually all the way to New Zealand. Despite this being the first time that either boy had seen the ocean, Scott summarised the voyage in about two sentences and Ian associated it mainly with helping his mother to change his new baby sister's nappies.[35] Likewise, Michael Orr tersely described the trip in these terms: 'On reaching Edinburgh after the now familiar three weeks steaming through Indian Ocean, Red Sea, Mediterranean and Bay of Biscay, courtesy of the Anchor Line, we stayed for a while with grandparents and aunts'.[36] For some, however, the memories are richer. In Jim's mind such voyages represented a 'marvellous three-week holiday', with children left to their own devices, hazardous dares like standing on the outside of the ship's railings and never-ending supplies of ice cream. This extended to wartime, in that travel afforded new and exciting experiences. While transiting through Japan to Canada, Joyce took great delight in constantly riding the lifts in her hotel.[37]

For children of the 1920s onwards, more significant difficulties were faced in the adjustments that had to be made at the other end. This was exacerbated in that such experiences were often repeated for those, like Jim, who travelled at least three times with his family between 1944 and 1955.[38] For some, it was the climate, and for others, the stark contrasts in living conditions. Landing at Tilbury, London, in January 1955 Jim 'could not believe the extraordinary appalling nature of the freezing cold ... I thought we were in the North Pole and it must have taken a year or more before I got used to the winter weather in Scotland'. After years in both Manchuria and Western Canada, the desolation of post-war Liverpool as a point of entry was 'horrendous' for Joyce. Glasgow was little better with its darkness, dreariness, 'soot and grime' and food rationing along with having to meet relatives who, from her perspective, were complete strangers.[39] Yet others took such transitions in their stride, like Dorothy Kirk, in New Zealand and Scotland for the first time in 1920 aged seven. In Edinburgh, she enjoyed six months of school and delighted in getting to know her grandfather ('6 ft 3" or 4" & wore size 12 shoes') and her 'Auntie Margo' who 'was a great character & graphic teller of stories'. Dorothy's written narrative is affirming and warm in tone.[40]

For other children, however, short transitional stints in school while their families were on furlough had the strongest imprint on memory, due perhaps to a mixture of personality and circumstances. Almost half of those interviewed experienced such transitional schooling (see further Table 5.2). In 1936 Dawn sailed with her family from Manchuria to Britain, via a visit to relatives in California. She was then placed in school at age four and a half while they resided in Aberdeen because her parents thought it good for her socialisation. She remembers that playing with other children was 'good fun'. However, she was teased by her playmates for using Chinese words:

> quite often they burst out into fits of laughter, not very nice laughter, and I suddenly realised that it was the words I was saying ... and I very quickly tried to find out which was the right word to say and since then I don't think I have spoken or learnt half a dozen Chinese words. I just realised that it was not done.

Dawn also struggled to understand what was expected of her in the classroom during instruction, given that in her mind she already knew the material from earlier home schooling.[41] Some thirty years later Kirsten experienced two such transitional school experiences in Edinburgh, with a

Table 5.2 Interview participants' schooling experiences, 1920s–50s

Name	Region	Years	Mission field schooling		Metropole schooling	
			Day school	Boarding school	Day school	Boarding school
Michael	South Asia	1920s–1930s	✓HS, W	–	✓F, G, CH	–
Scott Gray	South Asia	1920s–1930s	✓HS, W	✓	✓F	✓NZ
Ian Gray	South Asia	1920s–1930s	✓HS, W	✓	✓F	✓NZ
Unnamed	South Asia	1920s–1930s	✓HS, W	✓	✓	–
Amelia	South Asia	1930s	–	–	✓HH	–
David	East Asia	1930s	✓K	–	✓	–
Rose	Africa	1930s–1940s	✓	✓	✓	–
Louisa	Africa	1930s–1940s	✓	✓P, S	–	–
Robin W.	Africa	1930s–1940s	–	–	✓	–
Robin S.	South Asia	1930s–1940s	✓	–	✓E, F, HH, CH	–
Alan	South Asia	1930s–1940s	✓	–	✓F, HH, CH	–
Dawn	East Asia	1930s–1940s	✓	–	✓F, C, Sc	–
Joyce	East Asia	1930s–1940s	✓	–	✓C, Sc	–
Isabel	Africa	1930s–1950s	–	✓P, S	✓F	–
Janice Rowley	Pacific	1940s–1950s	✓HS	–	–	✓NZ
Joan Sutherland	Pacific	1940s–1950s	–	–	✓NZ	–
Marie	South Asia	1940s–1950s	–	✓	✓Sc	✓Sc
Jim	South Asia	1940s–1950s	✓	✓	✓F, CH	–
Unnamed	South Asia	1940s–1950s	–	–	✓CH	–
Veronica	Africa	1940s–1950s	–	✓	✓	–
Alison	Africa	1940s–1950s	✓	–	✓F, ✓G, ✓CH	–
Kirsten	Middle East, Africa	1950s–1960s	✓✓	–	✓F	–

Explanatory notes: C = Canada; CH and HH = Cunningham House or Home House; E = England; F = school attendance in country of origin while parents on missionary furlough; G = Glasgow; HS = home schooling; K = kindergarten; NZ = New Zealand; P = primary school; S = secondary school; Sc = Scotland; W = Woodstock.

clear juxtaposition of positively and negatively felt memories. Her primary school was remembered as 'nice' but not so the daily walk when, on one occasion, she was bullied by a local boy, giving her nightmares afterwards. A later brief high school experience stood out more because of peer teasing, being 'called Pakistani 'cos I used to speak with a Pakistani accent [laughs], or Indian accent. And also I was quite dark skinned 'cos I'd lived abroad.'[42] Isabel also remembers clearly an instance of schoolyard bullying while briefly at school in Auchterarder (near Perth, Scotland), before transferring to a school in Rothesay (Isle of Bute, western Scotland) with family on furlough from Nyasaland in 1945. At age six, this was her first unfortunate introduction to formal schooling.[43] As Ian Gray's story also indicated, the Western schoolyard could be a merciless arena for missionary children, as it was for migrant children more generally, either temporarily or permanently adjusting to what was essentially their parents' culture.[44]

Missionary children's lives were marked more regularly by repeated shorter-distance movements on an annual basis: seasonal relocations to higher altitudes or to more temperate coastal sites; holidays (both national and regional); accompanying parents on evangelistic winter-tours; and shifts between home and school for boarding, especially as children reached high school age. Geography and embodied senses demarcate these experiences for some. For Margaret Beetham these lived experiences were primarily apprehended through bodily senses of temperature and smell: the 'annual migrations to the hills' in southern India, marked by a transition from 'the plains – red, hot and dusty – to the green hills – cool, smelling of pine and eucalyptus'.[45] Propelled by a mixture of climatic and educational reasons, families often lived apart for significant chunks of a year and this was taken largely for granted. For Ian Gray a typical year in the Punjab was lived in two parts – the 'Cool Season when we stayed on the plains' and the 'Hot Season' spent 'at 7000 feet altitude' in Landour.[46] Over time various missions invested in hill-station properties, residences that were fondly remembered as second homes. Fathers were often absent from or sporadically present in children's lives at these times but were with their families for increasingly longer periods by the interwar years. Even when they joined their children for vacations, parents might fulfil professional duties, such as Scott and Ian's father James leading worship at Landour's Kellog Interdenominational Church or their mother Marion volunteering at the local hospital. In these settings, most children remember their mothers as a more stable or regular presence.

Different contexts, however, suggest other ways in which these seasonal migrations might be remembered. In the 1920s Dorothy Kirk adopted 'adventure' as a dominant narrative emphasis when writing about long-distance and seasonal travel. Her regular trips from Canton to Chefoo for school took a good five to six days, sometimes accompanied by her father

Dr John Kirk or some other adult from the New Zealand mission taking children by a mixture of train and cargo ship.[47] Similarly for Pat Booth, regularly returning to school in Darjeeling from 1949, this way of life was remembered as an adventure.[48] Logistics were not always easy. Louisa and Isabel's return travel to two different high schools in the late 1940s was a four- to five-day experience that took them from Nyasaland to Southern Rhodesia (Zimbabwe) via Mozambique, by road and rail plus a pontoon trip across the Zambesi River. Louisa remembered that this 'was a bit of a job really' which had to be endured, complete with dust, unreliable trains and delays caused by bad weather. Isabel's response was different – she recalled 'all the excitement' and narrated the journey as 'an adventure'. This included sections where the train went so slowly that they would 'leave the train and walk alongside it ... much against the rules and to the annoyance and worry of the school escorts who accompanied us throughout the travel'.[49] In this respect Judith Murphy (née Crozier) – travelling annually in the late 1940s between Western India and Perth (Western Australia) for boarding school with older brother Murray – perhaps spoke for many in wondering if all of this 'did have the effect of forcing us to become independent too'.[50]

Education

Discussion to this point reveals the extent to which furloughs, seasonal mobility, separation and the complications of life cohered most commonly around education. These were multiple experiences, made more complex in that children might experience more than one schooling mode over their educational lifetime (Table 5.2). This table indicates the great diversity of experience across a varied scale of distances and, when compared with similar stories in published memoirs, represents the wider range of missionary children's experiences. These varied from relatively stable and straightforward schooling situations – like Joan Sutherland (née Crump),[51] who only ever attended day school in New Zealand from the age of five when her family finally returned from the New Hebrides – to those, like Ian and Scott Gray who experienced the full gamut of schooling possibilities.

Yet the details given here could be illusory. Amelia, from India in the 1930s, spent much of her school life in Edinburgh, sometimes in the company of her parents but also including significant stints residing in Home House while attending George Watson's Ladies' College. What the table does not reveal, however, is that World War II added extra complexity for her. She was evacuated to Banff in Aberdeenshire, to live with relatives, and was unsettled by having to attend a co-educational school for the first time.[52] War also complicated school life for other children. For Robin S.

and his older brother, war was the catalyst for reuniting his whole family in India. England, where they were at school while living with relatives, was deemed to be unsafe as the scale of total war escalated in 1940 and so they were quickly recalled to India. In his view, war saved him from what he remembered to be an unhappy phase of early childhood in England. And for both Joyce and Dawn, extended experiences of yet another schooling system, in Vancouver, were the unexpected but fondly remembered product of wartime evacuation from Manchuria and a consequent long sequestering in Canada due to the dangers of further international travel.[53] Conversely, both Christopher and Faith Cook were sent to an alternative boarding school in western China between 1942 and 1944 – 800 miles distant from where their parents worked – because Chefoo was under Japanese occupation. From there the school's children were progressively relocated further west for safety reasons, first to Calcutta (Kolkata) and eventually to the Kalimpong school complex.[54] Faith later remembered this as a very unhappy phase of her life.

Wartime exigencies highlight the fact that this diversity of educational experiences can be explained by an equally wide range of micro- and macro-factors often specific to events, geography, mission policy, nationality and evolving contemporary attitudes towards children's welfare. For many, like Joyce Wilkins, years of separation reflected the long-standing mission policy of repatriation for education that was an enduring norm to which parents either readily assented or perhaps felt obliged to adhere.[55] For the interviewed Scottish Presbyterian children returning to Britain in this same period, most were not school boarders (even though they often still lived in an institutional environment), unlike many English children over the same period. Other missionary-sending nations also differed from this pattern, expediting specific policies for different geographical contexts. Late-nineteenth-century decisions about where Norwegian (NMS) children attended school are a good example. In South Africa, they boarded at a mix of local primary and secondary schools because parents perceived greater opportunities for them in the developing British colonies. More tropical Madagascar, however, was perceived to be a place of greater physical, mental or moral danger for children – influenced by contemporary medical thinking on children in tropical areas – and so the original missionary school and home at Antananarivo was relocated to Stavanger, Norway, in 1887.[56]

This complexity is further exemplified in the case of New Zealand. Early Presbyterian families in the New Hebrides routinely repatriated their children back to New Zealand for their education from the 1870s onwards, due to the simple lack of any schools and because of the disparate and isolated island contexts in which they lived. This was still the case, for example, for both Donald and Janice Crump in the 1950s.[57] By way of contrast,

Presbyterian missionary families in southern China and northern India from the 1900s sent their children to regional schools – namely Chefoo and Woodstock. Yet other factors played a key part in differentiating this pattern. Children of the Canton Villages Mission tended to have all of their education at Chefoo, whereas the Punjab Mission's children often were sent to New Zealand for high school. This pattern was further complicated by a child's place in the family (older children like Scott and Ian Gray being sent home) and, increasingly from the 1930s, parents' concerns about the American cultural influences of mission schools like Woodstock; a perception that a New Zealand high school education was better; and growing discomfort over the emotional and developmental impact of separation on their children.[58] As such, children's schooling experiences were dictated by circumstances mixed in with parental and organisational decisions or policies, over which they had little influence.

In her analysis of missionary children's memoirs, Vandrick helpfully observes that some 'loved boarding school, some hated it and some were merely resigned to it. Like it or not, they almost never had a choice.'[59] This same observation can be extrapolated for the wider range of educational experiences and transitions, although in this current study, there were at least two cases of children in the 1940s who were included in the decision-making process.[60] What is most noticeable, across many of those interviewed, is the degree to which children accepted and made these changes and transitions, while at the same time recognising the degree to which such changes could be difficult. In Veronica's mind – reflecting on her various schooling experiences in South Africa and Scotland and also drawing upon her extensive experience as an educator herself – 'I was just nine and nine you actually accept everything still. Not quite as much as three perhaps but you know that was just the way it was. You didn't question it at all.'

Veronica's oral testimony is interesting in that she indicates so clearly how very similar experiences of multiple educational transitions could have such varying responses, influenced by such things as personality and disposition. In her own case, she clearly differentiated her final transition to a Scottish school with respect to two things. On the one hand she found learning easy: 'after a few weeks I'd caught up with the rest of the class and that was fine and I was the kind of child that is so easy to teach'. That was not challenging. On the other hand, 'what was hugely challenging was changing the educational system, changing the language, just changing your peer group. All of that you know was different.'[61] Like so many of her missionary child peers, navigating the cultures and politics of school classrooms and playgrounds was central to Veronica's experience. Likewise, for all of those in Table 5.2 who boarded in a range of mission field and metropole settings, school was defined as much by what they experienced as by what they learnt, complicated further by the communal spaces of dormitories and dining rooms. Here the various stories indicate again as diverse a range of experiences as there were individuals.

Alongside the issues raised by Veronica and earlier by Ian Gray, two further features deserve comment. One was that initial struggles and adjustments were the norm, irrespective of age, gender or school level, or whether school was experienced in the mission field or metropole. Endurance was a common theme – some thrived and others simply toughed it out. Typical of many narratives is Janice Crump's experience as an eight-year-old in 1950s southern New Zealand, far from her childhood on tropical Nguna Island. She boarded for three years at Columba College for girls in Dunedin. Initially, Janice was meant to live with relatives in a small regional town, but her aunt could not drive and 'she said I was too gregarious to be kept at home [laughter] so I needed to go places and she couldn't take me places so that's why they decided Columba would be a better option for me [laughter]'. At the point of parting from her parents, the strongest emotional imprint for Janice was her puzzlement over her mother's crying, refracted through her own later experiences as a parent wherein she now apprehends the emotional cost for her mother of long-term separation. She remembers 'crying a lot and being very homesick that first term' and the consequent kindness shown to her by the school's principal and staff. At the same time, most of her memoir fleshes out her sense that 'in time I settled at Columba, and looking back, they were good days'. And unlike Jim's pejorative view of a Scottish winter, Janice's first experience of snow in Dunedin 'was an amazing sight', made more memorable by a teacher who sensitively prompted her to go and sit at the classroom window to watch it fall.[62]

Yet, a similar set of experiences for someone of a different personality, disposition or a particular stage of life might leave darker, unhappier traces in memory. Therefore, a second feature is that missionary children had to adjust, sometimes more than once, to the vagaries and idiosyncrasies of school cultures, and this was not always easy. Jim's introduction to Scottish schools was somewhat sobering. While not himself bullied, his sense was that children were constantly 'fighting and tousling on the concrete playground' and he wondered if he 'had come to some place where the law of the jungle pertained and that was quite disturbing I remember'. A teacher who one minute helped to 'tutor me in pounds, shillings and pence' but who later would 'occasionally give me the belt for not being able to do it' was equally perturbing to a young boy trying to find his way.[63] One case from southern Africa illustrates this further.[64] Isabel was introduced to the vagaries of school life in Scotland as a six-year-old with parents on furlough between 1945 and 1948. On return to Nyasaland, and a change of location for her father, Isabel and her sister boarded at a succession of primary and secondary schools in Salisbury. While she remembered the trips home as highly anticipated adventures, that anticipation was perhaps a reflection of school life as something to be endured: there was 'such a relief when it was time to go home at the school holiday[s]'. Her overall estimation that 'I was never very brilliant at school ... I never got very far' sums up her sense of academic achievement at that time, but it also belies a deeper-seated emotional memory that was more to do with boarding culture than the academic experience of school. She recalls the whimsies of boarding life such as gender segregation, meal-time etiquette, the strictness of a matron, separation from siblings, regimented weekends to the extent that 'your whole time was actually pretty much planned out' and limited money. One instance that stands out was being hit over the head with a soup ladle for talking during meals, while a primary school boarder. 'There was no way that the staff made us feel at home!', but at the time this kind of institutional behaviour was 'considered all part and parcel of being a school boarder and very much taken for granted'. Across the interviews, this was as bad as it got, in terms of institutional violence. Yet we know that abuses did occur when other memoirists and present-day institutional revelations are considered. This element of school and institutional life demands serious and careful attention within wider mission history.[65]

Separation – children's perspectives

Veronica did not question her schooling experiences and weekly separation, but she did qualify this in one important respect: 'I might have questioned it if we had been sent to this country [Scotland] leaving my parents in South Africa. That might have been another matter, but they didn't believe in having other people bringing up their children.'[66] As noted at various points through this book, from very early on missionary children's repatriation for education, and consequent familial separation, was normative for nineteenth- and early twentieth-century British missionary (and other Empire) families and was replicated by other nations. Enshrined early on in the life of the LMS, it formed an 'uneasy compromise' that balanced 'permanent settlement' with 'parental autonomy' and that was 'mediated by the missionary and evangelically philanthropic public'. In the process it emerged as the 'most powerful recurring motif of the missionary experience', but one that also 'provoked intense emotional suffering among missionary parents (and children)' and thus became 'embedded' as 'one of the many contradictions' within the Protestant missionary movement.[67] Veronica's parents' decision in the 1950s to return the family intact to Scotland for their children's education signified how this began to change over time. By the mid-twentieth century, there were other possibilities or trajectories and indeed discourses at play. Furthermore, previous discussion reveals the extent to which over time geographical and ideological contexts, refracted through the varying lenses of sending-nation cultures and politics, increasingly (re)shaped both parents' decisions and children's experiences.

Separation was a complex phenomenon and one that was not experienced the same by all. Some children did not experience any separation and so it did not define what it meant for them to be missionary children. For others, there were a number of variations on a theme: separation from family (or some family members) within a mission field setting for defined periods of time; separation from parents but sometimes in the company of siblings; long-term separation in metropole settings; and commonly children and mother living in the metropole but with fathers left in or returning to a mission field context. However this was configured, the information in Table 5.2 makes it very clear that different modes of separation did demarcate and inscribe the lives of many. Sixteen of the twenty-two interviewed from the 1920s to the 1950s experienced some degree of separation from parents and/or siblings. Some of this has already been canvassed both in this chapter and previously in Chapter 2. The following discussion addresses two further questions – to what extent did missionary children perceive separation to be an issue, And how did they navigate the complications of separation? – with the latter considered through a further consideration of emotional labour and happiness and emotional frontiers.

Children's responses to separation

The realities of separation are helpfully bookended by two memoirs from children in the Indian context who responded in quite different ways. One is that of Joyce Wilkins.[68] The moment of her initial separation in 1909 was but one episode in a longer autobiographical narrative that paints a wholly pejorative picture of what it meant to be a missionary child. At Sevenoaks railway station she recorded in her book that 'the full horror of the situation suddenly struck me. Mother and Father were leaving me behind, *and taking Phyllis and Eric with them* [emphasis original].' She chased the slowly moving train down the platform and onto the track, eventually caught up by a porter and older sister Dorothy; 'a very sad tearful little girl was taken back to school that day and left to cry herself to sleep in the night nursery'. This moment left a clearly felt emotional imprint on her adult memory. In an interview some eighty years later, she added that 'I can remember it even if I go through Sevenoaks station now, I get the feeling of it'. More importantly, she thought that this event marked 'the beginning of my really traumatic experience'. From an incident where she hid in her bedside locker and broke a chamber pot, to a constant struggle with schoolwork (which would now be identified as dyslexia), to a long litany of hated institutional strictures, Joyce's nine years of separation were unhappy ones. Of the many large posters of biblical stories on the nursery walls, she identified most with the one depicting the shepherd searching out the lost sheep. She wrote: 'The picture was probably called the Good Shepherd, but I thought of it as the Lost Sheep. And I felt such an affinity with that sheep!'

The second story of New Zealand children Judith and Murray Crozier both continues this theme and yet suggests other possible child responses. It is instructive because of its complexity and the way that it suggests that children, as much as parents, might perceive why hard decisions were made.[69] During the 1940s as children and then teenagers, they experienced two phases of separation from their parents: first to Hebron School in Tamil Nadu, three days travel south of their village near Pune, India; and then subsequently to boarding schools in Perth, Western Australia. Hebron School was set in a beautiful location but, wrote Judith, 'we were too young to be in boarding school'. It lacked domestic warmth and love and her main recollection was of 'lines of children doing things': medical treatments, school meals and 'sitting on rows of little commodes'. Added to this was what she later described as the 'theologically conservative' nature of the school, including the weekly occurrence of 'text day' wherein 'each child would have to stand up in the dining room in front of the whole school and say a [Bible] text by heart'. This was a 'traumatic experience'. Many children 'cried because they could not remember or say their verse properly'. This seems to have been the catalyst for their parents to send them to Perth for their high school years, from where they would return to India annually. In this decision the parents displayed some enlightenment: they worked within a theologically conservative mission (PIVM) and yet struggled with Hebron's approach, and they included the children in their decision-making.[70] In Judith's mind, while this was a hard decision, she and Murray 'were aware both of the depth of our parents' love for us, as well as their commitment to their chosen area of service in India, and hence did not resent their decision'.

In the broader mission history record and its consequent historiography, Joyce's story tends to be normative in how it represents missionary children's responses to separation, with Judith and Murray's story acting more as a counter-narrative. Historical change might be one way of explaining or positioning these differences, but another possibility is to see them as being two ends of a spectrum of negative to positive experiences and responses differentiated by a mix of other contextual or personal factors. Vandrick's analysis of American missionary child memoirs – less historicised – echoes this complexity. It emphasises the lifelong impact of separation and adjustment issues (exacerbated for many by the 'cycle of separation and departure'), while conceding that some either did not suffer or did not suffer too much and 'many if not most were and are able to adjust at least reasonably well eventually, and to celebrate the good aspects of their having lived in different countries' as children.[71]

The children in this study sat at a range of points along that spectrum, highlighting that their responses could be individually varied. Some, like Veronica, were able to rationalise shorter-term separations, while now realising that they would have struggled with longer-term separations. Joyce tellingly attested to this when she recounted a short separation from family on return to Scotland in 1944. While her parents sought an apartment to rent in Glasgow, she and a sister were 'farmed out with ancient missionaries that we didn't know' in Edinburgh, living for a month in a tenement flat that was 'very dark and very old fashioned'. Eventually reunited as a family in Glasgow she realised 'we had broken their [parents'] hearts I had never been separated from them in my life'. Isabel also considered herself to have been 'lucky' to have lived so long in southern Africa, to have had the company of siblings while away at boarding school in Southern Rhodesia and to have avoided what felt like a foreign education system in Scotland. At the same time, in hindsight and in a similar vein to Joyce, she thinks that the person hardest hit emotionally by their separation was her mother.[72]

For others, significant periods of separation seem not to have been a problem although, as one woman pondered this, she conceded that many details now eluded her. She experienced whole or partial family separation as a seasonal boarder at Woodstock School in the 1930s. On return to New Zealand in 1939, mother and children together were separated from their father for the length of the war while he did medical study and war service in England. However, she conveyed no regret, concern or unhappiness about this, unlike that of her older sister.[73] Likewise, others thought, in hindsight, that they accepted such transitions and separations without too much bother: Rose quite matter-of-factly recounted that her mother took her to Cape Town (from Nyasaland) 'and settled me into boarding school and then went home … [and] I seemed to manage to settle down'. This, she now thinks, 'helped me in life' with respect to facing or coping with later life transitions.[74]

At the other end of the spectrum, there were those for whom separation was more difficult, and their cases explain further why children's responses to separation could be so varied. Alison's experience of separation was complex (see next section) but her account of time spent in Cunningham House, Edinburgh, was positive and thorough. At the same time, she observed that others 'really suffered' wherein 'some children also just felt completely deprived of their mother's love and everything'.[75] The interview material, at least, does not reveal this as a gendered experience, but more one of age or life stage. Taken as a whole, this struggle resulted from just being too young to be sent off to boarding school or a child's place in the family. Often, but not always, those who struggled the least or who quickly adapted to changed circumstances were the oldest child of a family: people like Marie at boarding school in Pakistan and then Edinburgh; Scott Gray in India and Christchurch; Rose in South Africa; Jim and Michael each at different times in both India and Edinburgh; Louisa in Africa; and Alison in Glasgow and Edinburgh.[76] Conversely, often the next (second) sibling was the one who struggled more with the transitions away from the immediate family, epitomised in Ian Gray's narrative.

Separation was also precipitated by unexpected circumstances, which tended to elicit negative responses. One man experienced two periods separated from his parents while at school in Edinburgh and living in Cunningham House. The first was anticipated but the second resulted from a sudden change in family circumstances. He was ambivalent about the first stint of separation ('I think it wasn't the best period in my life 'cos I, at one stage I stole all the pocket money') but described it largely in positive terms. The second one he described as being 'dumped back in the house', with a younger brother, and that was a 'bitter experience I think … going back there for a second time, I think that was not good for me'.[77] The impact of political instability or war also caused unanticipated separations. Many missionary children in China experienced forced separations through the Boxer Rebellion period and a later succession of regional conflicts between warlords in the interwar period. Thomas Torrance along with five siblings and their mother – in Edinburgh and separated from their father for six years from 1928 to 1934 – were typical of many families in this period.[78]

War separation was epitomised further by the experiences of two of the Cook children (CIM) during World War II. Faith Cook joined brother Christopher as a school evacuee in Western China in 1944, where in the dormitories she remembers that 'many small children, disturbed by the sudden loss of parents and home, showed their distress by becoming bed-wetters. These unfortunate children were obliged to have a notice posted at the head of their beds that read in large letters, "I am a baby. I wet my bed."' Further evacuation in late 1944 to Kalimpong, India, further accentuated her own sense of loss and distress, recounting run-ins with school authorities (and subsequent corporal punishments 'that left bruises and welts'), as well as kindness shown by individual staff. Her overriding memory is of her emotional responses, embodied in the fact that

> like any other young child taken from the security of her home and parents, I craved attention. Among the youngest in the school, my homesickness was often acute; then I would cry quietly into my pillow at night, longing for my

father's loud cheery voice or my mother's goodnight kiss. The only way to obtain such individual care was through illness,

which she capitalised on as much as possible.[79]

Reflecting on his own experience of separation, through living in Cunningham House in the 1930s, Michael Orr asks 'What effect did the long separation from parents have on our lives [...]? The first answer must be that the effect varied widely from child to child; and the second that it was a good deal less than would have been the case with children in that situation today.' This perspective reflects a largely positive personal experience wherein he and his sister had 'little cause to complain'.[80] Yet Faith Cook's stated intent, in writing her autobiography, to touch on negative 'experiences shared by many other missionaries' children known to me', bears out Orr's recognition that it was not easy for others.[81] Together their accounts suggest that a 'whole family' approach might be a more satisfying way to further develop a history of missionary children's separation, exemplified further in the case of the Wilkins family (with three sisters experiencing separation in uniquely different ways)[82] and by the instances wherein interviewees reflected as much on the emotional toll for their parents as on their own struggles. At that point children's, parents and institutional narratives intersect. From children's perspectives, this intersection is usefully conceptualised as a set of emotional navigations and negotiations between and within age groups.

Children, separation and emotional management

Michael Orr's sense that family separation in the 1930s might have been more the norm, and therefore more acceptable, finds some resonance in wider scholarship on children, empire and nation. At the same time, there was tension, in that when set against the emerging cultural norm of the companionate family, 'British-Indian children in the metropole were commonly defined in terms of their *lack* of family [emphasis original]'. As such they were perceived often as 'analagous to orphans' and therefore came under the care of 'boarding school staff, other relatives, and non-familial guardians' acting as 'surrogate childrearers'.[83] Separation and re-adjustment to metropole settings therefore became an experience to be both negotiated and managed. To reiterate an earlier point, separation emerged primarily as an emotional issue for children as much as it did for their parents.[84] It was less about how much they liked or hated school and more about feeling the lack of immediate family and therefore searching for a locus of security and identity. Here discussion moves from one family's story to a brief focus on the Edinburgh missionary children's homes as emotionally managed sites within which children had to contend with, cross or negotiate spatially bounded and age-defined emotional frontiers.

Alison, aged eight, moved with her family to Africa's Gold Coast in 1948, as her father took up a teacher education position in a Presbyterian college in Akropong near Accra.[85] This was a positive period of her life described in colourful detail. In 1950 they travelled back to Scotland for furlough. Alison and her twin sister remained behind when the family returned to Africa. For the first year, they lived with family friends in South Glasgow, partly because this household spoke 'Scots' and her father wanted them 'to learn the Scots language'. Life continued more or less as normal. Then cataclysmically 'our whole life changed totally' when 'my mother died' unexpectedly in Africa. Initially swept out of school and taken to Edinburgh by 'well-meaning aunts', eventually they all resided together again as a family in Renfrew once their father and younger brother returned to Scotland. At this point, at around eleven or twelve years of age, Alison took on the role of mother, irrespective of her own grief: 'we just had to get on with it, there was no counselling for children in those days, my father was a wreck basically, a complete emotional wreck, he absolutely adored my mother and so I just became like little mother in the family'. She juggled domestic responsibilities with daily school, often turning up late which was understood by the headmaster. And then came a second, heart-rending blow. As Alison describes it:

> that was a tough old world, I mean our father just put us on the train [to Edinburgh] when he was going back to Ghana, he didn't tell us he was going back, he just put us on the train and said bye, remember don't drink tea out of your saucer and that was it and we didn't realise that that was him away to Ghana, he hadn't, I mean sure he couldn't tell us, sure he couldn't say anything, it would be impossible for him.

Cunningham House then became home for all three children.

Alison's adoption of the role of 'mother' issued partly from self-perceived character traits, in that she saw herself as 'a very capable little girl'. Her mother's death and ensuing events 'affected us all differently, I think it made me very capable, we didn't shed tears or I didn't shed tears then'. These events certainly had an impact but, in her memory as a child, she thinks that she was more 'heartbroken' at being whisked out of school by their Edinburgh aunts, thus missing the last day of term, the end-of-year school play and carol service and also because she had to leave behind 'all our childhood possessions'. At her father's unheralded return to Ghana, she muses that 'we did feel a bit let down, we felt he might've said that's me off to Ghana, you know it would've not been nearly so hard for us as it would've been for him to say it actually'. Of their move into Cunningham House, Alison understatedly observed that 'all was not lost, it was a good place and we just got on with it you know'. Again, she became the 'kind of steady reliable one who said c'mon boys, you know get the work done or whatever'. As children, they constantly seemed to be the physical and emotional meat in the sandwich. While 'in those days people didn't understand about asking the children what they would like to do', Alison now thinks that they should have been asked. They were not, and her narrative starkly outlines how she had to navigate a confusing pathway, between adults' expectations and children's desires.

Alison's telling of the story puts the spotlight back on the emotional dimensions of parent–child separation. Thoughts or feelings about separation often appear absent in the correspondence of British imperial families, for example, but 'may have come under deeper scrutiny only in retrospect'.[86] Oral history provides one such retrospective angle, accentuating here the extent to which separation required emotional management[87] by the children affected. Alison's family story was one such case, unique in its sobering details but also representative of many others. Here we return to a combination of emotional concepts to aid understanding – 'emotional labour', 'happiness' and 'emotional frontiers'.

While previous discussion outlined labour and happiness separately in relation to parents' and institutional narratives, their relevance is also evident through children's narratives. Recent scholarship on happiness, however, points to the efficacy of considering happiness and emotional labour together as interrelated concepts. Mary Hatfield argues that defining happiness is 'a vexed philosophical dilemma', a sentiment echoed by cultural commentator Sara Ahmed.[88] It is an emotion that therefore needs to be carefully historicised. For missionary children, this means thinking about issues of age and religious expectations. In the process, happiness emerges as a highly politicised emotion. As Ahmed notes in the work of Simone de Beauvoir, 'happiness translates its wish into a politics, a wishful politics, a politics that demands that others live according to a wish'.[89]

This observation is apposite for children in missionary homes, as further discussion suggests. Hatfield also draws general attention to the various 'emotional scripts specific to age and gender, class, and event'[90] that circumscribe or proscribe relationships, linking the enactment of happiness to the notion of 'emotional labour'. This reconfigures the management of emotions as both a private and public activity (considered in Chapter 2). I would suggest that, in the Scottish context, these 'scripts' can be rethought of as significations of the emotional frontiers confronted by and thus navigated by the children within the wider emotional community of the homes. While such frontiers have been conceived as marking lines in the sand between spatially separate communities (like school or home),[91] here they are spatially, temporally and institutionally bounded. Furthermore, there is great potential in seeing such frontiers not just as 'barriers' but also as productive 'contact zones' – in this case, the negotiations between adults and children. As such, then, a critical question might be: '[w]hat kind of potential was embedded in the experience and the space' of emotional frontiers encountered by children?[92] The interweaving of these concepts, when scrutinised for one significant site of separation – Scottish missionary children's homes – serves to highlight further both the interrelated and differentiated nature of the narrative lenses and to outline how children's homes constituted a problematic emotional community.

Up to 1939, at least 122 children lived in either of the Presbyterian Edinburgh homes (Duddingston Home House and Cunningham House) with an average annual intake of between ten and fifteen, encompassing an even spread of boys and girls ranging from five to sixteen years of age on entry.[93] Nearly 80 per cent of the children were there with siblings. Of the sixteen Scottish interviewees seven resided in one or other of these homes (see again Table 5.2). From a public and parental perspective, they were 'happy children' occupying 'happy homes'. A sustained adult-produced emotional discourse represented the two homes in terms of domestic stability and happiness, focused on reassuring both public supporters and the children's parents. Happiness was the expressed and hoped-for outcome: both homes were ideally represented as 'happy homes' or reflecting a 'happy family'. Alison and her sister were two such members of this supposedly 'big cheerful family'.[94]

When looked at from children's perspectives, however, the emotional labour of being 'happy' took on a potentially more onerous dimension. They were confronted by a frontier that demanded a two-fold set of emotional expectations: to effectively please three sets of adults (the wider public, their parents and the adult staff who acted *in loco parentis*); and to maintain the emotional order and well-being of the homes' community. Therefore, from their point of view, 'happiness' can be re-read as an imposed adult 'emotional script' – the key marker of the frontier that forced children to navigate their way between their own variably positive or negative experiences of separation and the wider social expectations and norms set by the adult world – that demanded regular, active emotional management.[95]

This is evidenced quite clearly when adult-produced sources are read against the grain. Cunningham House's matron Lily Wilkie, for instance, wrote at length in 1922 about the ways in which children managed their own emotions for the sake of others. One older boy 'kept his temper' when disturbed by younger children while doing his homework, 'although he was feeling so annoyed'. In the aftermath of parents leaving, children controlled their emotions: 'there wasn't a tear when the mother was in sight'; departing parents would get a 'smile – a very watery smile – and a cheery shout of "good-bye"'; and the boys would later head upstairs 'manfully whistling'. At bedtime, some were distressed while the older ones actively comforted younger children. She noted that the 'little ones are more easily comforted; but the older ones realize better what it means, and that years will pass before they see their parents again'. Yet in their 'sorrow' Wilkie witnessed mutual sympathy. She quoted one upset boy who told her that he would not go to his room '"yet for fear the others see that I have been crying, and it may make them feel sad and want their fathers and mothers too". There was no shame for the tears, but a desire not to make others unhappy.'[96] Clearly these stories would tug at readers' heartstrings to elicit more financial support. But they also reveal the cooperative efforts required by children to fulfil their emotional obligations and the extent to which this emotional community was mutually negotiated, practised and sustained by adults and children together over several decades.

At the same time, the interviews reveal emotional ambiguity, with children's memories flavoured by such variations as personality, family position and circumstances. For example, Alan remembers disliking school but loving his time in Cunningham House. His brother Robin S. was similar, recalling friends made and the use given him of an old air raid shelter to do chemistry experiments. Robin valued freedoms that he would not have had at home, where he thinks that he would have been told to 'do better' and 'work harder'. Alan found this detrimental and had to repeat a year of high school.[97] Another person related with a chuckle how he and a friend absconded from the home one evening dressed up as 'Red Indians'.[98] Alison spoke warmly of both her own experiences and the details of co-residents. She recounted duty rosters and responsibilities, but also communal activities like homework around the large dining room table, evening recreation and holding concerts. Older girls and boys helped to care for younger children in their respective dormitories and going to school.[99] During World War II, life was harder, perhaps, with rationing of food and bathwater and a lack of heating. Elaine McArthy remembers that for 'most of the winter my, and other children's fingers and toes were covered with painful chilblains'. She was a wartime evacuee resident, but noted that for many of the missionary children, 'it was very hard' because many of them were separated without relief for the duration of the war.[100]

There were difficulties, as Alison commented on previously. Noting the loss of connection of many with their mothers, she wonders for herself if 'we would've felt that, if we'd had a mother but having already lost our mother, we weren't used to that kind of attention'.[101] Annual reports note difficult residents whose families were advised to seek alternative arrangements. In context, this appears to have been a personnel issue, involving a matron of the late 1930s who was perhaps not suited to the position and who struggled with the teenage residents.[102] Along with the absconding 'Red Indians', however, these might also be read as juvenile forms of resistance at the frontier, asserting themselves demonstrably (while others, perhaps, kept their resistances and struggles to themselves).[103]

Ex-residents also indicated another point of difference from adult rhetoric. The earlier matron, Lily Wilkie, was lauded in official minutes and reports, especially for her motherly qualities and approach.[104] Children perhaps experienced or perceived this differently. They certainly respected her (and later kept contact), but in Michael's words, from their perspective, she 'was very strict' and 'ruled us with a rod of iron'. She 'was in charge of you, she wasn't your mother and she never asserted herself as such ... but she loved us I think'. Two decades later Alison's memory was of no-nonsense staff, who were 'strict' and yet caring, and a regime which had 'structure and form', but which was also 'flexible'.[105]

Taken as one iteration of the larger 'world' of missionary children's homes, children's experiences of or responses to the Edinburgh institutions bear witness to Hatfield's conclusion that 'happiness has to be contextualised, understood as part of a shared emotional lexicon, riddled with personal and social connotations, and described to others with consideration and a degree of intention'.[106] The homes emphasise the importance of understanding 'happiness' equally as a historicised and politicised concept. By placing this discussion at the intersections of the three overlapping narrative lenses a more dynamic picture of a spatially bounded emotional community emerges, as one that was produced through the acts of management and negotiation at the emotional frontier of adult and child expectations. It was shaped and produced both by children 'learning to feel' as well as 'feeling through practice' wherein, as noted by Hester Barron and Claire Langhamer in English schools, that 'practice was a process embedded in the material context, spaces and – particularly – the relationships of everyday life'. They make a case for differentiating the 'learned' elements of emotional community from the 'practice' of feeling. However, the evidence from the Edinburgh missionary children's homes suggests that both worked together to produce emotional community.[107] In this case that community was signified by an imposed 'emotional script' (which required certain responses), but also by shared expectations of mutual support among residents, and a balance between hard work, play and potentially gendered freedoms. Yet individuality led to different responses and abilities to cope, signposted further by varied acts of resistance. Separation worked for some but not for others.

Conclusion: identity and impact

This chapter has focused carefully on the ways by which missionary children negotiated the complicated elements of their lives spatially, cognitively, educationally and emotionally. It provides a more complex narration – based again largely on hindsight reflection via both oral history and published memoirs constructed doubly through remembered details and feelings – that both complements and complicates the equally important perspective that life was ordinary. In turn, the analysis conducted throughout the chapter has attempted to judiciously balance collective insights with the individuality of experience so clearly on view across the sources. Likewise, it has walked a careful line between either under- or over-emphasising parent–child separation as a critical descriptor or analytical category. Children's emotions and responses to separation were highly variable for a host of reasons, and the foregoing discussion attempts to capture that reality. David Hollinger makes a similar judgement juxtaposing the different fortunes of selected American missionary children in the twentieth century. On the one hand he is not convinced 'that missionary children as adults were disproportionately subject to emotional problems and mental illness' or that they were 'more likely to be depressed or to commit suicide than others in their age cohort'. Neither does he 'find reliable evidence that parental religious beliefs, parenting styles, the mission environment, encounters with "natives", or any other specific set of factors correlate more than others with the psychological stress of missionary children'. On the other hand, he is right in suggesting that the 'taken for granted' nature of such risks deserves further comment. 'The memoirs of even the most successful of missionary children', he observes, 'comment on the psychological challenges they experienced in adjusting to mainstream American life', which now forms a common and easily recognised trope in more recent non-fictional and fictional literature. He goes on to identify both the attendant 'casualties' of missionary childhood as adults alongside those 'high achievers' who went on to notable vocations and careers.[108]

By way of conclusion, then, brief comment is made on how the complicated contours of missionary children's lives might have shaped resulting identities and life trajectories. This is evidenced for individuals and families across a range of sources. Rose recognised this when she reflectively adjudged that the separation and changes in her childhood and teenage years helped her cope with later life transitions.[109] More controversially, Ron Malcolm, the only son of New Zealand CIM missionaries, attributed his uncompromised conscientious objection and pacifism during World War II to having seen 'the results of Chinese warfare' as a child. As such 'his conscience convinced him of the utter wrong and futility of war'.[110] Missionary child enculturation may also have contributed to young Willie Marwick's conscientious objection during World War I, made on 'ethical and intellectual grounds' as a graduate arts student. Marwick went on to an acclaimed career as a Scottish labour historian.[111]

Each of the Wilkins children pursued careers in professions or interests that may have been influenced in part by the crucible of Protestant religion and missionary lives as well as by personal responses to their individual experiences. Two became doctors (with one specialising in psychiatry and the other returning later to India as a medical missionary), one was a life-long teacher and educational leader and Joyce became a speech therapist and university lecturer.[112] There were other legacies too. The Wilkins sisters later used 'Freudian analysis to come to terms with their childhood experiences'.[113] Joyce documented a mix of anxieties developed through her childhood – further exacerbated by other adults' attempts to teach and regulate sexual issues as a young teenager and keenly felt hypocrisy over her baptism in 1916 – that 'psychoanalysis' then helped her to move beyond in the mid-1930s. Younger sister Phyllis also received similar therapeutic help in reconciling her sexuality as an adult. Joyce later insightfully concluded that their 'parents had a call and they made the big sacrifice; they went out to preach to the heathen. But the sacrifice was also of the children.'[114]

Brendon concedes that the Wilkins family was not typical, especially in the ways in which they articulated and later came to terms with their complicated lives. On a grander scale, historical missionary children may have gone on to be influential cultural icons or political leaders in America, to influence national politics (as in the case of ABCFM children in the Hawaiian Islands) or to morph into colonial citizens upholding the status quo as in the case of Norwegian children enculturated within the British schools of South Africa.[115] The interviews, however, reveal a more mundane spectrum of experiences and responses for many others, suggesting that for those children who 'came home' from such locations (or who only returned to mission locales later) issues of identity were sometimes only properly apprehended through adult hindsight. This is an important topic, but one that is still in its infancy. Final discussion sketches this out in preliminary form only, comparing New Zealand and Scottish ex-children's memories, because the interviews suggest a degree of differentiation.

The legacies of missionary childhoods for New Zealanders living in India and the New Hebrides from the 1920s to the 1950s were narrated mainly in terms of parental influence, resulting character traits or values and, to a lesser extent, the formation of cultural empathy. Maternal influences were prominent. One woman plainly stated that 'I don't think it [India] has influenced my life too much' and then directly proceeded to talk about her mother as a more significant influence: someone who was 'very interesting' and 'very kind-hearted', who she thought 'certainly did her best to make life good for us'. The burden of care fell on her mother, with her doctor father away so much.[116] For David, however, his father's dictum that a missionary should 'always work to make yourself dispensable' rubbed off on him, as he later proceeded to a medical missionary vocation in India.[117] Both Scott and Ian Gray directly thought of their mother's influence when asked this question, but for them, parental influence was thoroughly mixed up with identity. As the eldest two children born in India to Scottish parents (one of whom grew up in New Zealand), and who then went to an American-run school in India and a public boarding school in New Zealand, this was complex. Experiences as missionary children may have contributed to Scott's eventual vocation as a dentist and academic, and Ian's many positions within New Zealand and New Hebridean education. Yet they attributed most influence to their mother who embodied for them what it meant to be 'Scottish'. Ian reflected that 'while I feel proud of my Scottish ancestry the only impact it has had has been through the training, education of my mother really'. Her 'dour, her energetic absolutely honest Scottish approach to life has been valuable to me. And the little success that I've had … I put down really to the character strain that she sowed in me. So that's my Scottish background, true Scottish character I think.'[118]

A mixture of parenting and individual experiences fed into persistent character traits or values important in later adult life. Joan Sutherland and Janice Rowley simply viewed their years in the New Hebrides as being 'a part of my life' and 'normal', one of many pieces fitting into the mosaic of their identity.[119] Scott Gray thought of himself as independent, self-reliant and a 'perfectionist'. These were all traits that served him well as a dentist and later as a serious recreational painter. Yet independence and self-reliance, he conceded, could have been coping strategies learnt while separated from parents over many years.[120] Janice identified caring and thriftiness as positive and sustaining personal values inherited from her parents, but her tendency to be 'over-protective' as a parent was a consequence of her early boarding experiences. Although he returned to New Zealand at an early age, David similarly thought that his ability to be confident in his own 'individuality' was due largely to his infant and pre-school years in 1930s Japan.[121] For David, however, the missionary influence did not end there. He belonged to a wider family lineage of Protestant missionaries and, through his parents' interests and many international contacts or visitors, developed a 'global perspective' and 'international awareness'. He learnt that making friendships lay at the heart of cross-cultural understanding both overseas and at home. Cultural empathy was also a significant personal legacy for Ian Gray, who always 'delighted' in his contacts with South Asian people in New Zealand. He could say that like them, he was born in India and 'straight away you had a common bond'. The net effect of his years both in India and the New Hebrides, he thought, has been two-fold. On the one hand, 'I feel sympathetic to people outside their parent, their home culture' and 'am sensitive to other people's cultural differences'. On the other hand, this has bred in him a keen cultural critique of the New Zealand context where he thinks that until recently, 'New Zealanders don't accept other cultures kindly'. This might be 'an indication of people who themselves are not sure of their identity'.[122] That is a point worth pondering further, both for the culture under critique and as a corrective for the supposedly problematic identity of missionary children.

Scottish interviewees made similar observations which were refracted through children's individual circumstances or contexts, also signalling siblings or other family members with the same background but no interest in it. Kirsten made two observations for herself: that she identified as 'European' rather than 'Scottish', because of her mixed Danish-British parentage (exemplified by different national traditions followed at Christmas time); and that growing up in the Middle East and East Africa, along with the inheritance of Christian faith, has made her a 'much more tolerant person' with a 'warmth for people that are in the minority rather than the majority'.[123] Robin W. was very young when his parents returned definitively to Britain from the Belgian Congo in 1940, so has no memory of his African birthplace. Yet like David, he was one of many such children whose parents were at least second-generation missionaries along with wider family and thus were steeped in missionary narratives and outlooks. This spilled over into their lives in Scotland. For instance, he was brought up to regard everyone as equal, regardless of things like race. At school 'I could never understand … how there was a prejudice towards people who were not white'. During the war years, he found that he could relate to evacuated Jewish boys 'more readily than some of the other white boys could'. This derived from 'the whole family attitude. We were all God's children.' Like Kirsten, these elements combined with Christian faith meant that, as a businessman in later life, he was 'known for [his] ethics'. He mused that 'Christianity is a way of life for me. And so I suppose that's the same missionary principles.'[124] Yet he also observed that one brother has no interest in their earlier years, thus individuality also plays a part in responsive identity. For others identity, life trajectory and legacies were less clear-cut and therefore more diffuse. Again like Kirsten, for many, the mixed nationalities of their parents along with childhoods in other spaces have created a sense of being more than one thing. Jim framed it like this: 'In my case I have never had any sense of an Indian identity' (while much of that location still resonates). However, 'I do have a strong dual sense of identity. I am of course Scots, my father was Scots. I'm a British subject … With my American passport [due to his mother] in my hand I am as republican as the next man [*sic*].' He thinks of himself as completely 'Scots' and completely 'American'.[125]

One final brief vignette illustrates this further. Louisa's take on her own life journey was sophisticated and novel. She mused that 'there's never been a whole story that's come out neat and clean like that at all, I mean anything you pull out of my background leaves sort of sticky trails in all directions'. Her reflections on being African and being spiritual will preface the Conclusion. But her sense of being a contested person occupying equally contested spaces is worth noting here. After African high school, she moved to Aberdeen to do her medical degree, prompted in part by her mother's desire for her to stay with relatives as well as Louisa's own desire to gain an 'internationally recognised degree'. In that physical transition, 'I carried Africa with me and which comes first, I don't know really.' Her intention was always to return to Africa. As such she saw herself as a 'white African', albeit complicated then and later by apartheid and post-World War II decolonisation. 'I just knew in myself that this was what I was, I was more African than British, even than Scottish, I certainly, I was never English.' Yet others, like Dawn growing up in Manchuria, considered themselves to be nothing but British, perhaps shaped by different physical and mental experiences than those of Louisa in Malawi. This sense of living a contested life in contested spaces, and the spectrum of responses to what this meant (or did not mean), thus provides an appropriate segue into the final chapter's focus on missionary children inhabiting and navigating their way within imperial and colonial spaces.

Notes

1 Gray, *We Travel Together*, pp. 14–15.
2 *Ibid.*, p. 16.
3 Scott Gray interview. Children's proximity to and involvement with medical interventions were possibly quite common. Both Judith and Murray Crozier vividly remember watching or participating in minor dental or medical procedures and preparations in 1940s India. Murray went on to be a doctor. Crozier, *Will the Rajah?*, pp. 188–89.
4 Scott Gray interview.
5 Gray, *We Travel Together*, pp. 19, 30, 31.
6 Ian Gray interview.
7 Gray, *We Travel Together*, pp. 98–138.
8 Vandrick, *Growing Up*, pp. 9–10; in turn referencing American counsellor Walters, *Untold Story*. Similar contours of modern-day missionary children's adjustment difficulties are also portrayed or canvassed in moving detail in: Ostini et al., *Sent*; and Klemens and Bikos, 'Psychological Well-Being', 721–33.

9   Vandrick, *Growing Up*, p. 9. This intent is also corroborated in other published memoirs, exemplified in Cook, *Troubled Journey*.

10 Katajala-Peltomaa and Toivo, 'Introduction', pp. 10, 13.

11 The following details and quotes come from Fleming, 'Adjustment', pp. 15–49.

12 *Ibid.*, p. 28.

13 Vallgårda, *Imperial Childhoods*, p. 189.

14 Vandrick, *Growing Up*, pp. 80–88.

15 Dopirak, *Missionary Kid*, p. 21; Gray, *We Travel Together*, p. 11; Ian Gray interview; Jackson, *Indian Saga*, p. 74.

16 Pomfret, *Youth*, p. 58. Brendon notes a similar set of processes for British children in India, *Children*, p. 165.

17 Cook, *Troubled Journey*, p. 19.

18 Kirsten interview; David interview. In February 1943 a protest by Japanese prisoners of war in the Featherston Camp, New Zealand, resulted in a riot and the tragic deaths of forty-eight Japanese men – 'Featherston Prisoner of War Camp'.

19 Marie interview; Rose interview; Veronica interview.

20 Wilkins, *A Child's Eye View*, pp. 27–28.

21 Pomfret, *Youth*, pp. 57–58 and Brendon, *Children*, pp. 164–65; Martin, 'Play', p. 65.

22 Pomfret, *Youth*, pp. 60–61; Vallgårda, *Imperial Childhoods*, p. 192.

23 Indicated, for example, in the memoirs of North American ex-children. Vandrick, *Growing Up*, pp. 85–86.

24 Scott Gray interview.

25 Scholarship on the British child migrant schemes of the nineteenth and twentieth centuries is represented by: Boucher, *Empire's Children*; Lynch, *UK Child Migration*; and Sherington, 'Suffer Little Children', 461–76. One model for the integration of children's narratives into a history of migration is McCarthy, *Personal Narratives*.

26 Jobs and Pomfret, 'The Transnationality of Youth', p. 6; in turn referencing Byron and Condon, *Migration*, p. 12.

27 For example, see Buettner, *Empire Families*; Brendon, *Children*; Cleall, 'Far-Flung Families', 170–73; and Manktelow, *Missionary Families*.

28 Jobs and Pomfret, 'The Transnationality of Youth', p. 6.

29 Fraser, 'Memory', pp. 105–109; Toitū Otago Settlers' Museum, Research Centre, Dunedin, New Zealand, C 053, SEE AG-64, George Hepburn Diary 1850.

30 Moffat, *The Lives of Robert and Mary Moffat*, pp. 124–25, 211.

31 Wilkins, *A Child's Eye View*, pp. 33–34.

32 Alison interview; Joyce interview.

33 Angus Library, BMS, 'Ernest Whitby Burt', CH/56, 'Autobiography of Rev. E.W. Burt (China 1892–1933)', p. 65.

34 *Ibid.*, p. 44.

35 Scott Gray interview; Ian Gray, *We Travel Together*, pp. 20–22, 23.

36 Michael Orr, Unpublished memoir, Private Collection, Scotland.

37 Jim interview; Joyce interview.
38 Jim interview.
39 Jim interview; Joyce interview.
40 Dorothy Kirk, '80 Years of "Living"'.
41 Dawn interview.
42 Kirsten interview.
43 Isabel interview.
44 For migrant children see again McCarthy, *Personal Narratives*, pp. 188–90.
45 Beetham, 'Dust and Mangoes', p. 136.
46 The following details for the Gray family are from: Ian and Scott interviews; Gray, *We Travel Together*, pp. 13, 17; and PRC, GAO149 PM), Staff Files, 'James Gray' (6.06), James Gray to Rev. Mawson, 8 May 1930.
47 Dorothy Kirk, '80 Years of "Living"'; PRC, GAO148 Canton Villages Mission, Staff Files, 1901–1940, 'Herbert Davies' (6.08), Herbert Davies to Rev. H. H. Barton, 11 February 1924.
48 See next chapter. Booth, *Pat's India*, p. 57.
49 Louisa interview; Isabel interview.
50 Crozier, *Will the Rajah?*, p. 192.
51 Joan Sutherland interview.
52 Amelia interview, Scotland, 13 January 2015. 'Amelia' is a pseudonym as this person did not want to be identified.
53 Robin S. interview; Joyce interview; Dawn interview.
54 Cook, *Troubled Journey*, pp. 19, 30, 41.
55 For further elaboration see Buettner, *Empire Families*, pp. 154–62. The same expectation was operative for children of the Basel Mission who were all accommodated and schooled in Switzerland. Konrad, 'Lost', 219–23.
56 Tjelle, *Missionary Masculinity*, pp. 180–82.
57 Janice Rowley interview; Crump and McKenzie, *Christina's Story*, pp. 95–97.
58 These observations, for the New Zealand Presbyterian context, are gleaned from: *Proceedings of the General Assembly of the Presbyterian Church of New Zealand*, 1866–1901; *Proceedings of the Synod of the Presbyterian Church of Southland and Otago*, 1866–1901; *Proceedings of the General Assembly of the Presbyterian Church of New Zealand*, 1901–1939; and from a range of missionary correspondence found in the staff files of each of the Canton Villages Mission, the New Hebrides Mission and the Punjab Mission.
59 Vandrick, *Growing Up*, p. 68.
60 Louisa interview; Crozier, *Will the Rajah?*, p. 192.
61 Veronica interview.
62 Janice Rowley interview; Crump and McKenzie, *Christina's Story*, pp. 95–97.
63 Jim interview.
64 The following discussion is based on Isabel's interview.
65 Exemplars for this are found in Manktelow, *Gender, Power* and in Vandrick, *Growing Up*, pp. 73–75.
66 Veronica interview.
67 Manktelow, *Missionary Families*, p. 124.

68 This account is drawn from Wilkins, *A Child's Eye View*, pp. 44–46, plus the published transcript of an interview conducted for a BBC oral history project – Wood and Thompson (eds), *The Nineties*, pp. 134–40. The wider story of the Wilkins children is outlined in Brendon, *Children*, pp. 189–93.

69 Discussion here draws from Crozier, *Will the Rajah?*, pp. 191–92.

70 For context see: Welch, 'Poona'; Morrison, *Pushing Boundaries*, pp. 77–79.

71 Vandrick, *Growing Up*, pp. 9–11, particularly at pp. 10 and 11.

72 Joyce interview; Isabel interview.

73 Unnamed interview, New Zealand.

74 Rose interview.

75 Alison interview.

76 Marie interview; Scott Gray interview; Rose interview; Jim interview; Michael interview; Louisa interview; Alison interview; Ian Gray interview.

77 Unnamed interview, Scotland.

78 McGrath, *T.F. Torrance*, pp. 16–28.

79 Cook, *Troubled Journey*, pp. 31–50, particularly at pp. 31–32, 45–46, 50.

80 Michael Orr, Unpublished memoir.

81 Cook, *Troubled Journey*, p. x.

82 Brendon, *Children*, pp. 189–93. This view also finds support in Elizabeth Buettner's discussion of British Empire families separated between India and Britain, in *Empire Families*, pp. 110–45.

83 Buettner, *Empire Families*, pp. 111–12; in turn citing Davidoff et al., *The Family Story*, p. 55.

84 In Chapter 2 the reference point for this is Manktelow, *Missionary Families*, p. 149.

85 This narration is based on Alison's interview.

86 While there may be a variety of reasons for this, Buettner suggests that it is evidenced in published memoirs and was influenced by post-1945 decolonisation, the advent of air travel, changing social or cultural expectations, and the emergence of 'interest in the psychological dimensions of childhood'. Buettner, *Empire Families*, pp. 139–45, especially pp. 141–42.

87 Here 'emotional management' and 'emotional labour' are used synonymously through the discussion. In a sense 'management' is a more inclusive term, and is used by Rosenwein and Cristiani, for instance, with reference to performative and embodied elements of emotions. They write: 'The performance of emotions, which is largely about how people behave and the impact they have on others, shades quite naturally into concern about the orchestrators of such behaviors [*sic*]. Emotions, in this light, are "managed" from the outside ... [wherein] people must strive to perform their emotions as expected.' Rosenwein and Cristiani, *What Is?*, p. 21.

88 Hatfield, 'Introduction', p. 3. Ahmed, *The Promise*; Ahmed, *Cultural Politics*.

89 Ahmed, *The Promise*, p. 2. In this respect she quotes more extensively from de Beauvoir: 'It is not too clear just what the word *happy* [emphasis added by Ahmed] really means and still less what true values it may mask. There is no possibility of measuring the happiness of others, and *it is always easy to*

describe as happy the situation in which one wishes to place them.' de Beauvoir, *The Second Sex*, p. 28.

90 Hatfield, 'Introduction', p. 6.

91 For example – Olsen, 'Children's Emotional Formations', 644; Barron and Langhamer, 'Feeling', 104–105; Kaarninen, 'Red Orphans', p. 165.

92 See further Vallgårda, Alexander and Olsen, 'Emotions', pp. 25–26.

93 These details are extracted from reports and minutes for both Home House and Cunningham House: NLS, Acc. 12398/78, COSBWM, Cunningham House for Missionaries' Children 1919–1973; NRS, COSA, CH1/38/10/2, Home House for Missionaries' Children Reports, 1900–1947; NRS, COSA, CH1/5/245, Home House Council Minutes 1914–1922; NRS, COSA, CH1/5/246, Home House for Missionaries Children Reports, 1923–1933; NRS, COSA, CH1/5/247, Home House for Missionaries Children Reports, 1934–1947.

94 Beatrice Sawyer, 'Happy Family: Pakistan, Africa, Arabia Missionary "Juniors"', *Life and Work* [nd], pp. 54–57.

95 While this is historicised, here, for one particular context (of place and time), more recent scholarship indicates its applicability for understanding the lives of historical and modern third culture children living in other negotiated liminal spaces; for example: Bjørnsen, 'The Assumption?', 120–33.

96 The following details are quoted from Lily F. Wilkie, 'The Home That Is Like Home', *Other Lands* (January 1922), pp. 62–63.

97 Alan interview; Robin S. interview.

98 Unnamed interview, Scotland.

99 Alison interview.

100 McArthy, 'Growing up in Wartime Britain'.

101 Alison interview.

102 NLS, Acc. 12398/78, COSBWM, Cunningham House for Missionaries' Children 1919–1973, Cunningham House Committee Minute Book, 1938–1948, Meeting minutes 5 June 1938, 30 January 1939, and 5 February 1940.

103 This notion of resistance, or subversion, as another demarcation of the emotional frontiers encountered by children is yet to be developed fully, but is given initial shape in Kaarninen, 'Red Orphans', pp. 181–83.

104 NLS, Acc. 12398/78, COSBWM, Cunningham House for Missionaries' Children 1919–1973, Annual Reports, 1936.

105 Michael interview; Alison interview.

106 Hatfield, 'Introduction', p. 9.

107 Barron and Langhamer, 'Feeling', 117–18.

108 Hollinger, *Protestants Abroad*, pp. 16–17, 18.

109 Rose interview.

110 '"Prepared to Die". Advocate of Non-Violence. Conscience Appeal Dismissed', *Evening Post* (7 November 1941), p. 7.

111 NRS, HH30 Military Service Appeal Tribunal Records (Lothians and Peebles), William Marwick Appeal Tribunal Papers, 4 August 1916, HH30/6/2/20; MacDougall, *Essays*, pp. ix–xi; Marwick, 'Conscientious Objection', 157–64.

112 Wilkins, *A Child's Eye View*, pp. 127–31, 132–34.
113 Brendon, *Children*, p. 193.
114 Wilkins, *A Child's Eye View*, pp. 97–101, 114–17, 133; Brendon, *Children*, pp. 192–93.
115 Hollinger, *Protestants Abroad*; Schulz, *Hawaiian by Birth*; Tjelle, *Missionary Masculinity*.
116 Unnamed interview, New Zealand.
117 David interview.
118 Scott Gray interview; Ian Gray interview.
119 Joan Sutherland interview; Janice Rowley interview.
120 Scott Gray interview.
121 Janice Rowley interview; David interview.
122 David interview; Ian Gray interview.
123 Kirsten interview.
124 Robin W. interview.
125 Jim interview.

6

Private navigations: missionary children inhabiting imperial and colonial spaces

Pat Booth begins the published memoir of her missionary childhood in these terms, with an introductory chapter entitled 'If You Don't Eat Your Vegetables I Won't Cook You Dahl Baht':

> I was about six years old at the time, and eating dinner with my parents and three year old brother John in … North-East India. The threat was not from Mum or Dad, but from Sadhon (pronounced Shahdhon), our cook who had worked for the family ever since 1944, the year I was born. Sadhon was like a parent to me, and I grew up knowing that he cared about me as much as any parent would. That also gave him the right and responsibility to exert parental guidance when he thought it necessary. In fact I saw more of him than my Dad … But Sadhon was a 'servant'. When I talk about my childhood to New Zealanders, the issue that seems most foreign to them is this one of servants. How can supposedly poor missionaries afford them? And should they be employing them?[1]

Three things stand out from Pat's memoir that, among other things, serve to sharpen the focus of this final chapter on the spatial dimensions of empire as experienced by missionary children. One feature is a keen sense of her life lived in defined spaces. The memoir begins with a map of northeast India (now including Bangladesh), placing her town (Agartala) in clear relationship to wider geographical and political configurations of the 1940s, followed by her description above. She provides fine-grained details of her family home, the missionary compound, the mission school and church, holidays in Darjeeling and furloughs in New Zealand. Several chapters outline her ongoing residency at Mt Hermon School in Darjeeling, with the same attention to nuances of place. Another feature is her trenchant hindsight observations about the various people who shared those childhood spaces, including ambiguous feelings about having household servants, but perhaps taken for granted at the time; single women missionaries who were 'strong, highly focused on their vocations, working autonomously' and who became 'wonderful role models for a future 1960s and 1970s feminist'; male missionaries referred to as 'uncles' but now thought of as 'benevolent conservative sexists'; and home-sick missionaries eating Christmas fare sent from New Zealand.[2] A third feature is a focus on mobility. She did not simply inhabit these various spaces but regularly moved within and between them. While most of her early life was spent in and around the Agartala compound, there were summer trips to the hills and regular trips to the nearby mission base at Brahmanbaria which, from 1947 onwards, was across the border in East Pakistan (Bangladesh). At age fourteen she first did this latter trip alone, navigating not just modes of transport (train, rickshaw and walking) but also the gendered protocols of border crossing in a Muslim context.[3] Regular trips to school in Darjeeling involved an hour-long plane flight, a ferry crossing (over the Brahmaputra River), an overnight train and the final leg by American jeeps.[4] By her reckoning Pat did this return twenty-four-hour trip at least twelve times, one which also involved emotional navigation, but more for her mother. Pat remembers that at the halfway point, 'Mum would have to say goodbye. I have to confess that I was always dismissive of and embarrassed by her distress at the parting. I was always more excited with the adventure, I'm afraid.'[5]

Pat displays throughout her memoir an adult awareness of spatial and temporal context. She recognises a sense of temporal entrapment, in that her childhood was bounded by gendered, cultural and political norms now dissonant for her modern readers but, as she notes, all too familiar within the transitional political realities of 1940s and 1950s South Asia. Such navigations were not easy for a young girl. She remembers an incident at the end of her first year of boarding. At home she did not make her bed: 'I was on holiday, I argued. When Mum discovered that Sadhon had just quietly made it, she was furious and said I was to do it myself. He wasn't there to do such things for me.'[6] She further recognises that her life was located within a period of critical geopolitical fragmentation and re-configuration, sitting between Raj and republic and the newly created nations of East and West Pakistan. There were also dangers of a more immediate nature, with jackals and tigers prowling near the compound. Yet it was at boarding school that these larger tensions were embodied for Pat. By the 1950s missionary children were in the minority at Mt Hermon School, alongside a large cohort of South Asian students. In what was generally a very positive educational experience, Pat remembers one or two instances of bullying perpetrated by a group of older non-European girls: one with respect to body maturation and another aimed at her public embarrassment in the school community. While she navigated each of these (noting, for example, that the bullying was a 'formative experience' for later years), on reflection Pat now wonders if in these incidents there 'was an element of payback: perhaps the Asian girls saw a chance to treat the white girl the way the Brits had sometimes treated the Asians'.[7]

Pat's rich story suggests that space is an important and complicated factor to consider more specifically, bringing the focus to bear on how children experienced, perceived, were impacted by and responded to the spaces that framed their lives.[8] This final chapter therefore returns to the notion of missionary children inhabiting particular spaces. Chapter 1 emphasised literary spaces and missionary child representations created primarily by adults, even if the reading audiences were often children and young people. Those representations both reflected and reinforced narratives created by both their parents and their employing institutions. A dominant trope running through these was that where children lived could be dangerous – physically and morally – or at the very least disadvantageous for their longer-term development. Educational interventions with attendant family separations or dislocations were one way to mitigate such perceived dangers.

The previous two chapters, however, have clearly outlined the many ways in which missionary children experienced and responded to missionary life both in mission and metropole settings, narrated both factually and emotionally through such hindsight constructions as memoirs or oral history interviews. Among other things, sources indicate the spatial nature of children's lives, living in and between spaces that were geographically, culturally or politically unique and diverse. Children variously perceived these spaces as ordinary or extraordinary depending on their own settings and complexities. At the same time, these were places of emotional negotiation and navigation, particularly the missionary boarding schools or children's homes in which many children lived out significant chunks of their younger years but which threw up a variety of emotional frontiers which had to be managed.

Yet there is one further context to consider, hinted at sometimes in the interviews but brought centre-stage by Pat's narrative. In the period under study, many such spaces were defined by British imperialism and colonialism, further complicated for missionary children by the ways in which parents' religious dispositions, motivations and imperatives intersected, collaborated with or even militated against colonial processes. Linda Devereux makes this point explicit, in an academic exegesis of her memoir of growing up in 1960s Democratic Republic of Congo. She comments that 'one of the factors that has influenced how stories such as mine have been told, or not told, is the complex subject position that results from being a white child in colonial Africa'.[9] Spatial and temporal context mattered.

With the focus still on children's narratives, then, this chapter proceeds to ask how selected missionary children in these transitional decades navigated their way within and across various colonial spaces and to what effect. The chapter returns more explicitly to thinking of such spaces as complex 'sites' experienced by children and which were simultaneously physically, socio-spatially and emotionally constructed. As in the previous chapter, these were complex places of lived experience, riven within and between by frontiers that were physical, metaphysical and emotional. Discussion tentatively probes what Susan Broomhall conceives of as 'spaces for feeling'. These can be 'understood as communities formed by a shared identity or goal (or aspiration towards these), practised through a specific set of emotional expressions, acts or performances, and exercised in a particular space or site'.[10] Representative discussion from memoir and oral history sources focuses on children's relationships with Indigenous mission personnel (especially those with child-minding roles), mobility as a way of living in empire (creating porous boundaries between places and complicating such notions as 'home' and 'abroad') and missionary architecture (using one child's response to missionary parents' appropriation of traditional religious or cultural spaces as a case study).

Relationships with Indigenous staff

As for their lives in general, missionary children primarily experienced empire in the confines of the home and missionary compound. In evocative fashion, American Ida Pruitt, living in the Chinese province of Shantung in the 1890s, remembers thus: 'there was etched on my mind, line upon line, laid in my heart, layer upon layer, painted in my heart and in my mind, brush stroke after brush stroke, that compound where we lived and the people in it and the people who came to it. That was my world.'[11] The evidence from interviews and memoirs reveals that in this space children interacted with a great variety of people, including wet nurses in infancy, various types of child-minder, household servants or employees (often cooks and gardeners), school teachers and mission evangelists among others. Typically, too, children in metropole Sunday schools and churches saw photographs of missionary children in the arms or presence of their local carers – like New Zealand children Muriel Robertson in a pram with her Indian ayah in 1912 and sisters Ere and Marie Michelsen with their New Hebridean 'native nurse' Leipakoa on the island of Tongoa in 1913 – images which were ubiquitous in other colonial settings beyond both the British Empire and missionary contexts.[12] Thus in child readers' minds, missionary children might be identified as both white and 'other', but with local people represented in a secondary, servile role.

Here we return to an important observation made by Pomfret for British children in South and East Asia: that 'the home became a shared space of trans-cultural connection and multilingual competence'. However, as he also notes, this was complicated, in that such spaces could also be contested, wherein 'home life might generate linguistic distance between parents and their biological offspring'.[13] This 'distance' could be perceived as a threat by adults within imperial settings generally, and in missionary settings like India where child-minders for the LMS 'were often treated as a destabilising influence, and parents pondered how "to save the little ones around from the terrible influence of the heathen ayahs and bearers"'.[14] However, other missionary families foresaw advantages. Hannah Crook (LMS), in Tahiti in the 1820s, regularly engaged her daughters Mary and Hannah Jr as language assistants 'as they are well acquainted with it'. German missionary Immanuel Pfleiderer (Basel Mission) lauded such bilingual opportunities, for his children in India, noting non-defensively that 'experience shows that such children normally learn the native language more quickly and easily than German'. Vandrick recalls that she quickly learnt Telugu as a young pre-school child, largely from time spent with her Indian ayah, and that she sometimes 'translated for my parents, who as adults learned more slowly'.[15] Hence 'linguistic difference' could turn adult and child roles or capabilities on their head, wherein the child became the teacher or cultural intermediary for the missionary adults. It also brought younger missionary children and domestic staff into tighter circles of domestic intimacy.

These examples suggest a degree of difference between missionary domestic spaces and those of other colonial or imperial families. Danish missionary parents in southern India, for example, were quite relaxed over children's relationships with Indigenous and non-Christian carers. As a result, these were more intimate relationships than adults often had with their Indian counterparts.[16] Most literature therefore focuses on the role of female child-minders, and again more usually on the Indian 'ayah', identified by Suzanne Conway as 'one of the most significant and distinctive figures in Anglo-Indian childhood from the eighteenth century until the end of British rule in India in 1947'.[17] Their equivalent was to be found across a host of other settings and for different nationalities, both in Asia and further afield – for example within British and French Southeast Asian settings, Danish families in south India, the 'amah' in China and the 'nursemaid', 'nanny' or servant in southern Africa.[18]

Women like Peronjini and Hannah were constant company for missionary children from infancy through to school age, sometimes living within the household or mission compound.[19] Margaret Dopirak remembers that Hannah was 'like a second mother to us … she took us for walks … [and] sometimes she would take us to her little house off the compound, and we would play with her daughters'. It was in this setting that Margaret also first perceived racial difference with respect to her own skin colour compared to her ayah and family. In her mind, she pictured her mother's response framed theologically as 'God made people with lots of different colors of skin, Margie dear, and He loves everyone, no matter what color skin they have!'[20] Ranging in age from teenagers to older women, ayahs thus inhabited 'the most intense point of intersection between the colonial rulers and those they ruled', engaging 'continuously in intimate, private family spaces' and with whom young children in particular 'spent most of their time'.[21] In this respect scholarship also highlights other domestic spaces (gardens, compounds and workers' homes), within which children conversed with non-European adults or played with their children. Thus both 'the colonial home and compound became spaces of disorderly and trans-ethnic engagements, which young people themselves recognised as having a transgressive charge'.[22]

At the same time, scholarship also emphasises other elements of this relationship, about which children probably had less awareness, wherein ayahs and other local household employees were caught up in the cultural politics of empire. Danish missionary parents might have looked benignly on children's vernacular expertise, but they still encouraged modes of dress, eating and holidaying for their children that accentuated 'cultural and racial difference'.[23] Distrust was a common adult stance towards long-term influences on children mixed in with a fear of disease or contamination. Cleall cites a disturbing account of Elizabeth Price, LMS missionary in southern Africa, scrubbing a new servant girl Maméri 'till the perspiration streamed off me' before she could 'call her fit to take my beautiful little one'.[24] Longer-term, British concerns about the influences of child-minders on children's development and education fed into the practice of sending children to Britain for education, particularly from India.[25] Parenting literature aimed at new 'Anglo-India' wives and mothers represented the ayah 'as indispensable to the hour-by-hour care' of their children, 'but also simultaneously as a live-in threat to them'.[26] This sense of being indispensable translated, longer-term, into ayahs often accompanying children or families back to England, where they could be left stranded by their employers. This was still an ongoing problem in the 1910s.[27]

The 'stark' contrast between adult and child perspectives on the role or place of the ayah reveals the extent to which 'intimacy was at the heart of the issue'.[28] In the context of this study, it again highlights the degree to which adult and child narratives might be divergent, and that this is no less true of how to interpret children's responses to empire. Brendon captures this neatly in her observation, across many memoirs and sources, that in imperial India 'it was for comfort and support rather than for stern authority, that their charges remembered most ayahs' and other people in their daily ambit, to the extent that sometimes an ayah or servant might be fired for supposedly spoiling a child.[29] Her observations pertain equally to missionary children. Those growing up in India particularly remembered the ayah as a confidante or the person who ran interference when children got into trouble; an informal teacher of language, music, culture and, sometimes, 'the facts of life'; and as someone who engendered a sense of being 'safe and happy'. There were noted instances of 'mistreatment', including sexual abuse, and over-indulgence by servants could lead to spoilt and imperious adults in later life. And, more generally, with age there developed, in many instances, genuine friendships between British and Indian children or teenagers, especially from the 1930s with more mixed-race schooling.[30]

Children's experiences evident in this current study largely mirrored those of other imperial families. In a few instances, such as David's early childhood spent in Japan, servants did not feature. In Rose's case, at Blantyre, her mother did all the childcare, seeing her missionary role exclusively as a maternal one. The implication was that she did not trust non-white people to be involved in raising her own children. At the other end of the spectrum, Michael can remember at least six 'servants' for his household alone in their Indian compound and twenty servants at the local 'resident's palace' who were deployed to find a toy he lost at the annual party.[31] Ayahs, gardeners, cooks, bearers and other personnel widely inhabited the spaces in which most interviewees lived – many now as a memory rather than a name. A chubby infant Ian Gray and slightly older brother Scott, holding a stuffed toy, posed naturally for a family photograph with a smiling but anonymous 'ayah' in 1925, thus fulfilling the photographic stereotypes common in New Zealand children's missionary magazines and representing photos in countless missionary family albums.[32]

The anonymity of domestic staff in children's narratives might be interpreted as a function of the interviewee's memory and distance of time, or as an indication that such people were simply there, taken for granted. Place and context might also account for this. In Manchuria, Dawn played with the cook's daughter up until school age, visited them in the kitchen and clearly had an amah. Consistent with her narrative emphasis on growing up British, however, they were present but nameless throughout her narrative. Nearby childhood friend Joyce did not have an amah (her older sister did) but she also played with the children of Chinese personnel in her own compound.[33] Many others reiterated that they learnt vernacular language from mission staff and conversed with them as children, as well as engaging in extensive play with children of their own ages. In this, boys in India might have had more licence, particularly beyond the physical strictures of a compound. Sometimes they were referred to as 'good friends', as in Robin S.'s case in Ajmer.[34]

Children's narratives raise at least two points of interest that deserve fuller investigation beyond this present discussion. One is the relative lack of awareness at the time, that living in imperial or colonial spaces might be problematic. Some hinted at it. Ian Gray surmised that his and Scott's 'ayah' had a minimal level of literacy and 'could very well have been an outcaste woman' – highly influential in their early lives and language acquisition but sitting on the social margins of society, nation and empire.[35] Dorothy Kirk remembered that 'my life was often adventurous & at times very frightening' during the warlord period of conflict in China post-World War I, but with frustratingly few details and no further reflection.[36] This was also a hallmark of Dawn's recollections of life in northern China two decades later. Much was taken for granted from a child's standpoint in terms of the Japanese military occupation of Manchuria, limited contact with Chinese staff within her own compound and her own wholly British lifestyle in the midst of what was a very complex political and cultural milieu. What stands out for Dawn is the degree to which this was still not an apparent issue for reflection and the ongoing influence of 'being British'.[37] A common sense interpretation is that age was a determining explanation for this lack of awareness. Most experienced closer supervision or care as infants up to about school age. As such Brendon's sense that many remember their carers through feelings of being 'safe and happy', indicates again the emotionally constructed nature of memory.

Second, family culture and geographical context may have partly dictated degrees of awareness. Pat's expectation that Sadhon would make her bed, while home for school holidays, might have been teenage laziness or a reflection of a cultural expectation of household staff. Her mother's quick retort that this was not his job to do may have been a sharp lesson in changing imperial realities or a reminder of family values shaped previously in the ostensibly more egalitarian setting of New Zealand. The same was true for Louisa growing up in Malawi. Her mother made it abundantly clear that it was not the job of their male house servant to pick up after any of the children, girls or boys. With the onset of puberty, she remembers her mother then employing a woman instead.[38] For Dawn a combination of Mukden's security and changing fortunes and her parents' focus on retaining British ways of life help to explain much of her own responses. In South Africa, by way of contrast, Veronica's play with local children in northern South Africa was very much to the fore in her unfolding narrative, buttressed by her parents' rejection of apartheid and racial separation.[39]

Thus, parents' attitudes mattered – irrespective of particular settings – shaped variously by prior cultural imperatives or theological convictions. What parents did or said rubbed off on children and the attitudes that they then formed both as children and later as adults. This might be explicit, as in the cases referred to here. Jim recounts a specific instance that neatly captures this. Annual picnics for the community hosted by his father's mission in 1940s India included running races for all the boys. Jim ran in these, but as the only boy with shoes his father 'ordered me to remove my shoes'. He understood that fairness was the issue but must have been resentful at the time: 'now that I had no shoes on of course I was last in every race as I could hardly walk on the stones let alone run'.[40] But such influences might also be more subtle, not apprehended until later – more a matter of unconscious osmosis. Stephanie Vandrick and her brothers remembered Peronjini, their favourite ayah in 1950s India: 'We loved her but were also sometimes naughty and disobedient, and sometimes teased her.' More recently, Vandrick muses 'I wonder now if we would have been as naughty if she hadn't been an Indian; did we somehow absorb the idea that white missionaries were "superior", and that because of her "inferior" status, we didn't have to obey her?'[41] In this anecdote, she implicitly points to one of the more specifically stated aims of her book – to 'shed some light on various types of privilege in the colonial context'.[42] The domestic setting considered here was one locus of 'privilege' for missionary children; their mobility was another.

Mobility as a way of living in empire

Missionary children were among 'the millions of people' identified by historical geographer Robin Butlin as being 'caught up, some deliberately but many of them unwittingly, in the dynamics of imperialism and colonial development'[43]. One such 'dynamic' was their constant movement, multiple times and in ways that redefined what it meant to be 'family' over long distances of time and space. Missionary children were 'nomadic', to quote Scott Gray, but also more profoundly 'diasporic' in that their multiple geographic shifts helped to constitute new identities of self and to reconfigure intimacies of being family.[44] At the same time, other scholars have noted that constant or multiple movements (and consequent re-adjustments in terms of location, schools and people) contributed to missionary children having 'trouble developing deep and trusting relationships' longer term.[45]

Colonial contexts throw up other possible ways of further contemplating missionary children's mobility. Vandrick's focus on the privileges enjoyed generally by white missionary children in colonised spaces is one, especially with regard to the freedoms and varieties of travel that they regularly experienced. In the process, their movements helped to sustain an expectation that travel and access were normative. Another approach is to think about Pomfret's contention that 'the spaces in between "departure" and "arrival"' were important for the constitution of 'new subjectivities' and of 'a transnational perspective' among young people, irrespective of race.[46] Yet another is to think about how missionary children mediated 'empire' through their relocation to metropole spaces. Beyond the features of mobility canvassed in the previous chapter, here we focus on indicative ways by which mobility afforded missionary children ways of living in and across empire. Again, as with the domestic spaces considered previously, children often did so usually unaware of the politics of movement, only figured out in hindsight.

In the first instance, movement into and around local spaces was an extension of compound or home life, perhaps circumscribed by gender or setting. Daily or weekly trips to bazaars, shops, school or other missionary residences in the company of local mission staff were common experiences. In so doing the white child was kept safe by accompanying staff, in a way that inverted imperial racialised adult roles. Boys like Jim in India might also roam at large on their own, depending on circumstances or parental licence (or perhaps also due to parental ignorance). He walked and cycled along 'dusty roads', interacting exclusively with non-Europeans like shopkeepers and waved to by the passing maharajah driving in one of his many 'American cars'. In hindsight 'I was a boy living [a] sort of Rudyard Kipling paradise. I remember it very fondly.' Yet Jim's uncomfortable incident over talking Hindi with a local police officer, stepping the short distance between the front door of his house to the open door of the officer's car, indicates how quickly the transition from one physical and mental imperial space to another might be disconcertingly problematic.[47]

Jim's invocation of Kipling automatically brings to mind notions of racial or national privilege, in the Indian context. However, such privileges of movement were perhaps also permissible due to younger age and the cultural importance of children among Indigenous communities. In the process, children's local movements often resulted in the formation of both trans-ethnic friendships and a sense of self-identity. As a six-year-old living in a town near Pune, Judith remembers regularly walking on her own or with her brother Murray and making friends easily. She understood in hindsight that 'children are much loved in India', still at the time the overriding sense was of never 'feeling a stranger'; 'we must have known that we were different and yet we felt quite at home and accepted'.[48] What Jim and Judith's narratives do not reveal was the extent to which they unknowingly transgressed cultural spaces or mores on a daily basis. Isabel vaguely remembers an incident while holidaying with the family in East London, South Africa in the early 1940s. The racial politics were different from her home in Nyasaland but 'we couldn't really believe it and … I think we caused a bit of trouble because on buses, for instance, we liked to sit on the upper deck unaware that this was only specifically for blacks'.[49] Such occasions remain one of the frustrating silences in the historical record but are hinted at through oral history evidence. But Isabel's brief story does indicate that the complexities and subtleties of racial or ethnic colonial politics could envelop or buffet children's lives while sitting on a moving bus, walking a dusty village street or simply stepping out from the doorstep of one's home.

Second, missionary children moved within and across much larger spaces, typically on a seasonal basis (lowland to highland areas during hot summers), between school terms and between mission setting and metropole (for furloughs or longer-term education). Such trips were often framed as adventures in both memoirs and interviews. Pat's many return trips to Darjeeling were typical in this regard, with the multiple modes of transport and her disregard for her mother's sense of loss each time.[50] In a different decade and place, the same was true for Dorothy Kirk from the age of ten.[51] Trips to and from Chefoo (from Canton) involved trains, riverboats and coastal steamers. From Hong Kong to Chefoo was a five-to-seven-day trip, barring problems like pirates boarding the ship.[52] If unaccompanied by an adult, she might then travel under the 'captain's care', dining in the officer's mess and being treated more generously than when she was at school. These were clearly the travelling privileges of a white child, who otherwise would not have travelled in this class. Nearer home, both daughter and mother were constrained by the same vagaries of timetables as their Chinese compatriots when attempting to catch local trains from the mission station into Canton an hour or more away. Depending on the decade or mission policy, most children remember their longer sea voyages as variously comfortable or not, with many having to endure post-World War II troop ships yet to be converted back to full liner status. By the 1950s the annual trip to cooler climes for summer holidays could just as commonly be made in a private motor vehicle as on public transport, reflecting both changing transport technologies and expectations as to how missionary families might travel.

Across these longer travel experiences, missionary children moved through spaces and across borders that were both real and ideological, often in a way that was well beyond the abilities or imaginations of the national people among whom they lived. Indeed, with respect to return travel to/ from school within regions, it was possible for some to simply move from one European space to another, using existing 'aqueducts' of train or ship travel to effectively circumvent intervening non-European spaces. The African anecdotes offered previously by Isabel, Louisa and Rose – along with Pat's story – also afford a different view of this, with the crossing of national borders, the sharing of carriages with local people and multiple modes of transport subject to the vagaries of weather and river crossings.[53] Again, this is a subject worthy of research focus in its own right.

One point of reflection, that might inform such research, is to think further about the relationships between missionary children's seasonal movements and prevailing discourses around health and education. In particular, the extent to which children's mobility was a visible expression of European dual concerns about juvenile health in tropical climates and the efficacy of an education gained in metropole over colonial settings.[54] Both were certainly influential, for instance, in the repatriation of New Zealand missionary children 'home' from the New Hebrides from the 1890s onwards, complicated by the total lack of schooling opportunities on any of the islands in the group. The preponderance of hill stations in India reflected a general view that the climate's 'ill effects might be tempered if children (as well as adults) spent intervals' there because they were 'healthier than the plains'.[55] Missions and their families readily bought into the practicalities of this, if not always the medical reasoning for it. By the interwar years, missionary doctors and other health experts had moved well away from 'environmental paradigms of disease transmission',[56] focusing instead on public health strategies and knowledge. But the idea of seasonal relocations held sway for many decades more across a range of South, Southeast and East Asian settings.[57] In the process, schools and hill stations were often co-located and associated together in the collective mindset of missionary and other imperial parents, and in so doing took on a prolonged life of their own. In southern African settings preferred schools were not necessarily 'hill station' locations, but in both geographic spheres, the determining factor was that children might receive a 'British' style education. As the twentieth century developed, different national cultures began to exert their own pressures or demands, complicated perhaps by the addition of a number of American-influenced schools. New Zealand parents favoured an emerging free and compulsory national high school system, from the 1930s onwards, while expressing concerns about American cultural influences on the mission field. Scottish families like the Marwicks esteemed Scottish schooling over other 'British' alternatives. In decolonising Africa after 1945, local high schools of mixed-race students became the preferred norm for many families *in situ*.

Third and finally, through their longer-distance movements back to countries of origin for furloughs and education, missionary children mediated and personified the Empire for their peers in places like Britain, Canada, Australia, America and New Zealand. Again, this lacks in-depth scholarship, reflecting the dearth of historical research to date on the 'ordinary' migration experiences of children and young people. Missionary children provide a potentially important case, in this regard, because as migrants they went through this process repeatedly. In some senses, they transported and communicated different iterations of metropole and colonial culture that progressively and potentially evolved over time. In this process, they were more aware, or became so, of the implications of where they lived for the ways that their lives might be understood, primarily through the perceptions and reactions of others. Ian Gray stated this in stark terms, remembering his initial days at Christchurch's St Andrew's College, a Presbyterian boarding school in a part of New Zealand where the population was identifiably white and Anglo-centric in the 1930s. Among his group of boarders, there was a 'brawny fellow' who with a gang of others 'took a dislike to me'. Whenever they met, Ian was greeted with 'Gidday N_____' which was 'triggered by the facts that I spoke differently and I had come from India'.[58] Dawn's experience on furlough in Scotland in the 1930s and that of Kirsten in the 1950s also while on furlough – enduring the jibes or misperceptions in Scottish primary schools – echoed Ian's taunting.[59]

Today this would be called 'bullying', but in context, these were displays of cultural ignorance or reflections of stereotypes developed in the Empire's classrooms or depicted in juvenile literature. As such it was not easy to stand out from the crowd. As Catherine Hepburn remembered, even in 1950s Scotland, to be a missionary child was to stand out among a 'peer group who had never travelled across Scotland',[60] let alone further. At this point, a cross-cultural encounter occurred within a shared Western cultural ambit that now became complex and contested for missionary children. The presence of a child like Kirsten or Ian might then challenge or exacerbate existing cultural stereotypes operative in metropole schoolrooms or yards. At the same time, individuals like Dawn had to quickly adjust their language, accent or behaviour, in order to survive as Empire citizens within the controlling norms of that Empire, which was predominantly European or white in its orientation and not African, Indian or even Chinese as had been their own formative experience.

Attitudes to missionary architecture and cultural appropriation

To this point, the focus on spatiality has indicated diverse ways in which empire and colonialism were experienced by missionary children. It emphasises their relative lack of awareness of the contested nature of such spaces and the adjustments that they had to make. Discussion has been necessarily wide-ranging, in keeping with the comparative focus of the book. The downside of this is that specificities and peculiarities of place and time are easily missed. Therefore, the final discussion returns to the domestic spaces inhabited, and how children might respond to the appropriation of those spaces for religious purposes. More broadly, it again indicates a richer vein of scholarship yet to be properly developed, which focuses on place, architecture and colonial culture. There is substantial scholarship around the evolution of the 'Christian home' as a missiological strategy, but the relationship between 'home' and architecture is less well drawn.[61] Previous chapters indicate that children were keenly aware of the spaces around them – houses, gardens and compounds – and that they appreciated the consequent comfort, security and sense of belonging. Here we focus on one child's perceptions of her Chinese home and her personal response to how both mission and parents reappropriated its physical and religious functions.

Two scholarly threads give this discussion context. China was a complex society with sophisticated architecture, town planning and infrastructure. However, missionary attitudes more generally were often orientated towards the deprecation of non-Western architecture when compared with the established domestic and religious architecture of Western Christendom. This attitude prevailed in many different mission settings. For example, late nineteenth-century LMS commentators in southern Africa tended to equate perceived low standards of Kaonde domestic architecture with '"heathen" underdevelopment' and therefore a lack of 'civilisation'.[62] Differently, but reflecting similar cultural assumptions, Norwegian missionaries started evangelisation in 1850s South Africa by building a simple Scandinavian house to which Indigenous adults and children were invited for lessons and worship.[63]

A second, related thread runs out of a mixture of children's history and the application of emotions' history to empire. For instance, a similar note of cultural hegemony and appropriation carried across British culture more generally, visible for instance in public parks created for children in the late Victorian and Edwardian periods. Ruth Colton observes that parks' flora and buildings 'referenced aspects of Britain's imperial identity', simultaneously offering children the chance to 'culturally colonise and assimilate foreign and exotic items through labelling and display' and spaces in which to bodily display eugenic and militarist virtues through public gymnastics or uniformed drills.[64] Another trend noted is changing domestic architecture, especially from the nineteenth century, in response to the intersection of 'new ideals of childhood' with such 'revolutionary' social changes as 'separation of home and work' and the notion of 'public and private life'.[65] Finally, Margrit Pernau draws attention to the relationships that historically existed between spaces, bodies and emotions, with a focus on nineteenth-century Delhi. For the case outlined in this chapter, she helpfully highlights that spaces can profoundly impact their inhabitants through 'a long-drawn process of the creation of emotion knowledge through experience and learning' and that 'spaces and practices co-produce each other'.[66] In this respect, I suggest that the case study that follows fleshes out further the ways in which a spatially constrained emotional frontier (in this case created unwittingly by adults for theological reasons but responded or reacted to by a child from both an emotional and ideological perspective) could be a productive experiential 'space for feeling', rather than a barrier, which contributed in significant ways to one child's subsequent life trajectory.

Ida Pruitt's memoir records her childhood in China's Shantung province during the 1890s, as the child of American Southern Baptist missionary parents.[67] Originally published in 1973, this is a hindsight document, drawing perhaps on written records but also on memory. Noted American historian, John Fairbank, provided a foreword which helpfully foregrounds Pruitt's account – that it is about a girl who up to about the age of twelve 'has grown up more Chinese than American' and as such 'learned to see the world through the eyes of the nurse and of the Chinese community around her'.[68] Ida's own sense of self at an early age is also important in setting the scene. She remembered an early incident when she realised that 'this is not me' and then spent many years afterwards 'learning about "me" and "not me"', and began to understand that as a missionary child, she had 'the patterns of two very dissimilar ways of life from which to choose' both 'habits' and 'thoughts'.[69] She mused that she did not fully understand why she ended up with cultural thought patterns that were at odds with those of her parents (especially her mother). Yet she presciently sensed that 'I probably felt from the feelings and thoughts of the people around me, from Dada's feelings, perhaps, and the feelings of others' of the local Chinese community.[70] 'Dada' was her amah, who was a strategically important part of shaping Ida's attitudes and values. Through her, Ida learnt the nuances of both spoken and body language, and therefore was able to read the behaviours and conflicts of daily street life communicated through gestures and tone of voice. Ida's critique of her domestic spaces was directly related to the impact of her amah and other local people.

The Pruitt family inhabited part of a complex previously owned by a once-wealthy Chinese landowner 'bankrupted through opium addiction', and since purchased as a mission station and compound. Ida's description in full helps to background her further commentary. Her home was constructed as seven courtyards containing eleven one-storey houses, where the:

> main house of a courtyard was always on the north side and faced south to get the life-giving sunshine. The smaller houses were sometimes against the east wall and sometimes against the west wall. This left the courtyard space as solid a whole as possible. A high wall surrounded the whole compound, broken on the south by the Great Front Gate and on the north by the Great Back Gate. The compound was as long as a small city block and almost half as wide. A compound was laid out to serve all the needs of a Chinese family of that time. It was a place for the family to sleep, eat, talk, enjoy the flowers and the sunshine; for the ancestors to return to at stated intervals; where with due regard to hierarchy and as much as the income of the family allowed,

provision was made for all sides of living. A family tried to do as much of its work as possible within its own gates.[71]

In their purchase of the complex, her parents created room for visitors and a boys' school alongside accommodation and worship spaces. 'Where the Ting family had lived we now lived and where they had worshipped their ancestors we and the Chinese converts now held church services.'[72] Ida described these changes and the ways in which they fundamentally reconfigured the complex physically, spiritually and emotionally. In the family home, original brick floors were re-covered with wood, papered lattices were swapped for 'aggressive vertical windows ... two sashes, and twelve panes each' and a 'two-leafed' pivot door was replaced by a 'foreign door that swung on hinges'. The 'living room' had a furniture arrangement that was too informal for Ida and the north wall was adorned all year long with a family portrait, where traditionally only ancestral pictures should be hung at New Year.[73] Within the wider complex what she called the 'Hall of the Ancestors' – 'famous as one of the most beautiful in the Huang District' – was now a Christian worship space. Here she noted two alterations akin to a 'mutilation'. One was the erection of a curtain to separate men from women during worship – a 'temporary mutilation'. More egregious, however, was the baptistry dug between 'the western terrace and the south wall', disturbing and breaking the pattern of mosaic bricks and pebbles in the courtyard.[74] Against all of this, however, other features remained unchanged – the courtyard itself, the elegantly tiled roof of the veranda along the front of the house and the 'comforting' high walls which her mother conversely found oppressive. In all, Ida found in the layout of the compound an aesthetically pleasing geometric arrangement that was 'harmonious' and that afforded 'dignity, formality and privacy'.[75]

Ida's critique was a product of upbringing and of an intense identification with China as 'home', partly constructed in hindsight but also framed through the influences identified above. In her mind, Westerners were redrawn as 'barbarians' for covering the house's brick floors. Other architectural alterations upset the traditional balance and serenity of the house's rooms. Soft light from paper lattices was now replaced by the 'hard and cold' light of glass. She felt 'uncomfortable' with the furniture arrangement of the living room, realising later that this was an American arrangement with which she had no experience. As an adult she thought that American house roofs 'had no dignity and often the rooms were not of harmonious dimensions, the facades were confusing'. Chinese layouts, by contrast, were 'satisfying' and their high walls 'comforting'. The 'mutilation' of the baptistry 'hurt me – hurt as though it were my flesh that had been cut into'. In turn, the ceremony of baptism she felt to be a 'grotesque and somewhat indecent ceremony', and the baptistry had 'broken the harmony' and 'scarred' the flow to the courtyard. In worship, sometimes she would ask her mother, as organist, to play a hymn that 'was set to an old Buddhist chant. The deep Chinese chest tones then came out, and the invocation to deity rolled out as it should, in the pentatonic scale.' On Sundays, the Ancestral Hall was too full. She thought that it was most beautiful when empty and bare, imitating past times when 'people could stand and kneel and make patterns in their standing and kneeling, as they knelt one after the other before the tablet of their ancestors'.[76]

Two brief observations serve to bring this to a close. One is that a child's perspective brings welcome nuance to the historical record and our interpretation of it. It fleshes out insightfully the ways in which Western Protestant missions and practices converted non-Christian spaces into sites of exemplary Christian worship and family life. But more importantly, it does so through the eyes of someone who, unlike her American-born parents, was born and enculturated in China for at least the length of her childhood and teenage years. Ida is indicative, at least, of those many children who grew up both in colonial and religious contexts, and who then had to navigate their way towards a genuine sense of self. For Ida, that put her at odds with those around her, although it is not clear from her memoir how far that dislocation was articulated or enacted as a child or teenager. The other observation is that her narrative indicates the deeply profound ways in which this place was felt as much as known intellectually. Again, as with the many interviewees, Ida's narrative of her early years was constructed at the time and in hindsight through emotional as much as cognitive processes. It bears out Pernau's conviction that such 'knowledge can be cognitive and conscious, but can also become habitualized and embodied'.[77] Ida came to know her house and compound in ways that seeped into her feelings, that were at times visceral, and which contributed to a longer-term critique of Westernisation in China. She went on to work as a journalist and a social worker in China, at least sympathetic to the communist cause, and fundamentally rejected missionary work and aims.[78] Her story, therefore, is not necessarily representative, but at least indicative of the fruitfulness of paying attention to how children, as opposed to their missionary parents, might respond differently both to the colonial and religious air that they breathed.

Conclusion: children's perspectives in context

This chapter has canvassed a range of ways by which children of Protestant missionary families, particularly from the 1890s onwards, lived within, responded to or thought about the imperial/colonial contexts of their lives. It has considered this with respect to children's cross-cultural relationships within their domestic spaces, movements within empire and how those movements created dissonance and new identities, and how children thought about or reacted to the impact of Westernisation on the architectural spaces which they inhabited. There are, of course, other sites of empire that might be considered further, especially the ways in which Western ideals and imperatives were perpetuated through schools for missionary children and other British imperial expatriates. As such the chapter has traversed its way across a period in which British imperialism both waxed and waned, and also within which resulting colonialism was variously expressed. Joyce Wilkin's India in the 1900s was different from Pat Booth's in the late 1940s and 1950s. Louisa and Isabel's experiences of British colonialism in Nyasaland and Southern Rhodesia were different from Joyce and Dawn's in Japanese-occupied Manchuria. Each experienced the everyday realities or impacts of imperialism and colonialism in ways that also differed with respect to mission context, national origins, family culture and individual personality.

A dominant theme through the discussion is that for many missionary children, where they lived – and the political context of those places – was not always a major point for reflection at the time. Imperialism, colonialism and Protestant religion together provided the air that they breathed or, to use an older phrase, were unconsciously accepted elements of the 'mental furniture' that adorned their lives.[79] A lot of what we read about children in imperial spaces is adult produced or reflects what adults perceived to be advantageous or hazardous for children in given circumstances. Adult hindsight on childhood, however, provides the intellectual and emotional space within which children like Pat were later able to reflectively consider this more critically, and with a greater measure of contextual understanding. In the process, they drew out the various complexities of place and context. Of her Chefoo schooling between 1923 and 1928, Dorothy Kirk commented later, with a hint of sadness, that while the 'education was excellent' it was 'entirely "western" in outlook. Unfortunately, we learnt nothing of the surrounding Chinese culture, its history, literature & art. Looking back, I feel this was a great loss & missed opportunity.'[80] Dorothy's Chefoo experiences reflected the extent to which the school, its culture and its curriculum had become aligned with British public school norms by this period.[81] At the same time other memoirists, as children, did appreciate the cultural significance of places encountered. Rebecca Terry visited Agra as a seventeen-year-old, *en route* to America from Western China in 1943. She wrote in her diary:

there is certainly nothing I have ever seen as thrillingly beautiful as the famous old tomb, the Taj Mahal. Honestly it is dazzling white and so perfect in its formation and surroundings ... When I could stare no more, I felt as thought [*sic*] I should sit down and rest with my eyes closed; the feeling that they weren't big enough to see it all, the exertion of trying to stretch them, just wore me out.

What also struck her was that this was a structure that was eternal. In it 'simplicity and grandeur and delicate detail are combined to make it something that will never die'.[82] In the Taj Mahal, the wonders of the West had met their match.

For the New Zealand and Scottish participants, the interview process provided a vehicle for further reflection. In this respect, for example, Rose became progressively apologetic in her descriptions of life at Blantyre in the 1940s. She referred variously and in an increasingly self-conscious manner to the 'natives' or 'boys' who supported them by carrying water from the mission's dam and then outlined briefly how both her play and later schooling in South Africa were segregated. She qualified this by commenting 'I'm sorry but that was how it was, aha, even in Cape Town when I was at boarding school, it was them and us' and, further on, describing segregated transport, she once again commented, 'I'm sorry but that was the way it was'.[83] There was a distinct sense of embarrassment and an unstated fear that she was being offensive (which she was not), in a way that indicated that Rose understood the deep ideological gulf between her past and present. At the same time, different political spaces afforded different opportunities or challenges. In this respect the Manchurian setting in the 1930s was particularly problematic, but only recognised as such later on. In hindsight, the Japanese occupation of Manchuria now forms a matrix within which Joyce narrates her own story, formed over subsequent years through the accretions of family storytelling and her own reading as an adult. While she emphasised her parents' respect for Chinese people and culture throughout the interview, she thinks that as a child she was 'never kind of integrated into that system'. Dawn only mentioned the complexity of Japanese colonialism from a prompted question, thinking that as a child she took the military presence for granted. On one occasion, at a checkpoint, she acted unwittingly to distract a guard's attention from a missionary nurse carrying illegal medicine back into Mukden. The nurse attributed this to divine intervention, but Dawn was quite unaware of her role until told later. In the school next door to the mission house, she was vaguely aware that the Chinese students had to learn Japanese, alongside English and Mandarin. Yet the most memorable feature was the Japanese teacher at the school and his wife who 'had a lovely dog'.[84] In her mind, then, Japanese militarism and civility sat together in a way that is selectively conscious at best.

Collectively these moments in both memoirs and interviews raise further red flags about the dominant trope of 'life as ordinary', prompting us to think more carefully about the geographical and temporal spaces inhabited by missionary children – spaces that were complexly and simultaneously racial, cultural, gendered, colonial and religious. These ranged from the missionary house and compound to the various schools attended within missionary contexts, to being 'at home with the empire'[85] in such places as Scotland's missionary children's homes or New Zealand's predominantly single-sex high schools up to the 1950s. As Buettner so clearly outlines for the Indian colonial context, these kinds of spaces were fundamentally 'problematic', within which white girls and boys negotiated and navigated racial status among other things.[86] They could also be problematic spaces for other reasons – wittingly or unwittingly inhabited or transgressed – the significance of which oftentimes was only apprehended properly in later life.

One final example illustrates this further. As a young girl in China, Faith Cook was often left to her own devices and would 'frequently steal out unnoticed from the mission compound and into the hard-baked streets of the town', witnessing daily life in all its vibrancy and messiness. One time she was inadvertently caught up in a crowd outside the town gates and witnessed a public execution – 'an image I have never been quite able to erase from my memory'. In summer she 'ran shoeless across the hard mud of the compound yard'. At the same time, she pushed the boundaries of what was acceptable to her parents.

> Happy enough in my childish way, I also learned regrettable habits from my Chinese friends. Lying and stealing became routine, as my companions would dare me to raid the larder in my mother's kitchen and bring them out bread and other commodities – for food was often in short supply in their homes. With a jersey bulging with a hidden loaf, I would receive a rapturous welcome from my hungry friends.[87]

Perhaps done with an eye to her own youthful reputation among friends, Faith only fully understood later the economic and political circumstances that explained why her actions were so well received at the time.

This chapter thus prompts us to think more carefully about missionary children's spaces as sites set within the broader and infinitely problematic landscape of imperialism and colonialism. As such, we need to consider both the 'dynamics' and practices of particular places at particular times, as well as the 'wider socio-cultural matrix which shaped that practice and the multi-layered meanings in which it was embedded'.[88] For missionaries' children, more specifically, this conceptualisation helps us to think about ideological commonalities across distinctly different international sites (in particular, their perceptions of or responses to Indigenous child-minders) and the relationship between geographical mobility, cultural interstitiality and consequent identity formation (imperial, national and religious). It also potentially contributes to a more nuanced understanding of how children related to or thought about the physical spaces that they inhabited (especially domestic ones), the uses or appropriations of local spaces by their parents, and ultimately how imperial sites became 'spaces for feeling'[89] in ways that were constitutive of later life values and trajectories.

Notes

1 Booth, *Pat's India*, pp. 13–14.
2 *Ibid.*, pp. 14, 23, 26.
3 *Ibid.*, p. 45.
4 *Ibid.*, pp. 56–58.
5 *Ibid.*, p. 57.
6 *Ibid.*, pp. 19–20.
7 *Ibid.*, pp. 63–64. This same sense of positionality, and the attendant guilt associated with being white and privileged, is a key element of Devereux's analysis of her childhood in Democratic Republic of Congo, in 'Narrating', pp. 202–209, 274.
8 The historical geography of children's lives is a growing focus in scholarship, signalled for example by: Hamlett, 'Space', pp. 119–38; Kozlovsky, 'Architecture', pp. 95–118; Romero, Garcia and Jiménez (eds), *Children*; and Sleight, *Young People*.
9 Devereux, 'Narrating', p. 159.
10 Rosenwein and Cristiani, *What Is?*, pp. 90, 91; Broomhall, 'Introduction', p. 1.
11 Pruitt, *A China Childhood*, p. 4.
12 'A Little Letter from India', *The Break of Day* (November 1912), p. 14; and 'Our Missionaries' Children', *The Break of Day* (February 1913), p. 8. For a further example, see the photographs from Java used in Stoler, *Carnal Knowledge*, pp. 166–93.
13 Pomfret, *Youth*, p. 58.
14 Cleall, *Missionary Discourses*, p. 66, in turn citing from an article in the LMS *Chronicle* (August 1895), pp. 212–14.
15 Hannah Crook, quoted in Manktelow, 'Making Missionary Children', p. 54; Pfleiderer quoted in Konrad, 'Lost', 220; Vandrick, *Growing Up*, p. 82.
16 Vallgårda, *Imperial Childhoods*, p. 192.
17 Conway, '*Ayah*', p. 41.
18 Pomfret, *Youth*, pp. 55–74; Vallgårda, *Imperial Childhoods*, pp. 188–93; Cleall, *Missionary Discourses*, pp. 58–73.

19 Vandrick, *Growing Up*, p. 58; Dopirak, *Missionary Kid*, p. 21.
20 Dopirak, *Missionary Kid*, pp. 21–23.
21 Conway, 'Ayah', p. 41.
22 Pomfret, *Youth*, p. 73.
23 Vallgårda, *Imperial Childhoods*, p. 192.
24 Cleall, *Missionary Discourses*, p. 67.
25 Grimshaw, 'Faith', p. 268.
26 Conway, 'Ayah', p. 51.
27 *Ibid.*, pp. 52–55.
28 *Ibid.*, p. 55.
29 Brendon, *Children*, p. 164.
30 *Ibid.*, pp. 163–69.
31 David interview; Rose interview; Michael interview.
32 Gray, *We Travel Together*, p. 12.
33 Dawn interview; Joyce interview.
34 Robin S. interview. Wider play or recreation was evident in: India – Jim interview; South Africa – Veronica interview.
35 Ian Gray interview.
36 Dorothy Kirk, '80 Years of "Living"'.
37 Dawn interview.
38 Booth, *Pat's India*, pp. 19–20; Louisa interview.
39 Veronica interview.
40 Jim interview.
41 Vandrick, *Growing Up*, p. 58.
42 *Ibid.*, p. 16.
43 Butlin, *Geographies*, p. 119.
44 Scott Gray interview. Diasporic families, as reconstituted but still profoundly related or intimately connected over distances, is explored for more recent contexts in Long, 'Diasporic Families', 243–52. For British missionary families, especially through the nineteenth century, see also Cleall, 'Far-Flung Families', 163–79, particularly 173–76.
45 Devereux, 'Narrating', p. 199.
46 Pomfret, 'Colonial Circulations', p. 117.
47 Jim interview.
48 'Judith's Memories', in Crozier, *Will the Rajah?*, p. 187.
49 Isabel interview.
50 Booth, *Pat's India*, pp. 56–58.
51 The following details are based on Dorothy Kirk, '80 Years of "Living"'; and Ian Waldram, 'A 1920's Journey to and from School', Kirk Papers, Private Collection, Ian Waldram, Scotland.
52 For example, an unrelated, later incident of piracy affecting Chefoo children was reported in '70 British Children on Pirated Ship', *The Telegraph* [Queensland] (2 February 1935), p. 1.
53 Isabel interview; Louisa interview; Rose interview; Booth, *Pat's India*, pp. 56–58.
54 See further Buettner, *Empire Families*, pp. 31–33, 46–52; and Pomfret, *Youth*, pp. 147–48.

55 Buettner, *Empire Families*, p. 33.
56 Pomfret, *Youth*, p. 147.
57 *Ibid.*, pp. 147–48; Buettner, *Empire Families*, pp. 31–33, 46–52.
58 Gray, *We Travel Together*, pp. 29–30.
59 Dawn interview; Kirsten interview.
60 Hepburn, 'The Burning Rosebush', p. 127.
61 See again discussion in Chapter 2. For example, Dana Robert makes no explicit reference to architecture in her otherwise important explication of Christian homes/households in Western Protestant mission history, in 'The "Christian Home"', pp. 134–65. Two examples of approach include: Ballantyne, *Entanglements*; and Hovland, *Mission Station Christianity*.
62 Cleall, *Missionary Discourses*, p. 39.
63 Hovland, *Mission Station Christianity*, pp. 29–30. The further significance of this is elaborated on pp. 42–45.
64 Colton, 'Savage Instincts', pp. 267–68, particularly 267.
65 Gutman, 'The Physical Spaces', p. 251. Gutman proceeds to document how architecture, use of space and childhood have evolved with respect to the family home, schools, public spaces and play.
66 Pernau, 'Space', 541, 542.
67 The following details are taken from Pruitt, *A China Childhood*. Wider context and comment on her life story can be found in King, *China's American Daughter*, pp. 5–19.
68 Pruitt, *A China Childhood*, p. xiii.
69 *Ibid.*, pp. 1–2.
70 *Ibid.*, pp. 26–28.
71 *Ibid.*, pp. 4–5.
72 *Ibid.*, p. 6.
73 *Ibid.*, p. 7.
74 *Ibid.*, p. 26.
75 *Ibid.*, pp. 11–12.
76 *Ibid.*, pp. 7, 11–12, 26, 30, 32.
77 Pernau, 'Space', 542.
78 Hollinger, *Protestants Abroad*, pp. 241, 242, 260, 369n30. See further King, *China's American Daughter*, who describes Ida Pruitt as 'a woman uncomfortable with her colonial privilege', p. xvii.
79 Quoting from Roberts, *Europe*, p. 51. This phrase reflects the influence of the French *Annales* 'history of mentalities' that is outlined in Burke, 'Strengths', 439–51 and is further applied in the imperial educational context in Mangan, 'Introduction', pp. 1–22.
80 Dorothy Kirk, '80 Years of "Living"'.
81 See Semple, 'The Conversion', 29–50; and Semple, *Missionary Women*, pp. 167–88.
82 Terry, *Help Me*, pp. 21, 22.
83 Rose interview.
84 Joyce interview; Dawn interview.

85 Borrowing the phrase most aptly adopted by Hall and Rose (eds) in *At Home*.
86 Buettner, 'Problematic Spaces', 277–98.
87 Cook, *Troubled Journey*, pp. 29–30.
88 Morrison, 'Theorising Missionary Education', 9.
89 Introduced in the Introduction and referenced by Rosenwein and Cristiani, *What Is?*, p. 90.

Conclusion

This book began with Joyce Wilkin's memoir of her early years growing up in 1900s India and her adult commentary on the problematic and at times traumatic experience of parent–child separation. In her postscript, from many decades distant, she voiced some 'sympathy' for her parents' own sacrifice and for the labours of her teachers, despite school being less than easy for her. Indeed, she expressed 'real appreciation' of the school and gave thanks for 'all the advantages that it gave me in preparing me for life'.[1] Stephanie Vandrick finishes her book on North American missionary children's memoirs (a mix of academic analysis and personal memoir), voicing similar concerns about authorial balance:

> I worry that perhaps I have presented a too negative portrayal of the MKs [missionary kids] themselves, perhaps too heavily emphasizing that many have been sad, miserable and damaged both during their years away from their home countries and afterwards. It is clear that this was the experience, or at least part of the experience, of some of the MKs. However, I hope it comes through in the book that many MKs, perhaps most, also felt and feel privileged to have had the experience of living in different countries, experiencing different cultures, having adventures and in general gaining a first-hand sense of the largeness and variety of the world.[2]

In recent decades 'missionary children' have been considered as one group among the wider phenomenon of 'third culture kids'. This is a complex 'space', one that is now being addressed by both professionals and academics, through scholarship and practical interventions that address the particularities of children and young people who are more 'transnational' than 'national' in terms of lifestyle and identity. That broader work recognises that for such children, there are both positive and negative elements. Benefits might include cross-cultural immersion, multiple language acquisition, 'developing a broader world view' and becoming more 'flexible and adaptable'. The challenges involve 'difficulties forming a sense of identity', which Devereux links to the highly mobile and frequently changing circumstances of children's lives that militate against stability and 'belonging'. In particular, the issue of family separation is being addressed, both in the present and retrospectively for children who, as adults, find their lives qualitatively impacted by experiences of separation.[3]

For missionary children in history, both memoirs and historiography to date have tended to accentuate the 'challenges', although not exclusively. That view is legitimate but there are also other possibilities, out of which emerge a much more complex picture than simply 'it was good' or 'it was bad'. Louisa's final reflections on evolving identity as a young woman bring these complexities into sharper relief. After her childhood years in Nyasaland and then in school in Southern Rhodesia in the 1930s and 1940s, she went to Aberdeen University as a medical student. At that point, she self-identified as being a 'white African' or at least 'more African than British, even than Scottish'. During her university years, two memories cemented this conviction and yet also muddied the waters.[4] One was a set of interactions with a Jamaican woman also in her class. Louisa had picked up from her African background particular ways of talking about dying and death. In conversation, her Jamaican friend commented, 'Ah you're talking like a Jamaican now you see so that's how I feel you know about things.' Yet Louisa's immediate response to this was 'no I'm not really, I'm talking like an African'. Here was a point of connection, between two cultures (Jamaican and British) but mediated by a third (African). She then connected this to an earlier memory from her school days, where she thinks that 'the fact of who I was, a missionary's child in an African setting meant something different from some of the other people around about me'. It was during that period that she had to settle, for herself, the conflicting messages about race that swirled around her and which, in Southern Rhodesia, were embodied in expectations of separate spaces for white and non-white Africans. For Louisa, the crucible for this was the servants' quarters of her school hostel, to which she would gravitate at day's end and where she would converse with the women and girls her own age. She knew that her presence there was against the social grain, yet she felt uncomfortable with expectations of segregation, while still wrestling with the mixed messages that permeated everyday life. By the time she reached university this internal struggle had come to an end. The clear sign of that was 'when I discovered that one of the people in my class was this black Jamaican woman, I thought good, you know there's somebody here who's going to understand me a bit'.

Hopefully this book has showcased in an appropriately detailed, comparative and sensitive manner both the complexities of missionary children's historical lives, like that of Louisa, and the further complexities involved in interpreting those lives. It has deliberately taken a comparative view and focused especially on the first half of the twentieth century, in order to complement and extend scholarship that to date has focused on more discrete, single-mission-focused settings mostly in the nineteenth century. This periodisation therefore throws the spotlight on children and their families living in and across spaces dynamically and variously shaped: by the British Empire at its zenith; by other colonial projects such as that of Japan in Manchuria; by the creeping cultural imperatives of Westernisation more generally; and by the emerging complexities of decolonisation after World War II. The focus on that slightly later period has also afforded the opportunity to use oral history interviews as well as archival and published sources, to sketch out a holistic picture that canvasses the perspectives of children, of their parents and of the institutions that embraced them.

Central to this approach has been the application of the concept of overlapping narrative lenses, book-ended by the notion of missionary children inhabiting defined public and private spaces. Throughout the book, I have argued that while each lens reveals pertinent details and expedites certain understandings, only through all three lenses do we arrive at a more satisfying overall picture. All three are linked. For example, parents' narratives help to explain institutional narratives as responsive and developmental, but which framed some of how children then narrated their own lives (at least for their earlier childhood years). Institutional narratives, in turn, created frameworks within which parents' narratives (especially about education) became calcified over the *longue durée* and thus locked children into repeated cycles of movement and separation. Children's narratives, shaped within or by those of parents and institutions, also took on shades of their own as they grappled with the complexities of being boys or girls, infants or teenagers, Scots or New Zealanders, while growing up in spaces of greater or lesser familiarity. This approach is critiqued further on.

Inhabited space is the other concept employed throughout the book, with a focus on public representations (through literature) and on discrete and transitional spaces defined by the parameters, dictates and inconsistencies of imperialism and colonialism (namely domestic spaces, the influences of cross-cultural interactions in those spaces and mobility as a way of living in empire). These spaces have been doubly conceptualised both as contested 'sites' of 'lived experience' (geographic, textual, figurative, ideological, theological) in which children were shaped by or responded to operative discursive influences and as contested 'spaces for feeling' wherein and between, at a range of scales, children had to navigate various forms of emotional frontier. Integral to both concepts is an emphasis on missionary children's lives as embodied emotional and cognitive experiences that had variable influences on their lives as children and later as adults.

The trajectory of the chapters therefore has moved from: the ways that missionary children might be 'known' by the wider public (especially through enduring imperial textual commons of newsprint and magazines) and by the church-going public (especially metropole children who were something of a captive audience and for whom reading material formed a virtual cross-cultural contact zone but also as a potential, if not realised, transnational juvenile theological-cum-emotional community); through the interrelated narratives of parents and institutions (drawing on concepts of parents and children's 'emotional labour' and a public discourse of 'happiness' to indicate how one fed off the other), in the process elaborating how children's well-being had emerged by the 1930s as a central concern for both parties; through two interwoven iterations of children's narratives elaborated through notions of 'life as ordinary' and 'life as complicated' (wherein separation emerges as one key narrative thread, but which was variously seen as problematic or not by children juxtaposed with parents' anxieties); and finally to children as inhabitants of imperial and colonial spaces, both as often unwitting imperial subjects but also as agents with respect to their own responses to those spaces. Conceptually and in historical detail, the chapters bear out a two-fold conviction stated in the book's Introduction: that the subject of missionary children is so broad as to require a 'global-historical' comparative and multi-centred approach; and that a 'relational' and 'contextual' approach that thinks about childhoods as created within a nexus of meaningful relationships and different contexts is ultimately a more productive historical approach.[5]

Four comments are worth making about this overlapping-lenses concept and approach that potentially feed into further discussion as to its efficacy or shortcomings. First, the strengths are noted above but can be restated thus. While each lens accentuates its own specificities, together they more sharply focus attention on the extent to which children's lives were rich, complex and intricate. In so doing they provide one answer, perhaps, to the continually vexed issue of finding, discerning and interpreting children's historical voices and experiences.[6] This is a legitimate concern and is commented on further. I also continue to think about the resulting pitfalls for historians, in the temptation to potentially reify one perspective (that of children's) to the detriment of other equally important perspectives. Therefore, a potential strength of the overlapping narratives approach is that it (hopefully) avoids one being dominant over another (as elaborated in previous paragraphs). It takes a triangulated approach in order to properly understand each perspective uniquely but also comparatively excavating both commonalities and discontinuities and their relationship to one another.

Second, the application of this concept across the various historical players, in tandem with insights from the history of emotions, serves to elaborate the emotionally constructed nature of memory and narrative. This was most visibly drawn out in the context of children's explication of their lives as variously 'ordinary' and 'complicated', in that their lives were remembered as much through feelings (at the time but more especially elaborated as residual emotional imprints on memory) as through the recollected or collected details of quotidian life. Interviews tended to elicit, in general, more nuanced life stories than those of published memoirs. The latter lean more towards negative memories and pejorative judgements (but note Vandrick's caution about authorial balance), acting among other things as ways of working out feelings and values in a public forum, or as therapeutic gifts to enable other readers to process their own unarticulated or traumatic life stories. Yet parents' narratives – about their children and their responses to what were seen as children's needs – were also constructed partially through emotional practices (emotional labour precipitated by anxiety over children's welfare and possible guilt over what they saw as the inevitability of separation). Similarly, institutional narratives were partially constructed around a prevailing childhood-oriented discourse of 'happiness' in response to both parents' stated needs and the cultural imperatives operative within wider society with respect to the domestic family unit. In turn, children also had to manage emotions, enacting 'happiness' for example in the residential homes, to fulfil the demands of parents and institutions, but in doing so helped to create their own emotional communities of mutual self-support. While this residential community was bisected by a clear and sometimes traumatic emotional frontier (between adult expectations and children's responses), this oftentimes became a productive space or a point of resistance for children, rather than a categorical barrier.

Third, one potential weakness is the uneasy tension to be maintained between reading multiple narratives discretely or relationally, to the extent that individual narratives are elided, subsumed by others or indeed analysed to such an extent that their authors' legitimate grievances are side-lined or negated. Therefore, differentiation within and between the narrative lenses remains an important and unfinished task. This book has tried to model this by giving careful attention to each narrative lens as well as seeking to comment on the overlaps between each. Two chapters that focus on one narrative – children's perspectives – were equally a response to the ongoing clarion call by children's historians that children's voices are important to hear and were also a result of the quality of the data collected. While the archival material eliciting missionary parents' and institutions' views on, feelings about and responses to their children was rich, even more so were the selected oral history interviews and selected published memoirs. From immersion in these data, there emerged a complex set of interwoven narratives that I have tried to capture in the two narrative threads – 'life as ordinary' or 'complicated' – about which I hope that justice has been done in a sensitive and professional manner. They contain much more potential yet, not the least being their further differentiation along lines of national origin. While I have tried to compare and contrast, for example, children from New Zealand and Scottish backgrounds, there is much yet to think about with respect to national origins and their impact on parenting.

A fourth point, therefore, is that there may well be more than just these three narrative lenses to be considered and that, in reality, different combinations of lenses were possibly of varying importance at different times or in different places. One obvious omission, for example, is the lens of Indigenous or local people with respect to their interactions with and views of missionary children. This is partly an issue of sources, in that written sources from long-past decades or indeed oral sources from more recent decades are hard to come by. Some of this can be gotten at, perhaps, by reading against the grain of existing sources. For example, at a number of points through the written and oral evidence, ex-children referred to friends made at the time, and to friendships that have lasted over distances of space and time. Furthermore, inferences might be made from the many sources derived from children of empire (for example, those many cases noted by Brendon for British India),[7] that warm relationships between ayah or amah and child were indicative of mutually caring, warm and emotionally significant relationships.

However, a caveat is found in the work of Laura Ann Stoler concerning imperial domesticities in Dutch Java (Indonesia). She quotes from two Dutch memoirs in which the relationship between European child and Javanese nanny was described in intimate and visceral terms – recalling the touch of a body or clothing, fragrance inhaled, caresses and peacefulness. Their meaning was clear – here was someone who cared intimately and carefully for the child. In contrasting fashion, she then quotes from a Javanese *babu* (nursemaid) who matter-of-factly remembered that she was 'told to take care of the child. At ten at night I'd go back in and give it something to drink, some milk, then a change of clothes, whatever clothes were wet, you know, ... then I'd return to the back [servants' quarters] again, like that.'[8] The disparities between perspectives are stark, even if these three people quoted were completely unrelated to one another. At the same time, Ida Pruitt's narrative, which clearly tied the influence of her amah to her own developing sense of self and attitudes towards Western responses to Chinese culture – and the critical manner in which the local community reacted when her amah was sent off by the family to look after another European family's baby – indicates the potential of looking for such narratives more carefully.

Finally, then, we return to the question 'how can we talk meaningfully about missionary children in history?' This book very deliberately advances the importance of taking a carefully historicised view of missionary children. Thus, it has worked within a given time frame (1870s to the 1950s), paying particular attention to the first half of the twentieth century. It has also deliberately and carefully worked with selected missionary materials and used oral history material collected from participants within the relatively cohesive and representative denominational framework of Scottish and New Zealand Presbyterianism. And it has carefully and deliberately taken a comparative approach across a number of different missionary settings or points of operation. It has thus sought to distinguish itself from previous scholarship confined mostly to the nineteenth century or to discrete geographical locations. Herein lies both the strength and weakness of this book.

To restate the point more constructively, perhaps here is the point at which this book might now provide a constructive bridge between previous scholarship and that which is yet to come. Most immediately it moves discussion into more comparative directions, seeking to draw lines between particular case studies and broader studies and to ask to what extent we can talk about 'missionary children' across time. For example, to what extent can we legitimately draw a straight line from the Crook children in 1820s Tahiti to the Marwick children of 1900s Jamaica, to the Gray children of 1920s India and to Kirsten in 1950s Yemen/Kenya? What are the continuities and discontinuities? Can we say, for example, that the experiences of ABCFM children, born in Hawaii but who initially had to spend months sailing back to the eastern coast of America for education, bear any relationship to the experiences of Michael Orr or Jim travelling three weeks by boat to Britain or to Marie flying the same distance in a matter of hours? In these respects, lines drawn around specificities of time and place seem important, demarcating very different experiences of being 'missionary children' in each case. This kind of approach is also integral to a 'global-historical' hermeneutic which should not simply subsume everything within one historical view or metanarrative, but which instead factors in 'a multi-centred world, characterized by ambiguity and contradiction', through which 'contingency and cultural temporal-specificity' are 'key concepts' in a 'geographically broad approach to the past'.[9]

Therefore, I hope that this book might contribute helpfully in both expanding current understanding and, more importantly, identifying fruitful avenues for further research. For missions history, it affirms existing scholarship that highlights the importance of children's perspectives about historical missionary life and work. Pomfret argues that in thinking about colonial history in the Southeast Asian sphere, 'youthful activities, mobilities and identities were central to the fashioning of empire and global modernity'.[10] The same goes for the future historiography of missions, wherein age (as well as gender and the family) needs to be placed more centrally – both as an important category of analysis and as a compelling explanatory factor for policy making and different place-based strategies among other things. To this are added perspectives from two national entities – Scotland and New Zealand – that in the period under study were constitutively and culturally a part of the British Empire and integral to the Western Protestant missionary movement. Myriad examples across the three narratives of children, adults and institutions serve to reinforce our understanding of mission and childhood history but, at the same time, indicate culturally and politically nuanced differences within that movement and its children that require further scrutiny. For example, that a male missionary (James Gray), born in Scotland but raised in New Zealand, married a Scot (Marion Scott) and then raised his own Indian-born sons within the direct ambit of the British Empire, sent them to an American-run school which he then criticised for its cultural impact, and so sent them off to boarding school in New Zealand is indicative of a movement that was more kaleidoscopic than monochrome.

On a wider front, I suggest that this book contributes to the further pursuit of children and young people in history, and the application of the history of emotions to this endeavour. Two broad comments can be made here. In the first instance, it points to the complexities of thinking about the historical religiosity of children and youth and the value in employing insights from the emerging 'history of experience' field, with its stated affinities to histories of emotion. For these children, religion was not configured the same for all, as the families to which they belonged inhabited a number of spots along a religious or theological continuum. Even to be 'Presbyterian', as many of those represented in this book were, meant different things depending on different denominational configurations (especially within Scotland) and changing theologies over time. Some were acutely aware of this, accepted it or reacted against it. Some accepted this but rejected it in later life. For others, religion was taken for granted and not remembered to any great extent. The same pertained to the extent to which they were aware of or reflected on the fact that they lived in the midst of other religious communities quite different to their own. That had a profound effect on some, but certainly not on many others depending, in part, on the extent to which they were sheltered from or exposed to the communities within which they lived. Changes in religious disposition became more of a factor as children became teenagers, were exposed to different or prescriptive religious cultures (especially at boarding schools) and then later made significant adjustments to Western settings as young adults. All of this, I suggest, is a part of thinking about 'religious childhoods' or 'religious adolescence'. It is not just about individuals and explicit religious experiences or awareness, but also about the geographical, mental, emotional and theological spaces inhabited.

As such, further work on this could benefit from thinking about religion as a complexly 'lived experience' that includes 'the relationship between individual subjective and shared collective or communal experience' and that addresses 'questions of producing, sharing, cultivating, curating, and modifying experiences' and 'how those processes influence social/societal structures'.[11]

Secondly, this book has implicitly wrestled with such questions as: what makes children's and young people's historical experiences unique, how do we genuinely discern juvenile voices and to what extent is it helpful to create essentialising analytical categories (such as 'missionary children'), which potentially privilege some, hide others and worse, do damage to many? To this end, a wide-ranging 'history of emotions' approach has been employed as both an analytical tool bag and a way to understand this group of youngsters more carefully and sensitively in the historical record. Yet that is inherently problematic, given the noted 'heterodoxy of approaches' and often the 'theoretically inchoate' nature of the field, and its until recently adult-centric conceptualisation.[12] There is a confusing array of ideas, but perhaps that is just a way for scholars to position themselves more prominently, or whose concerns are particular to different periods, groups, societies or nations. I am comfortable with drawing on a range of concepts without asserting that these should be privileged in any way. Furthermore, there is now a growing body of scholarship (as indicated throughout the book) that aims to write a more nuanced history of children's and young people's emotions. To that end, I suggest that this book contributes usefully to that body of scholarship. It focuses on children's embodied experiences and voices – especially through their memory and meaning-making – discerned in and emerging from both discrete and shared emotional spaces in which self-identity was dynamically forged through inter-age relationships and responses to context. Those spaces were complexly constructed – impacted for this period by ongoing processes of imperialism and colonialism – ranging from the micro to the macro, traversing almost mind-blowing dynamic combinations of culture, religiosity, politics, gender and age among many others. A focus on emotions and spaces throws into high relief, I think, the contested and negotiated nature of being a child or young person. These spaces were bisected by a multiplicity of emotional frontiers, which acted as life barriers for some and for others were productive spaces with respect to identity, resilience and life trajectories. This more focused survey of missionary children, however, reveals a group for whom emotional navigation was variably exciting, precarious, life-enhancing or life-threatening precisely because of where they were born, where they grew up and where they later had to move.

Perhaps what this book most powerfully indicates, through both its inherent strengths and weaknesses, is that a key ongoing task is to identify and elucidate what was core to historical missionary children's lives and experiences and what was context-specific. That is, to look further at what binds them together across these great distances of time and place, between big-picture comparisons and localised studies. Maybe that means thinking about national origins and denominational distinctions. Maybe that means looking for shared lifestyles within larger spaces like 'British India' in the late nineteenth century or 'Japanese North China' in the 1930s. Maybe that means excavating more carefully the gendered and age-specific experiences of going to boarding school or living in missionary children's homes. Maybe it requires a careful paring away of the experiences of separation and the analysis of these for children from religious compared with non-religious backgrounds, but also across national settings within the wider ambit of Western Protestantism. Maybe it is the task of grappling with the equally important observation, by so many of the participants, that missionary childhoods were as infinitely variable as the number of individuals, but thinking further about this with respect to discursive influences of historical context, family, theology, ecclesiology, cultural locale or political frameworks. Maybe it is about bringing analysis of missionary children back into the histories of missionary families, longitudinally as well as in discrete moments or places. These are some of the scholarly spaces that still remain, among many others, in which further research and thinking will be valuable – hopefully opened up through the pages of this book but, most certainly, still awaiting further exploration.

Notes

1 Wilkins, *A Child's Eye View*, p. 135.
2 Vandrick, *Growing Up*, p. 122.
3 Devereux, 'Narrating', pp. 197–98; and presented in richly evocative and thought-provoking detail through the narratives curated in Ostini et al., *Sent*.
4 Louisa interview.
5 Referencing again concepts from: Vallgårda, Alexander and Olsen, 'Emotions', p. 14; and Gleason, 'Avoiding', 457.
6 Indicative literature for this issue is canvassed in the Introduction, but was usefully foregrounded by Stearns, 'Challenges', 35–42.
7 Brendon, *Children*, pp. 163–70.
8 Stoler, *Carnal Knowledge*, pp. 164–65.
9 Vallgårda, Alexander and Olsen, 'Emotions', p. 14.
10 Pomfret, *Youth*, p. 277.
11 Katajala-Peltomaa and Toivo, 'Introduction', p. 2.
12 Olsen, 'The History of Childhood', 1, 2.

Bibliography

Primary material

Unpublished material

Canada

The Rare Books Collection, University of British Columbia, Vancouver

China

*Special Collections and Archives, Au Shue Hung Memorial Library, Hong Kong
    Baptist University, Hong Kong*

New Zealand

Alexander Turnbull Library, Wellington
    Phyllis Long Papers
Carey Baptist College Library, Auckland
    New Zealand Baptist Missionary Society Archives
Hocken Library, University of Otago, Dunedin
    McNeur Family Papers
    Malcolm Papers
John Kinder Theological Library, St John's College, Auckland
    New Zealand Church Missionary Society Archives
*Presbyterian Church of Aotearoa New Zealand Archives, Presbyterian Research
    Centre, Dunedin*
    Canton Villages Mission Staff Files
    New Hebrides Mission Staff Files
    Presbyterian Foreign Missions Committee Archives
    Punjab Mission Staff Files
    Rev Dr Rutherford Waddell Personal Papers
Toitū Otago Settlers' Museum, Research Centre, Dunedin
    George Hepburn Diary

United Kingdom

Angus Library and Archives, Regent's Park College, University of Oxford, Oxford
  Baptist Missionary Society Archives
Cadbury Research Library, University of Birmingham, Birmingham
  Church Missionary Society Archives
Centre for the Study of World Christianity, School of Divinity, University of Edinburgh, Edinburgh
  Alexander and Elizabeth McKenzie Collection
  Joseph Ross Collection
Centre for Research Collections, University of Edinburgh, Edinburgh
  Collections Relating to Winifred Rushforth
  Material Relating to John W.L. Spence
National Library of Scotland, Edinburgh
  Church of Scotland Board of World Mission (Cunningham House)
  Church of Scotland Foreign Missions Committee
  Church of Scotland Overseas Council
  Scottish Foreign Mission Records
  William Hutton Marwick Papers
National Records of Scotland, Edinburgh
  Church of Scotland CH1 (Home House)
  Church of Scotland CH3 (Letters from Foreign Missionaries)
  Military Service Appeal Tribunal Records (Lothian and Peebles)
Private collections
  Dorothy Kirk Papers, Ian Waldram, Scotland, used with family permission
  Michael Orr Memoir (unpublished), Scotland, used with family permission
School of Oriental and African Studies, University of London, London
  Christian World Mission/London Missionary Society Archives

United States of America

SIM International Archives, Fort Mill, South Carolina
  Bolivian Indian Mission Archives

Oral history interviews

New Zealand

Scott Gray, 15 June 2014 (South Asia)
Ian Gray, 29 December 2014 (South Asia)
Janice Rowley, 19 March 2015 (Pacific)
Joan Sutherland, 19 March 2015 (Pacific)
David, 27 March 2015 (East Asia)
Unnamed, March 2015 (South Asia)

Scotland

Kirsten, 3 January 2015 (Middle East/Africa)
Marie, 7 January 2015 (South Asia)

Rose, 8 January 2015 (Africa)
Robin W., 9 January 2015 (Africa)
Veronica, 10 January 2015 (Africa)
Jim, 12 January 2015 (South Asia)
Louisa, 12 January 2015 (Africa)
Alison, 13 January 2015 (Africa)
Amelia, 13 January 2015 (South Asia)
Robin S., 14 January 2015 (South Asia)
Dawn, 15 January 2015 (East Asia)
Alan, 17 January 2015 (South Asia)
Joyce, 19 January 2015 (East Asia)
Michael, 20 January 2015 (South Asia)
Isabel, 21 January 2015 (Africa)
Unnamed, January 2015 (South Asia)

Official published material

The Baptist Handbook, 1927–1956
BMS Reports of Committee and Abstracts, 1890–1891
Presbyterian Women's Missionary Union Annual Reports [New Zealand], 1905–1940
Proceedings and Debates of the General Assembly of the Free Church of Scotland, 1850–1900
Proceedings of the General Assembly of the Presbyterian Church of New Zealand, 1866–1901
Proceedings of the Synod of the Presbyterian Church of Southland and Otago, 1866–1901
Proceedings of the General Assembly of the Presbyterian Church of New Zealand, 1901–1939
Reports to the General Assembly of the Church of Scotland, 1879–1939
Reports to the General Assembly of the United Free Church of Scotland, 1901–1939

Contemporary published material

Anonymous, *Charles Dwight: or, the Missionary's Son* (London: Religious Tract Society, [1853]).
Anonymous, *The Missionary's Daughter. A Brief Memoir of Emily Judson Lillie* (London: John Snow, Paternoster Row, [1865]).
Anonymous, *Presbyterian Homes for Children of Foreign Missionaries, Wooster, Ohio* (Pittsburgh, PA: Presbyterian Board of Foreign Missions of the Presbyterian Church, USA, 1893).
Baird, James, *Nyono at School and at Home: The Story of an African Boy* (Edinburgh and London: Oliphant, Anderson, & Ferrier, 1906).
Baketel, Oliver S. (ed.), *The Methodist Yearbook 1921* (New York and Cincinnati, OH: The Methodist Book Concern, 1921).
Bird, Handley H., *Carol 'A Sweet Savour of Christ': The Memoir of a Missionary Child* (London, Edinburgh and New York: Marshall Brothers Ltd., 1910).

Brummitt, Dan B., 'The Fate of Missionaries' Children', *The Missionary Review of the World* (January 1934), pp. 37–38.

Christie, Mrs., *Dugald Christie of Manchuria Pioneer and Medical Missionary: The Story of a Life with a Purpose* (London: James Clarke & Company, Limited, 1932).

Church of Scotland, *Home-House for Foreign Missionaries' Children* (Edinburgh: Church of Scotland, [1897]).

Cummings, A.P., *The Missionary's Daughter: A Memoir of Lucy Goodale Thurston of the Sandwich Islands* (New York: American Tract Society, [1842]).

Curnock, Nehemiah (ed.), *Fanny Hurd or, the Story of a West Indian Missionary's Daughter* (London: T. Woolmer, 1886).

Don, Alexander, *Light in Dark Isles: A Jubilee Record and Study of the New Hebrides Mission of the Presbyterian Church of New Zealand* (Dunedin: Foreign Missions Committee, P.C.N.Z., 1918).

Editorial Committee, *Ecumenical Missionary Conference New York, 1900: Report of the Ecumenical Conference on Foreign Missions, Held in Carnegie Hall and Neighbouring Churches, April 21 to May 1*, 2 vols (New York: American Tract Society, 1900).

Ewing, Rev William, *Annals of the Free Church of Scotland 1843–1900*, 2 vols. (Edinburgh: T. & T. Clark, 1914).

Ewing, W., *Paterson of Hebron 'the Hakim': Missionary Life in the Mountain of Judah*, 2nd ed. (London: Jame Clarke & Company, Limited, 1930).

Fraser, Agnes R., *Donald Fraser of Livingstonia* (London: Hodder and Stoughton, 1934).

Fraser, Donald, *African Idylls: Portraits & Impressions of Life on a Central African Mission Station* (London: Seeley, Service & Co. Limited, 1923).

Hartley, Emily, *Ruth Allerton: The Missionary's Daughter* (Philadelphia, PA: American Sunday-School Union, 1871).

Hocking, William Ernest, *Re-Thinking Missions: A Laymen's Inquiry after One Hundred Years* (New York and London: Harper & Brothers Publishers, 1932).

Huntington, Ellsworth, 'The Success of Missionary Children', *The Missionary Review of the World* (February 1935), pp. 74–75.

Huntington, Ellsworth, and Leon F. Whitney, *The Builders of America* (New York: William Morrow, 1927).

Johnston, Rev James, *Report of the Centenary Conference on the Protestant Missions of the World Held in Exeter Hall (June 9th–19th), London, 1888* (London: James Nisbet & Co., 1898).

King, Rev Joseph, *W.G. Lawes of Savage Island and New Guinea* (London: The Religious Tract Society, 1909).

Lamb, John Alexander, *The Fasti of the United Free Church of Scotland 1900–1929* (Edinburgh and London: Oliver and Boyd, 1956).

Lee, Ada, *Seven Heroic Children: A Great Sorrow and a Great Victory* (London: Morgan and Scott, 1903).

Lee, Ada, *The Darjeeling Disaster: Its Bright Side* (Harrisburg, PA: Fred Kelker, 1912).

Lennox, William G., *A Comparative Study of the Health of Missionaries in Japan and China and a Selected Group in the United States* (Denver, CO: University of Denver Colorado, 1921).

Lennox, William G., *The Health of Missionary Families in China* (Denver, CO: University of Denver Colorado, 1920).

Lennox, William G., *The Health and Turnover of Missionaries* (New York: Advisory Committee of the Foreign Missions Conferences, 1933).

Lovett, Richard, *The History of the London Missionary Society, 1795–1895*, 2 vols ([S.I.]: Frowde, 1899).

Moffat, John S., *The Lives of Robert and Mary Moffat*, 3rd ed. (London: T. Fisher Unwin, 1885).

Mullens, Rev Joseph, 'Previous Conferences on Missions', in The Secretaries to the Conference (eds), *Conference on Missions Held in 1860 at Liverpool: Including the Papers Read, the Deliberations, and the Conclusions Reached* (London: James Nisbet & Co., [1860]), pp. 65–74.

Myers, John Brown, *The Centenary Volume of the Baptist Missionary Society 1792–1892* (Holborn: The Baptist Missionary Society, 1892).

Phillips, E.C., *Peeps into China; or, The Missionary's Children* (London, Paris, New York and Melbourne: Cassell & Company, Limited, nd).

The Secretaries to the Conference (eds), *Conference on Missions Held in 1860 at Liverpool: Including the Papers Read, the Deliberations, and the Conclusions Reached* (London: James Nisbet & Co., [1860]).

The Secretaries to the Conference (eds), *Proceedings of the General Conference on Foreign Missions Held at the Conference Hall, in Mildmay Park, London, in October, 1878* (London: John F. Shaw & Co., Paternoster Row, 1879).

Scott, H., *Fasti Ecclesiae Scoticanae: The Succession of Ministers in the Church of Scotland from the Reformation*, vol. 7 (Edinburgh: Oliver and Boyd, 1928).

Stock, Eugene, *The History of the Church Missionary Society, Its Environment, Its Men and Its Work*, 3 vols (London: Church Missionary Society, 1899).

Tyndale-Biscoe, E.D., *Fifty Years against the Stream: The Story of a School in Kashmir 1880–1930* (Mysore: Wesleyan Mission Press, 1930).

Published missionary children's autobiographies

Barnes, Albert E., *The Life Journey of a Missionary's Son* (Bloomington, IN: Balboa Press, 2012).

Beetham, Margaret Newbigin, *Home Is Where: The Journeys of a Missionary Child* (London: Darton, Longman & Todd, 2019).

Beetham, Margaret Rachel, 'Dust and Mangoes: Plain Tales and Hill Stations', in Jackie Stacey and Janet Wolff (eds), *Writing Otherwise: Experiments in Cultural Criticism* (Manchester: Manchester University Press, 2013), pp. 135–50.

Booth, Patricia, *Pat's India: Memories of Childhood* (Wellington: Philip Garside Publishing Ltd., 2017).

Cook, Faith, *Troubled Journey: A Missionary Childhood in War-Torn China* (Edinburgh: The Banner of Truth Trust, 2004).

Crozier, John P., *Will the Rajah Say No?* (Nelson: John P. Crozier, 1985).

Dopirak, Margaret H. Essebaggers, *Missionary Kid: Born in India, Bound for America* (Margaret H. Essebaggers Dopirak, 2016).

Gray, Ian, *We Travel Together: Lesley's and Ian's Journey* (Nelson: The Copy Press, 2014).

Hepburn, Catherine, 'The Burning Rosebush: Africa, Ecumenism and Country Parishes', in Robert D. Kernohan (ed.), *The Realm of Reform: Presbyterianism and Calvinism in a Changing Scotland* (Edinburgh: The Handsel Press, 1999), pp. 123–32.

Hopkins, Justin B., 'Coming "Home": An Autoethnographic Exploration of Third Culture Kid Transition', *Qualitative Inquiry* 21:9 (2015), 812–20.

Jackson, Elva, *Indian Saga* (Devonport, New Zealand: E.M. Jackson, 1980).

Miller, Sheila, *Pigtails, Petticoats and the Old School Tie* (Sevenoaks: Overseas Missionary Fellowship, 1981).

Moore, Margaret (ed.), *Daughter of China: An Autobiography Jean Moore (1907– 1992)* (Margaret Moore, 1992).

Ostini, Jenny, Bernard Dainton, John Chenoweth, Janet Smith and Bernice Watkins (eds), *Sent: Reflections on Missions, Boarding Schools and Childhood* (Chefoo Reconsidered Book Committee, 2020).

Pruitt, Ida, *A China Childhood* (Beijing: Foreign Languages Press, 2003).

Scholberg, Henry, *That's India: The Memoirs of an Old India Hand* (New Delhi: Bibliophile South Asia and Promilla & Co., 2002).

Terry, Rebecca Jean, *Help Me Be a Good Girl Amen: My Journey from Missionary Kid to Truth* (Custer, WA: Brandy Wine Press, 2011).

Van Reken, Ruth E., *Letters Never Sent: One Woman's Journey from Hurt to Wholeness* (Indianapolis, IN: Letters, 1988).

Wilkins, Joyce, *A Child's Eye View, 1904–1920* (Sussex: The Book Guild Ltd., 1992).

Contemporary journals and newspapers

Adelaide Observer
Advertiser
Age
Auckland Star
Australian Christian Commonwealth
The Ballarat Star
The Barrier Miner
Birmingham Daily Post
The Break of Day
Chefoo Magazine
Chefusian
The Children's Missionary Magazine of the United Free Church of Scotland
Children's Missionary Record of the Free Church of Scotland
The Children's Record

The Children's World
The China Press
The Chinese Recorder
The Chinese Recorder and Missionary Journal
Chronicle of the London Missionary Society
Church Missionary Gleaner
Church Missionary Intelligencer
The Church Missionary Juvenile Instructor
CMS Juvenile Intelligencer
Daily News
The Evening News
Evening Star
The Irish Times
John McGlashan School Magazine
The Juvenile Missionary Herald
The Juvenile Missionary Record and the Sabbath Scholars' Magazine
Life and Work
Macleay Argus
The Methodist
The Message
The Missionary Messenger
The Missionary Monthly
Missionary Record
The Monthly Leaflet
Moose Jaw Herald
Newcastle Morning Herald and Miner's Advocate
Newcastle Sun
News
New York Times
New Zealand Mail
New Zealand Missionary Record
On Continent and Island
Otago Daily Times
Otago Witness
Other Lands
The Outlook
Poverty Bay Herald
The Press
Quarterly Token for Juvenile Subscribers
Reynold's Newspaper
The Round World
Samoa Weekly Herald
The Scotsman
South Australian Register
Southland Times
Sydney Morning Herald

The Telegraph
The Times
Wagga Wagga Advertiser
The Watsonian
The Wesleyan Juvenile Offering
Young Scotland

Secondary material

Published

Addleton, Jonathan S., 'Missionary Kid Memoirs: A Review Essay', *International Bulletin of Missionary Research* 24:1 (2000), 30–34.

Adogame, Afe and Andrew Lawrence (eds), *Africa in Scotland, Scotland in Africa: Historical Legacies and Contemporary Hybridities* (Leiden and Boston: Brill, 2014).

Ahmed, Sara, 'Collective Feelings or, the Impressions Left by Others', *Theory, Culture and Society* 21:2 (2004), 25–42.

Ahmed, Sara, *The Cultural Politics of Emotion* (New York: Routledge, 2004).

Ahmed, Sara, *The Promise of Happiness* (Durham, NC: Duke University Press, 2010).

Anderson, Gerald, 'American Protestants in Pursuit of Mission, 1886–1986', *International Bulletin of Missionary Research* 12:3 (1988), 98–118.

Ask, Lene, *Dear Rikard* (London: Centrala, 2015).

Austin, Clyde and Billy van Jones, 'Re-Entry among Missionary Children: An Overview of Re-Entry Research from 1934 to 1986', *Journal of Psychology and Theology* 15:4 (1987), 315–25.

Ballantyne, Tony, *Entanglements of Empire: Missionaries, Māori, and the Question of the Body* (Auckland: Auckland University Press, 2015).

Ballantyne, Tony, 'Review Essay: Religion, Difference and the Limits of British Imperial History', *Victorian Studies* 47:3 (2005), 427–55.

Ballantyne, Tony, *Webs of Empire: Locating New Zealand's Colonial Past* (Wellington: Bridget Williams Books, 2012).

Barclay, Katie, 'Happiness: Family and Nation in Nineteenth-Century Ireland', *Nineteenth-Century Contexts*, 43:2 (2021), 171–90.

Barrett, David and Maria Kukhareva, 'Family Relationships', in Joseph M. Hawes and N. Ray Hiner (eds), *A Cultural History of Childhood and Family in the Modern Age* (London, New Delhi, New York, Sydney: Bloomsbury Academic, 2014), pp. 21–37.

Barron, Hester, and Claire Langhamer, 'Feeling through Practice: Subjectivity and Emotion in Children's Writing', *Journal of Social History* 51:1 (2017), 101–23.

Bateman, Grace, 'Signs and Graces: Children's Experiences of Confirmation in New Zealand, 1920s–1950s', in Hugh Morrison and Mary Clare Martin (eds), *Creating Religious Childhoods in Anglo-World and British Colonial Contexts, 1800–1950* (London and New York: Routledge, 2017), pp. 201–21.

Behlmer, G.K., *Friends of the Family: The English Home and Its Guardians 1850–1940* (Palo Alto, CA: Stanford University Press, 1998).

Bellenoit, Hayden J., *Missionary Education and Empire in Late Colonial India, 1860–1920* (London: Pickering & Chatto, 2007).

Bennett, Andy, *Culture and Everyday Life* (London: Sage, 2005).

Berner, Tali, '"For the Pleasure of Babies": Children and Emotions in Early Modern Jewish Communities', in Claudia Jarzebowski and Thomas Max Safley (eds), *Childhood and Emotion: Across Cultures 1450–1800* (London and New York: Routledge, 2014), pp. 28–41.

Bjørnsen, Ragnhild Holmen, 'The Assumption of Privilege? Expectations on Emotions When Growing Up in the Norwegian Foreign Service', *Childhood* 27:1 (2020), 120–33.

Boddice, Rob, 'The History of Emotions: Past, Present and Future', *Revista de Estudios Sociales* 62 (2017), 10–15.

Boddice, Rob, *The History of Emotions* (Manchester: Manchester University Press, 2018).

Bornat, Joanna, 'Remembering and Reworking Emotions: The Reanalysis of Emotion in an Interview', *Oral History* 38:2 (Autumn 2010), 43–52.

Boschmann, Kathryn, 'Speaking of the Sacred: Exploring Religion, Spirituality, and the Boundaries of Emotional Communities through Oral History', *Oral History Forum d'histoire orale* (2017), 1–23.

Boucher, Ellen, *Empire's Children: Child Emigration, Welfare, and the Decline of the British World, 1869–1967* (Cambridge: Cambridge University Press, 2014).

Bourke, Johanna, 'Fear and Anxiety: Writing about Emotion in Modern History', *History Workshop Journal* 55:1 (2003), 111–33.

Bourke, Johanna, '"Frightened and Rather Feverish": The Fear of Pain in Childbirth', in Daniel McCann and Claire McKechnie-Mason (eds), *Fear in the Medical and Literary Imagination, Medieval to Modern: Dreadful Passions* (Basingstoke: Palgrave Macmillan, 2018), pp. 55–78.

Bowersox, Jeff, 'Boy's and Girl's Own Empires: Gender and the Uses of the Colonial World in Kaiserreich Youth Magazines', in Michael Parraudin and Jurgen Zimmerer (eds), *German Colonialism and National Identity* (New York: Routledge, 2011), pp. 57–69.

Breitenbach, Esther, *Empire and Scottish Society: The Impact of Foreign Missions at Home, c.1790 to c.1914* (Edinburgh: Edinburgh University Press, 2009).

Brendon, Vyvyen, *Children of the Raj* (London: Phoenix, 2006).

Bretsch, Howard S., 'A Study of Intercultural Adjustment Problems of Missionary Children', *The Journal of Educational Research* 47:8 (1954), 609–16.

Brookes, Barbara, Annabel Cooper and Robyn Law, 'Situating Gender', in Barbara Brookes, Annabel Cooper and Robyn Law (eds), *Sites of Gender: Women, Men and Modernity in Southern Dunedin, 1890–1939* (Auckland: Auckland University Press, 2003), pp. 1–14.

Broomhall, Susan, 'Introduction', in Susan Broomhall (ed.), *Spaces for Feeling: Emotions and Sociabilities in Britain, 1650–1850* (Abingdon: Routledge, 2015), pp. 1–11.

Bruce, Emily, 'Encountering Emotions in the Archive of Childhood and Youth', in Deborah Levison, Mary Jo Maynes and Frances Vavrus (eds), *Children and Youth as Subjects, Objects, Agents: Innovative Approaches to Research Across Space and Time* (Cham: Palgrave Macmillan, 2021), pp. 33–45.

Buettner, Elizabeth, *Empire Families: Britons and Late Imperial India* (Oxford: Oxford University Press, 2004).

Buettner, Elizabeth, 'Parent-Child Separations and Colonial Careers: The Talbot Family Correspondence in the 1880s and 1890s', in Anthony Fletcher and Stephen Hussey (eds), *Childhood in Question: Children, Parents and the State* (Manchester and New York: Manchester University Press, 1999), pp. 115–32.

Buettner, Elizabeth, 'Problematic Spaces, Problematic Races: Defining "Europeans" in Late Colonial India', *Women's History Review* 9:2 (2000), 277–98.

Bunge, Marcia J. (ed.), *The Child in Christian Thought* (Grand Rapids, MI: William B. Eerdmans Publishing Company, 2001).

Bunge, Marcia J. and Don S. Browning, 'Introduction', in Don S. Browning and Marcia J. Bunge (eds), *Children and Childhood in World Religions: Primary Sources and Texts* (New Brunswick, NJ: Rutgers University Press, 2009), pp. 1–14.

Burke, Peter, 'Strengths and Weaknesses of the History of Mentalities', *History of European Ideas* 7:5 (1986), 439–51.

Butlin, Robin A., *Geographies of Empire: European Empires and Colonies c. 1880–1960* (Cambridge: Cambridge University Press, 2009).

Byron, M., and S. Condon, *Migration in Comparative Perspective: Caribbean Communities in Britain and France* (London: Routledge, 2008).

Chen, Shih-Wen Sue, *Representations of China in British Children's Fiction, 1851–1911* (Burlington, VT: Ashgate, 2013).

Chen, Shih-Wen Sue, '"Give, Give; Be Always Giving": Children, Charity and China, 1890–1939', *Papers: Explorations into Children's Literature* 24:2 (2016), 5–32.

Chiu, Patricia Pok-kwan, '"A Position of Usefulness": Gendering History of Girls' Education in Colonial Hong Kong (1850s–1890s)', *History of Education* 37:6 (2008), 789–805.

Choi, Hyaeweol, 'The Missionary Home as a Pulpit: Domestic Paradoxes in Early Twentieth-Century Korea', in Hyaeweol Choi and Margaret Jolly (eds), *Divine Domesticities: Christian Paradoxes in Asia and the Pacific* (Canberra: ANU Press, 2014), pp. 29–55.

Clapp-Itnyre, Alisa, *British Hymn Books for Children, 1800–1900: Re-Tuning the History of Childhood* (London and New York: Routledge, 2018).

Clarke, Alison, *Holiday Seasons: Christmas, New Year and Easter in Nineteenth-Century New Zealand* (Auckland: Auckland University Press, 2007).

Cleall, Esme, 'Far-Flung Families and Transient Domesticity: Missionary Households in Metropole and Colony', *Victorian Review* 39:2 (2013), 163–79.

Cleall, Esme, *Missionary Discourses of Difference: Negotiating Otherness in the British Empire, 1840–1900* (Basingstoke: Palgrave Macmillan, 2012).

Clemmons, Linda, '"Our Children Are in Danger of Becoming Little Indians": Protestant Missionary Children and Dakotas, 1835–1862', *Michigan Historical Review* 25:2 (1999), 69–90.

Colton, Ruth, 'Savage Instincts, Civilizing Spaces: The Child, the Empire and the Public Park, 1880–1914', in Simon Sleight and Shirleene Robinson (eds), *Children, Childhood and Youth in the British World* (Basingstoke: Palgrave Macmillan, 2016), pp. 255–70.

Connor, Dylan Shane, 'Poverty, Religious Differences, and Child Mortality in the Early Twentieth Century: The Case of Dublin', *Annals of the American Association of Geographers* 107:3 (2017), 625–46.

Conway, Suzanne, '*Ayah*, Caregiver to Anglo-Indian Children, c. 1750–1947', in Simon Sleight and Shirleene Robinson (eds), *Children, Childhood and Youth in the British World* (Basingstoke: Palgrave Macmillan, 2016), pp. 41–58.

Cottam, Susan, 'Small and Scattered: Poor Law Children's Homes in Leeds, 1900–1950', *Family & Community History* 20:3 (2017), 175–92.

Cox, Jeffrey, *The British Missionary Enterprise since 1700* (New York and London: Routledge, 2008).

Crane, Jennifer, *Child Protection in England, 1960–2000: Expertise, Experience, and Emotion* (Basingstoke: Palgrave Macmillan, 2018).

Crocq, Marc-Antoine, 'A History of Anxiety: From Hippocrates to DSM', *Dialogues in Clinical Neuroscience* 17:3 (2015), 319–25.

Cross, Gary, 'Play, Games, and Toys', in Paula S. Fass (ed.), *The Routledge History of Childhood in the Western World* (London and New York: Routledge, 2015), pp. 267–82.

Crump, Chris and Dorothy McKenzie, *Christina's Story: Realities of Family Life on an Isolated Pacific Island, 1938–1956* (Wellington: Ngaio Press, 2000).

Cummins, Stephen and Joel Lee, 'Missionaries: False Reverence, Irreverence and the Rethinking of Christian Mission in China and India', in Benno Gammerl, Philipp Nielsen and Margrit Pernau (eds), *Encounter with Emotions: Negotiating Cultural Differences since Early Modernity* (New York, Oxford: Berghahn, 2019), pp. 37–60.

Davey, Gwenda Beed, Kate Darian-Smith and Carla Pascoe, 'Playlore as Cultural Heritage: Traditions and Change in Australian Children's Play', in Kate Darian-Smith and Carla Pascoe (eds), *Children, Childhood and Cultural Heritage* (London: Routledge, 2013), pp. 40–54.

de Beauvoir, Simone, *The Second Sex*, transl. H.M. Parshley (London: Vintage, [1949], 1979).

de Bellaigue, Christina, 'Charlotte Mason, Home Education and the Parents' National Education Union in the Late Nineteenth Century', *Oxford Review of Education* 41:4 (2015), 501–17.

de Gruchy, John W., '"Who Did They Think They Were?" Some Reflections from a Theologian on Grand Narratives and Identity in the History of Missions', in Andrew Porter (ed.), *The Imperial Horizons of British Protestant missions, 1880–1914* (Grand Rapids, MI and Cambridge: William B. Eerdmans Publishing Company, 2003), pp. 213–25.

Dodd, Lindsey, *Feeling Memory: Remembering Wartime Childhoods in France* (New York: Columbia University Press, 2023).

Duff, S.E., *Changing Childhoods in the Cape Colony: Dutch Reformed Church Evangelicalism and Colonial Childhood, 1860–1895* (Basingstoke: Palgrave Macmillan, 2015).

Elleray, Michelle, 'Little Builders: Coral Insects, Missionary Culture, and the Victorian Child', *Victorian Literature & Culture* 39:1 (2011), 223–38.

Elleray, Michelle, *Victorian Coral Islands of Empire, Mission, and the Boys' Adventure Novel* (London and New York: Routledge, 2019).

Eustace, Nicole, 'Emotional Life', in Paula S. Fass (ed.), *Encyclopedia of Children and Childhood in History and Society*, vol. 1 (New York: Macmillan Reference USA, 2004), pp. 313–21.

Fass, Paula (ed.), *Encyclopedia of Children and Childhood in History and Society*, 3 vols (New York: Macmillan Reference USA, 2004).

Fass, Paula (ed.), *The Routledge History of Childhood in the Western World* (London and New York: Routledge, 2015).

Fisher, Fiona, 'Viewing the Early Twentieth-Century Institutional Interior through the Pages of *Living London*', in Jane Hamlett, Lesley Hoskins and Rebecca Preston (eds), *Residential Institutions in Britain, 1725–1970: Inmates and Environments* (London: Pickering & Chatto, 2013), pp. 17–33.

Fraser, Lyndon, 'Memory, Mourning and Melancholy: English Ways of Death on the Margins of Empire', in Lyndon Fraser and Angela McCarthy (eds), *Far from Home: The English in New Zealand* (Dunedin: Otago University Press, 2021), pp. 99–122.

Frevert, Ute, Pascal Eitler, Stephanie Olsen et al., *Learning How to Feel: Children's Literature and Emotional Socialization, 1870–1970* (New York: Oxford University Press, 2014).

Galbraith, Gretchen, *Reading Lives: Reconstructing Childhood, Books, and Schools in Britain, 1870–1920* (Basingstoke and London: Macmillan, 1997).

Ganter, Regina and Patricia Grimshaw, 'Introduction: Reading the Lives of White Mission Women', *Journal of Australian Studies* 39:1 (2015), 1–6.

Garrett, Eilidh, Alice Reid, Kevin Schurer, and Simon Szreter, *Changing Family Size in England and Wales, 1891–1911* (Cambridge: Cambridge University Press, 2001).

Gauvreau, Danielle, 'Religious Diversity and the Onset of the Fertility Transition: Canada, 1870–1900', in Renzo Derosas and Frans van Poppel (eds), *Religion and the Decline of Fertility in the Western World* (Dordrecht: Springer, 2006), pp. 235–58.

Gibson, Mary Ellis, 'The Perils of Reading: Children's Missionary Magazines and the Making of Victorian Imperial Subjectivity', in James Holt McGavran (ed.), *Time of Beauty, Time of Fear: The Romantic Legacy in the Literature of Childhood* (Iowa City, IA: University of Iowa Press, 2012), pp. 105–27.

Gleason, Mona, 'Avoiding the Agency Trap: Caveats for Historians of Children, Youth and Education', *History of Education* 45:4 (2016), 446–59.

Goodall, Norman, *A History of the London Missionary Society 1895–1945* (London, New York and Toronto: Oxford University Press, 1954).

Grant, Julia, 'Parent-Child Relations in Western Europe and North America, 1500–Present', in Paula S. Fass (ed.), *The Routledge History of Childhood in the Western World* (London and New York: Routledge, 2015), pp. 103–24.

Grenby, M.O., *The Child Reader 1700–1840* (Cambridge: Cambridge University Press, 2011).

Green, Anna and Megan Hutching (eds), *Remembering: Writing Oral History* (Auckland: Auckland University Press, 2004).

Grigg, Russell, "Wading through Children's Tears": The Emotional Experiences of Elementary School Inspections, 1839–1911', *History of Education*, 49:5 (2020), 597–616.

Grimshaw, Patricia, 'Christian Woman, Pious Wife, Faithful Mother, Devoted Missionary: Conflict in Roles of American Missionary Women in 19th Century Hawaii', *Feminist Studies* 9:3 (1983), 489–521.

Grimshaw, Patricia, 'Faith, Missionary Life, and the Family', in P. Levine (ed.), *Gender and Empire* (Oxford: Oxford University Press, 2007), pp. 260–80.

Grimshaw, Patricia, *Paths of Duty: American Missionary Wives in Nineteenth-Century Hawaii* (Honolulu, HI: University of Hawaii Press, 1989).

Gunson, Neil, 'The Deviations of a Missionary Family: The Henrys of Tahiti', in J.W. Davidson and D. Scarr (eds), *Pacific Island Portraits* (Wellington and Auckland: A.H. & A.W. Reed, 1973), pp. 31–54.

Gutman, Marta, 'The Physical Spaces of Childhood', in Paula S. Fass (ed.), *The Routledge History of Childhood in the Western World* (London and New York: Routledge, 2015), pp. 249–66.

Hafez, Rania. 'Playing on the Boundaries: A Childhood across Cultural and Geographical Lines', *Childhood in the Past* 7:2 (2014), 117–32.

Haggis, Jane, and Margaret Allen, 'Imperial Emotions: Affective Communities of Mission in British Protestant Women's Missionary Publications C1880–1920', *Journal of Social History* 41:3 (2008), 691–716.

Hall, Catherine, *Civilising Subjects: Colony and Metropole in the English Imagination, 1830–1867* (Cambridge: Polity Press, 2002).

Hamlett, Jane, *Material Relations: Domestic Interiors and Middle-Class Families in England, 1850–1910* (Manchester: Manchester University Press, 2010).

Hamlett, Jane, 'Space and Emotional Experience in Victorian and Edwardian English Public School Dormitories', in Stephanie Olsen (ed.), *Childhood, Youth and Emotions in Modern History: National, Colonial and Global Perspectives* (Basingstoke: Palgrave Macmillan, 2015), pp. 119–38.

Hamlett, Jane, Lesley Hoskins and Rebecca Preston, 'Introduction', in Jane Hamlett, Lesley Hoskins and Rebecca Preston (eds), *Residential Institutions in Britain, 1725–1970: Inmates and Environments* (London: Pickering & Chatto, 2013), pp. 1–15.

Harding, Jenny, 'Looking for Trouble: Exploring Emotion, Memory and Public Sociology', *Oral History* 42:2 (Autumn 2014), 94–104.

Hatavara, Mari, Lars-Christer Hydén and Matti Hyvärinen, 'Introduction, or Another Story of Narrative', in Matti Hyvärinen, Mari Hatavara and Lars-Christer Hydén (eds), *The Travelling Concept of Narrative* (Amsterdam and Philadelphia, PA: John Benjamins Publishing Company, 2013), pp. 1–10.

Hatfield, Mary, 'Introduction', in Mary Hatfield (ed.), *Happiness in Nineteenth-Century Ireland* (Liverpool: Liverpool University Press, 2021), pp. 1–13.

Hewat, Elizabeth G.K., *Vision and Achievement 1796–1956: A History of the Foreign Missions of the Churches United in the Church of Scotland* (Edinburgh, London, Melbourne, Johannesburg: Thomas Nelson and Sons, 1960).

Hill, Myrtle, 'Women in the Irish Protestant Foreign Missions c.1873–1914: Representations and Motivations', in Pieter N. Holtrop and Hugh McLeod (eds), *Missions and Missionaries* (Woodbridge: Boydell Press, 2000), pp. 170–85.

Hillel, Margot, '"Give Us All Missionary Eyes and Missionary Hearts": Triumphalism and Missionising in Late-Victorian Children's Literature', *Mousaion* 29:3 (2011), 179–92.

Hillel, Margot, '"Nearly All Are Supported by Children": Charitable Childhoods in Late-Nineteenth and Early-Twentieth-Century Literature for Children in the British World', in Hugh Morrison and Mary Clare Martin (eds), *Creating Religious Childhoods in Anglo-World and British Colonial Contexts, 1800–1950* (London and New York: Routledge, 2017), pp. 163–80.

Hochschild, Arlie Russell, 'Emotion Work, Feeling Rules, and Social Structure', *American Journal of Sociology* 85:3 (1979), 551–75.

Hochschild, Arlie Russell, *The Managed Heart: Commercialization of Human Feeling* (Berkeley and Los Angeles, CA: University of California Press, 1983).

Hofmeyr, Isabel, 'Introduction: World Literature and the Imperial Textual Commons', *English Studies in Africa* 57:1 (2014), 1–8.

Hofmeyr, Isabel and Antoinette Burton (eds), *Ten Books That Shaped the British Empire: Creating an Imperial Commons* (Durham, NC: Duke University Press, 2014).

Hollinger, David A., *Protestants Abroad: How Missionaries Tried to Change the World But Changed America* (Princeton, NJ and Oxford: Princeton University Press, 2017).

Holmes, Katie, 'Does It Matter If She Cried? Recording Emotion and the Australian Generations Oral History Project', *The Oral History Review* 44:1 (2017), 56–76.

Houlbrooke, Ralph, 'Death in Childhood: The Practice of the "Good Death" in James Janeway's *A Token for Children*', in Anthony Fletcher and Stephen Hussey (eds), *Childhood in Question: Children, Parents and the State* (Manchester and New York: Manchester University Press, 1999), pp. 37–56.

Hovland, Ingie, *Mission Station Christianity: Norwegian Missionaries in Colonial Natal and Zululand, Southern Africa 1850–1890* (Leiden and Boston: Brill, 2013).

Hudspith, M.A., *Ripening Fruit: A History of the Bolivian Indian Mission* (Harrington Park, NJ: Harrington Press, 1958).

Ingram, Allan and Clarke Lawlor, '"The Gloom of Anxiety": Fear in the Long Eighteenth Century', in Daniel McCann and Claire McKechnie-Mason (eds), *Fear in the Medical and Literary Imagination, Medieval to Modern: Dreadful Passions* (Basingstoke: Palgrave Macmillan, 2018), pp. 55–78.

Jackson, Stephen, *Constructing National Identity in Canadian and Australian Classrooms: The Crown of Education* (Cham: Palgrave Macmillan, 2018).

Jackson, William, and Emily J. Manktelow (eds), *Subverting Empire: Deviance and Disorder in the British Colonial World* (Basingstoke: Palgrave Macmillan, 2015).

Jay, Elisabeth, '"Ye Careless, Thoughtless, Worldly Parents, Tremble While You Read This History!": The Use and Abuse of the Dying Child in the Evangelical

Tradition', in Gillian Avery and Kimberley Reynolds (eds), *Representations of Childhood Death* (Basingstoke: Macmillan, 1999), pp. 111–32.

Jensz, Felicity, 'Hope and Pity: Depictions of Children in Five Decades of the *Evangelisch-Lutherisches Missionsblatt*, 1860–1910', in Judith Becker and Katharina Stornig (eds), *Menschen – Bilder – Eine Welt Ordnungen Von Vielfalt in Der Religiösen Publizistik Um 1900* (Göttingen: Vandenhoeck & Ruprecht, 2018), pp. 259–81.

Jensz, Felicity, *Missionaries and Modernity: Education in the British Empire, 1830–1910* (Manchester: Manchester University Press, 2022).

Jensz, Felicity, 'Origins of Missionary Periodicals: Form and Function of Three Moravian Publications', *Journal of Religious History* 36:2 (2012), 234–55.

Jensz, Felicity, and Hanna Acke, 'Introduction', in Felicity Jensz and Hanna Acke (eds), *Missions and Media: The Politics of Missionary Periodicals in the Long Nineteenth Century* (Stuttgart: Franz Steiner Verlag, 2013), pp. 9–15.

Jobs, Richard I., and David M. Pomfret, 'The Transnationality of Youth', in Richard I. Jobs and David M. Pomfret (eds), *Transnational Histories of Youth in the Twentieth Century* (Basingstoke: Palgrave Macmillan, 2015), pp. 1–19.

Johnson, Ryan, 'European Cloth and "Tropical" Skin: Clothing Material and British Ideas of Health and Hygiene in Tropical Climates', *Bulletin of the History of Medicine* 83:3 (2009), 530–60.

Jones, Kathleen W., 'Child Guidance', in Gary McCulloch and David Crook (eds), *The Routledge International Encyclopedia of Education* (London and New York: Routledge, 2008), pp. 87–88.

Jones, O., '"True Geography [ ] Quickly Forgotten, Giving Away to an Adult-Imagined Universe". Approaching the Otherness of Childhood', *Children's Geographies* 6:2 (2008), 195–212.

Kaarninen, Mervi, 'Red Orphans' Fatherland: Children in the Civil War of 1918 and Its Aftermath', in V. Kivimäki et al. (eds), *Lived Nation as the History of Experiences and Emotions in Finland* (Cham: Palgrave Macmillan, 2021), pp. 163–85.

Kagan, Jerome, 'Child Psychology', in Paula S. Fass (ed.), *Encyclopedia of Children and Childhood in History and Society*, vol. 1 (New York: Macmillan Reference USA, 2004), pp. 167–70.

Kashay, Jennifer Fish, 'Problems in Paradise: The Peril of Missionary Parenting in Early Nineteenth-Century Hawaii', *The Journal of Presbyterian History* 77:2 (1999), 81–94.

Katajala-Peltomaa, Sari, and Raisa Maria Toivo, 'Introduction: Religion as Historical Experience', in S. Katajala-Peltomaa and R.M. Toivo (eds), *Histories of Experience in the World of Lived Religion* (Cham: Palgrave Macmillan, 2022), pp. 1–35.

Kennedy, Elizabeth Lapovsky, 'Telling Tales: Oral History and the Construction of Pre-Stonewall Lesbian History', in Robert Perks and Alistair Thompson (eds), *The Oral History Reader* (London and New York: Routledge, 1998), pp. 344–55.

Kenny, Sarah, '"Basically You Were Either a Mainstream Sort of Person or You Went to the Leadmill and the Limit": Understanding Post-War British Youth Culture

Through Oral History', in Kristine Moruzi, Nell Musgrove and Carla Pascoe Leahy (eds), *Children's Voices from the Past: New Historical and Interdisciplinary Perspectives* (Cham: Palgrave Macmillan, 2019), pp. 233–59.

King, Marjorie, *China's American Daughter: Ida Pruitt (1888–1985)* (Hong Kong: The Chinese University Press, 2006).

Kivimäki, Ville, Sami Suodenjoki and Tanja Vahtikari, 'Lived Nation: Histories of Experience and Emotion in Understanding Nationalism', in V. Kivimäki et al. (eds), *Lived Nation as the History of Experiences and Emotions in Finland* (Cham: Palgrave Macmillan, 2021), pp. 1–28.

Kleinau, Elke, 'Autobiographical Writing, Autobiographical Narration: Memories of a "Child of the Occupation" in the Mirror of Two Genres', *Paedagogica Historica* 58:3 (2022), 378–89.

Klemens, Michael J., and Lynette H. Bikos, 'Psychological Well-Being and Sociocultural Adaptation in College-Aged, Repatriated, Missionary Kids', *Mental Health, Religion and Culture* 12 (2009), 721–33.

Koller, Hans-Christoph, *Bildung anders denken. Einführung in die Theorie transformatorischer Bildungsprozesse* (Stuttgart: Kohlhammer, 2012).

Konrad, Dagmar, 'Lost in Transition: Missionary Children of the Basel Mission in the Nineteenth Century', *International Bulletin of Missionary Research* 37:4 (2013), 219–23.

Kozlovsky, Roy, 'Architecture, Emotions and the History of Childhood', in Stephanie Olsen (ed.), *Childhood, Youth and Emotions in Modern History: National, Colonial and Global Perspectives* (Basingstoke: Palgrave Macmillan, 2015), pp. 95–118.

Kwon, Jungmin, 'Third Culture Kids: Growing Up with Mobility and Cross-Cultural Transitions', *Diaspora, Indigenous, and Minority Education* 13:2 (2019), 113–22.

Landahl, Joakim, 'Emotions, Power and the Advent of Mass Schooling', *Paedagogica Historica* 51:1/2 (2015), 104–16.

Langford, Mary, 'Global Nomads, Third Culture Kids and International Schools', in Mary Hayden and Jeff Thompson (eds), *International Education: Principles and Practice* (London: Logan Page, 1998), pp. 28–43.

Langmore, Diane, *Missionary Lives: Papua, 1874–1914* (Honolulu, HI: University of Hawaii Press, 1989).

Langmore, Diane, 'The Object Lesson of a Civilised, Christian Home', in Margaret Jolly and Martha Macintyre (eds), *Family and Gender in the Pacific: Domestic Contradictions and the Colonial Impact* (Cambridge: Cambridge University Press, 1989), pp. 82–94.

Lassonde, Stephen, 'Age, Schooling, and Development', in Paula S. Fass (ed.), *The Routledge History of Childhood in the Western World* (London and New York: Routledge, 2015), pp. 211–28.

Latourette, Kenneth Scott, *A History of the Expansion of Christianity*, 7 vols (London: Eyre and Spottiswoode, 1938).

Laurie, N., C. Dwyer, S.L. Holloway and F.M. Smith, *Geographies of Femininities* (Harlow: Longman, 1999).

Lester, Allan, *Imperial Networks: Creating Identities in Nineteenth-Century South Africa and Britain* (London and New York: Routledge, 2001).

Lineham, Peter J., 'The New Zealand Christmas and the Interweaving of Culture and Religion', in Geoffrey Troughton and Stuart Lange (eds), *Sacred Histories in Secular New Zealand* (Wellington: Victoria University Press, 2016), pp. 154–70.

Long, Joanna C., 'Diasporic Families: Cultures of Relatedness in Migration', *Annals of the Association of American Geographers* 104:2 (2014), 243–52.

Lynch, Gordon, *UK Child Migration to Australia, 1945–1970: A Study in Policy Failure* (Cham: Palgrave Macmillan, 2021).

Macdonald, Lesley A. Orr, *A Unique and Glorious Mission: Women and Presbyterianism in Scotland, 1830–1930* (Edinburgh: John Donald Publishers, 2000).

MacDougall, Ian, *Essays in Scottish Labour History: A Tribute to W.H. Marwick* (Edinburgh: John Donald Publishers, 1978).

Majumdar, Boria, 'Tom Brown Goes Global: The "Brown" Ethic in Colonial and Post-Colonial India', in John J. MacAloon (ed.), *Muscular Christianity in Colonial and Post-Colonial Worlds* (Oxford and New York: Routledge, 2008), pp. 105–20.

Mangan, J.A., *The Games Ethic and Imperialism: Aspects of the Diffusion of an Ideal* (London and Portland, OR: Frank Cass Publishers, 1998).

Mangan, J.A., 'Introduction: Making Imperial Mentalities', in J.A. Mangan (ed.), *Making Imperial Mentalities: Socialisation and British Imperialism* (Manchester and New York: Manchester University Press, 1990), pp. 1–22.

Mangan, J.A., *Manufactured Masculinity: Making Imperial Manliness, Morality and Militarism* (London and New York: Routledge, 2012).

Manktelow, Emily J., 'Forging the Missionary Ideal: Gender and the Family in the *Church Missionary Society Gleaner*', *Journal of Religious History* 43:2 (2019), 195–216.

Manktelow, Emily J., *Gender, Power and Sexual Abuse in the Pacific: Rev. Simpson's 'Improper Liberties'* (London: Bloomsbury Academic, 2018).

Manktelow, Emily, 'Making Missionary Children: Religion, Culture and Juvenile Deviance', in Hugh Morrison and Mary Clare Martin (eds), *Creating Religious Childhoods in Anglo-World and British Colonial Contexts, 1800–1950* (London and New York: Routledge, 2017), pp. 41–60.

Manktelow, Emily J., *Missionary Families: Race, Gender and Generation on the Spiritual Frontier* (Manchester: Manchester University Press, 2013).

Manktelow, Emily J., 'Rev. Simpson's "Improper Liberties": Moral Scrutiny and Missionary Children in the South Seas Mission', *Journal of Imperial and Commonwealth History* 40:2 (2012), 159–81.

Marten, James, 'Family Relationships', in Colin Heywood (ed.), *A Cultural History of Childhood and Family in the Age of Empire* (London: Bloomsbury Academic, 2014), pp. 19–38.

Martin, Mary Clare, 'Play, Missionaries and the Cross-Cultural Encounter in Global Perspective, 1800–1870', in Hugh Morrison and Mary Clare Martin (eds), *Creating Religious Childhoods in Anglo-World and British Colonial Contexts, 1800–1950* (London and New York: Routledge, 2017), pp. 61–84.

Martin, Mary Clare, 'The State of Play: Historical Perspectives', *International Journal of Play* 5:3 (2016), 329–39.

Martin, Mary Clare, 'Women and Philanthropy in Walthamstow and Leyton 1740–1870', *The London Journal* 19:2 (1994), 119–50.

Marwick, William H., 'Conscientious Objection in Scotland in the First World War', *Scottish Journal of Science* 1:3 (1972), 157–64.

Maß, Sandra, 'Constructing Global Missionary Families: Absence, Memory, and Belonging before World War I', *Journal of Modern European History* 19:3 (2021), 340–61.

Maxwell, David, 'The Missionary Home as a Site for Mission: Perspectives from Belgian Congo', in John Doran, Charlotte Methuen and Alexandra Walsham (eds), *Religion and the Household* (Woodbridge: Ecclesiastical History Society by Boydell Press, 2014), pp. 428–55.

May, Helen, 'Recollecting Childhood at School in the Early Twentieth Century,' in N. Higgins and C. Freeman (eds), *Childhoods: Growing Up in Aotearoa New Zealand* (Dunedin: Otago University Press, 2013), pp. 95–109.

Maynes, Mary Jo, 'Age as a Category of Historical Analysis: History, Agency, and Narratives of Childhood', *Journal of the History of Childhood and Youth* 1:1 (2008), 114–24.

McCabe, Jane, *Race, Tea and Colonial Resettlement: Imperial Families, Interrupted* (London and New York: Bloomsbury Academic, 2017).

McCann, Daniel, and Claire McKechnie-Mason (eds), *Fear in the Medical and Literary Imagination, Medieval to Modern: Dreadful Passions* (Basingstoke: Palgrave Macmillan, 2018).

McCarthy, Angela, *Personal Narratives of Irish and Scottish Migration, 1921–65: 'For Spirit and Adventure'* (Manchester and New York: Manchester University Press, 2007).

McDowell, Kathleen, 'Toward a History of Children as Readers, 1890–1930', *Book History* 12 (2009), 240–61.

McGeorge, Colin, 'Childhood's Sole Serious Business: The Long Haul to Full School Attendance', *The New Zealand Journal of History* 40:1 (2006), 25–38.

McGrath, Alister E., *T.F. Torrance: An Intellectual Biography* (Edinburgh: T&T Clark, 1999).

McLisky, Claire, and Karen Vallgårda, 'Faith through Feeling: An Introduction', in Claire McLisky, Daniel Midena and Karen Vallgårda (eds), *Emotions and Christian Missions: Historical Perspectives* (Basingstoke: Palgrave Macmillan, 2015), pp. 1–21.

Millei, Zsuzsa, Iveta Silova and Susanne Gannon, 'Thinking through Memories of Childhood in (Post)socialist Spaces: Ordinary Lives in Extraordinary Times', *Children's Geographies* 20:3 (2022), 324–37.

Mishler, Elliot, 'Narrative and Identity: The Double Arrow of Time', in Anna D. Fina, Deborah Schiffrin and Michael Bamberg (eds), *Discourse and Identity* (Cambridge: Cambridge University Press, 2006), pp. 30–47.

Moessener, Jeanne Stevenson, 'Missionary Motivation', *Sociological Analysis* 53:2 (1992), 189–200.

Montgomerie, Deborah, 'New Women and Not-So-New Men: Discussions about Marriage in New Zealand, 1890–1914', *New Zealand Journal of History* 51:1 (2017), 36–64.

Moran, Jeffrey P., 'Sex Education', in Paula S. Fass (ed.), *Encyclopedia of Children and Childhood in History and Society*, vol. 3 (New York: Macmillan Reference USA, 2004), pp. 739–43.

Morrison, Heidi, *The Global History of Childhood Reader* (London and New York: Routledge, 2012).

Morrison, Hugh, 'Colonial Archives: Protestant Missionary Magazines, Images and Children', in Judith Becker and Katharina Stornig (eds), *Menschen – Bilder – Eine Welt Ordnungen Von Vielfalt in Der Religiösen Publizistik Um 1900* (Göttingen: Vandenhoeck & Ruprecht, 2018), pp. 283–304.

Morrison, Hugh, '"I Feel That We Belong to the One Big Family": Protestant Childhoods, Missions and Emotions in British World Settings, 1870s–1930s', in Claire McLisky, Daniel Midena and Karen Vallgårda (eds), *Emotions and Christian Missions: Historical Perspectives* (Basingstoke: Palgrave Macmillan, 2015), pp. 218–39.

Morrison, Hugh, '"It Is Well with the Child": Changing Views on Protestant Missionary Children's Health, c.1870s–1930s', *Studies in Church History* 58 (2022), 306–29.

Morrison, Hugh, '"It's Really Where Your Parents Were": Differentiating and Situating Protestant Missionary Children's Lives, c. 1900–1940', *Journal of Family History* 42:4 (2017), 419–39.

Morrison, Hugh, *Protestant Children, Missions and Education in the British World* (Leiden: Brill, 2021).

Morrison, Hugh, *Pushing Boundaries: New Zealand Protestants and Overseas Missions, 1827–1939* (Dunedin: Otago University Press, 2016).

Morrison, Hugh, 'Reimagining the Missionary Family: The Malcolms of the China Inland Mission', *Journal of Religious History* 45:3 (2021), 465–88.

Morrison, Hugh, 'Settler Childhood, Protestant Christianity and Emotions in Colonial New Zealand, 1880s–1920s', in Stephanie Olsen (ed.), *Childhood, Youth and Emotions in Modern History: National, Colonial and Global Perspectives* (Basingstoke: Palgrave Macmillan, 2015), pp. 76–94.

Morrison, Hugh, 'Theorising Missionary Education: The Bolivian Indian Mission 1908–1920', *History of Education Review* 42:1 (2013), 4–23.

Morrison, Hugh, 'Three Variations on a Theme: Writing the Lives of Scottish and New Zealand Missionary Children, ca. 1900–1950', *Journal of the History of Childhood and Youth* 12:2 (2019), 199–218.

Morrison, Hugh, and Mary Clare Martin, 'Introduction: Contours and Issues in Children's Religious History', in Hugh Morrison and Mary Clare Martin (eds), *Creating Religious Childhoods in Anglo-World and British Colonial Contexts, 1800–1950* (London and New York: Routledge, 2017), pp. 1–20.

Murray, Jocelyn, 'Tyndale-Biscoe, Cecil Earle (1863–1949)', in Gerald H. Anderson (ed.), *Biographical Dictionary of Christian Missions* (Grand Rapids, MI and Cambridge: William B. Eerdmans Publishing Company, 1998), p. 686.

Musgrove, Nell, and Deidre Michell, *The Slow Evolution of Foster Care in Australia* (Basingstoke: Palgrave Macmillan, 2018).

Musgrove, Nell, Carla Pascoe Leahy and Kristine Moruzi, 'Hearing Children's Voices: Conceptual and Methodological Challenges', in Kristine Moruzi, Nell

Musgrove and Carla Pascoe Leahy (eds), *Children's Voices from the Past: New Historical and Interdisciplinary Perspectives* (Cham: Palgrave Macmillan, 2019), pp. 1–25.

Neill, Stephen, *A History of Christian Missions*, rev. ed. (Harmondsworth: Penguin Books, 1986).

Nys, Laura, '"I Am F.B.": Historians, Ethics and the Anonymisation of Autobiographical Sources', *Paedagogica Historica* 58:3 (2022), 424–38.

O'Dochartaigh, Eavan, '"Exceedingly Good Friends": The Representation of Indigenous People During the Franklin Search Expeditions to the Arctic, 1847–1859', *Victorian Studies* 61:2 (2019), 255–67.

O'Hara, Glen, 'New Histories of British Imperial Communication and the "Networked" World of the 19th and Early 20th Centuries', *History Compass* 8:7 (2010), 909–25.

Olsen, Stephanie, 'The Authority of Motherhood in Question: Fatherhood and the Moral Education of Children in England, c. 1870–1900', *Women's History Review* 18:5 (2009), 765–80.

Olsen, Stephanie, 'Children's Emotional Formations in Britain, Canada, Australia and New Zealand, around the First World War', *Cultural and Social History* 17:5 (2019), 643–57.

Olsen, Stephanie, 'Daddy's Come Home: Evangelicalism, Fatherhood and Lessons for Boys in Late Nineteenth-Century Britain', *Fathering* 5:3 (2007), 174–96.

Olsen, Stephanie, 'The History of Childhood and the Emotional Turn', *History Compass* 15:11 (2017), 1–10.

Olsen, Stephanie, *Juvenile Nation: Youth, Emotions and the Making of the Modern British Citizen, 1880–1914* (London: Bloomsbury, 2014).

Olssen, Erik, 'Towards a New Society', in W.H. Oliver (ed.), *The Oxford History of New Zealand* (Oxford: Oxford University Press, 1981), pp. 250–78.

Olssen, Erik, 'Truby King and the Plunket Society, An Analysis of a Prescriptive Ideology', *New Zealand Journal of History* 15:1 (1981), 3–23.

Orr, Brian J., *Bones of Empire* (Raleigh, NC: LULU Enterprises, 2013).

Ottewill, Roger, 'The Early Years of the Christian Endeavour Movement: Innovation and Consolidation at a Local Level, 1881–1914', *Studies in Church History* 57 (2021), 300–17.

Pande, Ishita, 'Feeling Like a Child: Narratives of Development and the Indian Child/Wife', in Stephanie Olsen (ed.), *Childhood, Youth and Emotions in Modern History: National, Colonial and Global Perspectives* (Basingstoke: Palgrave Macmillan, 2015), pp. 35–55.

Paul, Diane B., John Stenhouse and Hamish G. Spencer, 'Introduction: Eugenics as a Transnational Subject: The British Dominions', in Diane B. Paul, John Stenhouse and Hamish G. Spencer (eds), *Eugenics at the Edges of Empire: New Zealand, Australia, Canada and South Africa* (Cham: Palgrave Macmillan, 2018), pp. 1–19.

Peat, Jo, 'Child Development', in Gary McCulloch and David Crook (eds), *The Routledge International Encyclopedia of Education* (London and New York: Routledge, 2008), pp. 85–87.

Pedersen, Poul, 'Anxious Lives and Letters: Family Separation, Communication Networks and Structures of Everyday Life', *Culture and History* 8 (1990), 7–19.

Perks, Robert and Alistair Thomson (eds), *The Oral History Reader* (London and New York: Routledge, 1998).

Pernau, Margrit, 'Great Britain: The Creation of an Imperial Global Order', in Margrit Pernau, Helge Jordheim et al., *Civilizing Emotions: Concepts in Nineteenth Century Asia and Europe* (Oxford: Oxford University Press, 2015), pp. 45–62.

Pernau, Margrit, 'Space and Emotion: Building to Feel', *History Compass* 12:7 (2014), 541–49.

Pernau, Margrit, and Helge Jordheim, 'Introduction', in Margrit Pernau, Helge Jordheim et al. (eds), *Civilizing Emotions: Concepts in Nineteenth Century Asia and Europe* (Oxford: Oxford University Press, 2015), pp. 1–24.

Pernick, Martin S., 'Eugenics', in Paula S. Fass (ed.), *Encyclopedia of Children and Childhood in History and Society*, vol. 1 (New York: Macmillan Reference USA, 2004), pp. 318–29.

Pietsch, Tamson, *Empire of Scholars: Universities, Networks and the British Academic World, 1850–1939* (Manchester: Manchester University Press, 2013).

Piggin, Stuart, *Making Evangelical Missionaries, 1789–1858: The Social Background, Motives and Training of British Protestant Missionaries in India* (Abingdon: Sutton Courtenay Press, 1984).

Pike, Elsie, Constance E. Curryer and U.K. Moore, *The Story of Walthamstow Hall*, rev. ed. (Sevenoaks: Longmore Press, 1973).

Pitman, Julia, *'Our Principle of Sex Equality': The Ordination of Women in the Congregational Church in Australia, 1927–1977* (Melbourne: Australian Scholarly Publishing, 2016).

Plamper, Jan, 'The History of Emotions: An Interview with William Reddy, Barbara Rosenwein, and Peter Stearns', *History and Theory* 49:2 (2010), 237–65.

Plamper, Jan, *The History of Emotions: An Introduction* (Oxford: Oxford University Press, 2012).

Pocock, J.G.A., 'Tangata Whenua and Enlightenment Anthropology', *New Zealand Journal of History* 26:1 (1992), 28–53.

Pollock, David C., and Ruth E. Van Reken, *Third Culture Kids: The Experience of Growing Up among Worlds* (Yarmouth, ME and London: Intercultural Press, 2001).

Pomfret, David M., '"Colonial Circulations": Vietnamese Youth, Travel, and Empire, 1919–40', in Richard I. Jobs and David M. Pomfret (eds), *Transnational Histories of Youth in the Twentieth Century* (Basingstoke: Palgrave Macmillan, 2015), pp. 115–43.

Pomfret, David M., 'Imperial Rejuvenations: Youth, Empire, and the Problem of Accelerated Aging in "Tropical" Colonies, ca. 1800–1914', *Journal of Social History* 53:4 (2020), 939–62.

Pomfret, David M., *Youth and Empire: Trans-Colonial Childhoods in British and French Asia* (Stanford, CA: Stanford University Press, 2016).

Pooley, Siân, '"All We Parents Want Is That Our Children's Health and Lives Should Be Regarded": Child Health and Parental Concern in England, c. 1860–1910', *Social History of Medicine* 23:3 (2010), 528–48.

Porter, Andrew, *Religion Versus Empire? British Protestant Missionaries and Overseas Expansion, 1700–1914* (Manchester and New York: Manchester University Press, 2004).

Pratt, Mary Louise, *Imperial Eyes: Travel Writing and Transculturation* (London and New York: Routledge, 1992).

Prevost, Elizabeth E., *The Communion of Women: Missions and Gender in Colonial Africa and the British Metropole* (Oxford: Oxford University Press, 2010).

Prochaska, F.K., 'Little Vessels: Children in the Nineteenth-Century English Missionary Movement', *Journal of Imperial and Commonwealth History* 6:2 (1978), 103–18.

Proctor, J.H., 'Scottish Missionaries in India: An Inquiry into Motivation', *South Asia* 13:1 (1990), 43–61.

Punch, Keith, *Introduction to Social Research: Quantitative and Qualitative Approaches*, 2nd ed. (London: Sage, 2009).

Raftery, Deirdre, 'Religions and the History of Education: A Historiography', *History of Education: Journal of the History of Education Society* 41:1 (2012), 41–56.

Raftery, Deirdre, 'Themes and Approaches in Research on Religion in the History of Education: Missionaries, Monasteries, Methodologies', in Stephen G. Parker, Jenny Berglund, David Lewin and Deirdre Raftery (eds), *Religion and Education: Framing and Mapping a Field* (Leiden: Brill, 2019), pp. 17–25.

Reddy, William, *The Navigation of Feeling: A Framework for the History of Emotions* (Cambridge: Cambridge University Press, 2001).

Reese, W.J., 'Education', in Joseph M. Hawes and N. Ray Hiner (eds), *A Cultural History of Childhood and Family in the Modern Age* (London: Bloomsbury, 2014), pp. 99–116.

Richards, Jeffrey, 'Introduction', in Jeffrey Richards (ed.), *Imperialism and Juvenile Literature* (Manchester: Manchester University Press, 1989), pp. 1–11.

Riddle, T.E., *The Light of Other Days* (Christchurch and Dunedin: Presbyterian Bookroom, 1949).

Robert, Dana L., 'The "Christian Home" as a Cornerstone of Anglo-American Missionary Thought and Practice', in Dana Robert (ed.), *Converting Colonialism: Visions and Realities in Mission History, 1706–1914* (Grand Rapids, MI and Cambridge: William B. Eerdmans Publishing Company, 2008), pp. 134–65.

Robert, Dana L., *Christian Mission: How Christianity Became a World Religion* (Chichester: Wiley-Blackwell, 2009).

Robert, Dana L., 'From Missions to Mission to Beyond Missions: The Historiography of American Protestant Foreign Missions since World War II', *International Bulletin of Missionary Research* 18:4 (1994), 146–62.

Roberts, J.M., *Europe 1880–1945* (London: Longman, 1969).

Robertson, Yvonne, *'Girdle Round the Earth': New Zealand Presbyterian Women's Ideal of Universal Sisterhood, 1870–1910* (Auckland: Presbyterian Historical Society of New Zealand, 1993).

Romero, Margarita Sánchez, Eva Alarćon Garcia and Gonzalo Aranda Jiménez (eds), *Children, Spaces and Identity* (Oxford and Philadelphia, PA: Oxbow Books, 2015).

Romesburg, Don, 'Making Adolescence More or Less Modern', in Paula S. Fass (ed.), *The Routledge History of Childhood in the Western World* (London and New York: Routledge, 2015), pp. 229–48.

Rosenwein, Barbara H., *Emotional Communities in the Early Middle Ages* (Ithaca, NY: Cornell University Press, 2006).

Rosenwein, Barbara H., *Generations of Feeling: A History of Emotions, 600–1700* (Cambridge: Cambridge University Press, 2016).

Rosenwein, Barbara H., 'Worrying about Emotions in History', *American Historical Review* 107:3 (2002), 821–45.

Rosenwein, Barbara H., and Riccardo Cristiani, *What Is the History of Emotions?* (Cambridge, UK and Medford, MA: Polity Press, 2018).

Ryrie, Alec, 'Facing Childhood Death in English Protestant Spirituality', in Katie Barclay and Kimberley Reynolds with Ciara Rawnsley (eds), *Death, Emotion and Childhood in Premodern Europe* (Basingstoke: Palgrave Macmillan, 2016), pp. 109–27.

Salesa, Damon, 'New Zealand's Pacific', in Giselle Byrnes (ed.), *The New Oxford History of New Zealand* (Oxford and Melbourne: Oxford University Press, 2009), pp. 149–72.

Samson, Jane, *Race and Redemption: British Missionaries Encounter Pacific Peoples, 1797–1920* (Grand Rapids, MI: William B. Eerdmans Publishing Company, 2017).

Sandin, B., 'Education', in Colin Heywood (ed.), *A Cultural History of Childhood and Family in the Age of Empire* (London: Bloomsbury, 2014), pp. 91–110.

Scheer, Monique, 'Are Emotions a Kind of Practice (and Is That What Makes Them Have a History)? A Bourdieuian Approach to Understanding Emotion', *History and Theory* 51 (May 2012), 193–220.

Schulz, Joy, *Hawaiian by Birth: Missionary Children, Bicultural Identity, and U.S. Colonialism in the Pacific* (Lincoln, NE: University of Nebraska Press, 2017).

Semple, Rhonda A., '"The Conversion and Highest Welfare of Each Pupil": The Work of the China Inland Mission at Chefoo', *The Journal of Imperial and Commonwealth History* 31:1 (2003), 29–50.

Semple, Rhonda A., 'Making Missions through (Re-)Making Children: Non-Kin Domestic Intimacy in the London Missionary Society's Work in Late-Nineteenth-Century North India', in Hugh Morrison and Mary Clare Martin (eds), *Creating Religious Childhoods in Anglo-World and British Colonial Contexts, 1800–1950* (London and New York: Routledge, 2017), pp. 23–40.

Semple, Rhonda A., *Missionary Women: Gender, Professionalism and the Victorian Idea of Christian Mission* (Woodbridge, Suffolk and Rochester, NY: Boydell Press, 2003).

Seriu, Naoko, 'Deserters' Voices on Childhood and Emotion in Eighteenth-Century France', in Claudia Jarzebowski and Thomas Max Safley (eds), *Childhood and Emotion: Across Cultures 1450–1800* (London and New York: Routledge, 2014), pp. 171–86.

Seymour, Mark, 'Emotional Arenas: From Provincial Circus to National Courtroom in Late Nineteenth-Century Italy', *Rethinking History: The Journal of Theory and Practice* 16:2 (2012), 177–97.

Sherington, Geoffrey, '"Suffer Little Children": British Child Migration as a Study of Journeyings between Centre and Periphery', *History of Education* 32:5 (2003), 461–76.

Sköld, Johanna, and Shurlee Swain (eds), *Apologies and the Legacy of Abuse of Children in Care: International Perspectives* (Basingstoke: Palgrave Macmillan, 2015).

Sleight, Simon, *Young People and the Shaping of Public Space in Melbourne, 1870–1914* (Farnham and Burlington, VA: Ashgate, 2013).

Stacey, Elizabeth, 'The History of Distance Education in Australia', *Quarterly Review of Distance Education* 6:3 (2005), 253–59.

Stanley, Brian, *Christianity in the Twentieth Century: A World History* (Princeton, NJ and Oxford: Princeton University Press, 2018).

Stanley, Brian (ed.), *Missions, Nationalism and the End of Empire* (Grand Rapids, MI and Cambridge: William B. Eerdmans Publishing Company, 2003).

Stearns, Peter N., *American Fear: The Causes and Consequences of High Anxiety* (New York: Routledge, 2006).

Stearns, Peter N., *Anxious Parents: A History of Modern Childrearing in America* (New York: New York University Press, 2003).

Stearns, Peter N., 'Challenges in the History of Childhood', *Journal of the History of Childhood and Youth* 1:1 (2008), 35–42.

Stearns, Peter N., 'Childhood Emotions in Modern Western History', in Paula S. Fass (ed.), *The Routledge History of Childhood in the Western World* (London and New York: Routledge, 2015), pp. 158–73.

Stearns, Peter N., *Childhood in World History*, 1st ed. (New York: Routledge, 2006).

Stearns, Peter N., 'Defining Happy Childhoods: Assessing a Recent Change', *Journal of the History of Childhood and Youth* 3:2 (2010), 165–86.

Stoler, Ann Laura, *Carnal Knowledge and Imperial Power: Race and the Intimate in Colonial Rule* (Berkeley and Los Angeles, CA: University of California Press, 2002).

Strhan, Anna, Stephen G. Parker and Susan B. Ridgeley, 'Introduction', in Anna Strhan, Stephen G. Parker and Susan B. Ridgeley (eds), *The Bloomsbury Reader in Religion and Childhood* (London: Bloomsbury Academic, 2017), pp. 1–13.

Studdert-Kennedy, Gerald, 'Christian Imperialists of the Raj: Left, Right and Centre', in J.A. Mangan (ed.), *Making Imperial Mentalities: Socialisation and British Imperialism* (Manchester: Manchester University Press, 1990), pp. 127–43.

Swain, Shurlee, 'Introduction', *Journal of the History of Childhood and Youth* 8:1 (2015), 2–3.

Swain, Shurlee, and Margot Hillel, *Child, Nation, Race and Empire: Child Rescue Discourse, England, Canada and Australia, 1850–1915* (Manchester: Manchester University Press, 2010).

Swartz, Rebecca, 'Educating Emotions in Natal and Western Australia, 1854–1865', *Journal of Colonialism and Colonial History* 18:2 (2017), https://doi.org/10.1353/cch.2017.0022

Swartz, Rebecca, *Education and Empire: Children, Race and Humanitarianism in the British Settler Colonies, 1833–1880* (Cham: Palgrave Macmillan, 2019).

Thompson, Andrew S. (ed.), *Britain's Experience of Empire in the Twentieth Century* (Oxford: Oxford University Press, 2012).

Thompson, Andrew S., *The Empire Strikes Back?: The Impact of Imperialism on Britain from the Mid-Nineteenth Century* (Harlow: Pearson Education, 2005).

Thompson, Paul, *The Voice of the Past: Oral History*, 3rd ed. (Oxford: Oxford University Press, 2000).

Thorne, Susan, *Congregational Missions and the Making of an Imperial Culture in 19th-Century England* (Stanford, CA: Stanford University Press, 1999).

Thorne, Susan, 'Religion and Empire at Home', in Catherine Hall and Sonya Rose (eds), *At Home with the Empire: Metropolitan Culture and the Imperial World* (Cambridge: Cambridge University Press, 2006), pp. 143–65.

Thurlow, Jessica, 'Review of *Missionary Families: Race, Gender and Generation on the Spiritual Frontier*, by Emily J. Manktelow', *Journal of British Studies* 54:1 (2015), 236–67.

Tjelle, Kristin Fjelde, *Missionary Masculinity, 1870–1930: The Norwegian Missionaries in South-East Africa* (Basingstoke: Palgrave Macmillan, 2013).

Vallgårda, Karen, *Imperial Childhoods and Christian Mission: Education and Emotions in South India and Denmark* (Basingstoke: Palgrave Macmillan, 2015).

Vallgårda, Karen, Kristine Alexander and Stephanie Olsen, 'Emotions and the Global Politics of Childhood', in Stephanie Olsen (ed.), *Childhood, Youth and Emotions in Modern History: National, Colonial and Global Perspectives* (Basingstoke: Palgrave Macmillan, 2015), pp. 12–34.

Vandrick, Stephanie, *Growing Up with God and Empire: A Postcolonial Analysis of 'Missionary Kid' Memoirs* (Bristol and Blue Ridge Summit, PA: Multilingual Matters, 2019).

Van Gent, Jacqueline, 'Emotions, Missions and Colonial Histories: An Epilogue', in Claire McLisky, Daniel Midena and Karen Vallgårda (eds), *Emotions and Christian Missions: Historical Perspectives* (Basingstoke: Palgrave Macmillan, 2015), pp. 240–50.

Van Poppel, Frans, and Renzo Derosas, 'Introduction', in Renzo Derosas and Frans van Poppel (eds), *Religion and the Decline of Fertility in the Western World* (Dordrecht: Springer, 2006), 1–19.

Wallace, Lee, 'A House Is Not a Home: Gender, Space and Marquesan Encounter, 1833–34', *The Journal of Pacific History* 40:3 (2005), 265–88.

Walsham, Alexandra, 'Introduction', in John Doran, Charlotte Methuen and Alexandra Walsham (eds), *Religion and the Household* (Woodbridge: Ecclesiastical History Society by Boydell Press, 2014), pp. xxi–xxxii.

Walters, Doris L., *The Untold Story: Missionary Kids Speak from the Ends of the Earth* (Chapel Hill, NC: Chapel Hill Press, 2007).

Walters, K., and A. Auton-Cuff, 'A Story to Tell: The Identity Development of Women Growing Up as Third Culture Kids', *Mental Health, Religion and Culture* 12:7 (2009), 755–72.

Wanhalla, Angela, 'Family, Community and Gender', in Giselle Byrnes (ed.), *The New Oxford History of New Zealand* (Melbourne: Oxford University Press, 2008), pp. 447–64.

Ward, Ted Warren, 'The Anxious Climate of Concern for Missionary Children', *International Bulletin of Missionary Research* 13:1 (1989), 11–13.

Weir, Christine, '"Deeply Interested in These Children Whom You Have Not Seen": The Protestant Sunday School View of the Pacific, 1900–1940', *Journal of Pacific History* 48:1 (2013), 43–62.

Williams, Raymond, *Orwell* (London: Fontana, 1971).

Wood, Gloria, and Paul Thompson (eds), *The Nineties: Personal Recollections of the 20th Century* (London: BBC Books, 1993).

Zelizer, Viviana A., *Pricing the Priceless Child: The Changing Social Value of Children* (New York: Basic Books), 1985.

Unpublished

Devereux, Linda, 'Narrating a Congo Missionary Childhood (1958–1964): Memory and Meaning Examined through a Creative Non-Fiction Text and Exegesis' (PhD thesis, Australian National University, 2015).

Fleming, Robert L., 'Adjustment of India Missionaries' Children in America' (PhD dissertation, University of Chicago, 1947).

Johnston, Ewen, '"Cannibals for Christ!": Oscar Michelsen Presbyterian Missionary in the New Hebrides, 1878–1932' (MA thesis, University of Auckland, 1995).

Keon, Hayley, 'Making Americans: Missionary Childhood and US Imperialism in Republican Shanghai' (PhD thesis, University of Hong Kong, 2023).

List, Elizabeth Ann, 'A Critical Analysis of "Missionary Kid" Literature: Past, Present, and Future Implications' (Doctoral dissertation, Azusa Pacific University, 2001).

Martin, M.C.H., 'Children and Religion in Walthamstow and Leyton c.1740–1870' (PhD thesis, University of London, 2000).

Mason, Sarah R., 'Missionary Conscience and the Comprehension of Imperialism: A Study of the Children of American Missionaries to China, 1900–1949' (PhD dissertation, Northern Illinois University, 1978).

McColl, Julie Anne, 'Imagining the Missionary Hero: Juvenile Missionary Biographies, c. 1870–1917' (PhD thesis, University of Liverpool, 2017).

Morrison, Hugh, '"It Is Our Bounden Duty": The Emergence of the New Zealand Protestant Missionary Movement, 1868–1926' (PhD dissertation, Massey University, 2004).

Parker, Allen Ellsworth, 'An Analysis of the Factors in Personality Development of the Children of Missionaries' (MA thesis, University of Chicago, 1936).

Stanley, Brian, 'Home Support for Foreign Missions in Early Victorian England c.1838–1873' (PhD thesis, University of Cambridge, 1979).

Van Evera, Louise, 'A Study of the Problems Involved in the Education of Children of Missionaries Serving under the Board of Foreign Missions of the Presbyterian Church, U.S.A., As Revealed in the Experience of a Selected Group of Undergraduate Students' (MA thesis, Presbyterian College of Christian Education, 1940).

Internet sources

'American Eugenics Society – Members, Officers and Directors Database', https://archive.org/stream/AMERICANEUGENICSSOCIETYMEMBERS/AMERICAN%20EUGENICS%20SOCIETY%20MEMBERS_djvu.txt (accessed 13 March 2019).

Baena, Rosalia, 'Of Missess and Tuan Kechils: Colonial Childhood Memoirs as Cultural Mediation in British Malaya', *ARIEL* 39:1–2 (2008), 89+. *Gale General OneFile*, https://link.gale.com/apps/doc/A190340826/ITOF?u=otago&sid=bookmark-ITOF&xid=66182a45 (accessed 13 October 2021).

'Baptist Missionary Children's Home Association of the Pacific Coast Records, circa 1895–1913', http://archiveswest.orbiscascade.org/ark:/80444/xv61087/pdf (accessed 4 February 2019).

Boddice, Rob, 'What Is the History of Experience?', www.tuni.fi/alustalehti/2019/04/18/what-is-the-history-of-experience/ (accessed 13 February 2023).

'Church Missionaries' Home, Islington/Limpsfield Common', www.childrenshomes.org.uk/ChurchMissionaries/ (accessed 8 October 2018).

Dodd, Lindsey, '"It's Not What I Saw, It's Not What I Thought": Challenges from Below to Dominant Versions of the French Wartime Past', *Conserveries mémorielles: Revue transdisciplinaire de jeunes chercheurs* 25 (2022), https://journals.openedition.org/cm/5169 (accessed 13 February 2023).

'Ellsworth Huntington Papers', https://archives.yale.edu/repositories/12/resources/4892?stylename=yul.ead2002.xhtml.xsl&pid=mssa:ms.0001&query=ellsworth%2520huntington&clear-stylesheet-cache=yes&hlon=yes&big=y&filter=&hitPageStart=1 (accessed 13 March 2019).

'Featherston Prisoner of War Camp', https://teara.govt.nz/en/photograph/1216/featherston-prisoner-of-war-camp (accessed 31 March 2022).

'Fleming, Robert Leland (1905–)' https://plants.jstor.org/stable/10.5555/al.ap.person.bm000376810 (accessed 11 March 2019).

'Guide to the Parker Family Photographs', https://history.pcusa.org/collections/research-tools/guides-archival-collections/rg-229 (accessed 13 March 2019).

Hamer, David, 'Stout, Robert', *Dictionary of New Zealand Biography*, first published in 1993. Te Ara – the Encyclopedia of New Zealand, https://teara.govt.nz/en/biographies/2s48/stout-robert (accessed 14 September 2021).

'The History of Experience: A History Like Anything Else?', www.oulu.fi/en/blogs/philosophy-history-now/history-experience-history-anything-else (accessed 13 February 2023).

'The Home That Eliza Built', www.walkerctr.org/history.html (accessed 4 February 2019).

McArthy, Elaine, 'Growing Up in Wartime Britain: 1939–1945 Chapter 3: Victory and the Aftermath', www.bbc.co.uk/history/ww2peopleswar/stories/67/a5231567.shtml (accessed 17 August 2018).

'Our History', Te Aho o Te Kura Pounamu – The Correspondence School, www.tekura.school.nz/about-us/who-we-are/our-history/ (accessed 22 November 2021).

'Papers of William Hutton Marwick', http://test.archiveshub.ac.uk/features /0605marwick.html (accessed 17 July 2015).

Preston, Lesley, and Jenny Campbell, 'Correspondence School of Victoria – Its First 60 Years', https://dehanz.net.au/entries/correspondence-school-of-victoria-its -first-60-years/ (accessed 22 November 2021).

'Register of New Zealand Presbyterian Ministers, Deaconesses & Missionaries 1840 to 2015', www.archives.presbyterian.org.nz/page143.htm (accessed 12 May 2022).

'Rev. William Marwick', http://histfam.familysearch.org/getperson.php?personID =I89235&tree+Fasti (accessed 16 October 2012).

Semple, Rhonda A., 'Christian Model, Mission Realities: The Business of Regularizing Family in Mission Communities in Late Nineteenth-Century North India', *Journal of Colonialism and Colonial History* 14:1 (2013), http://muse.jhu .edu/journals/journal_of_colonialism_and_colonial_history/v014/14.1.semple .html#f57-text. (accessed 20 June 2018).

Useem, Ruth Hill, 'A Third Culture Kid Bibliography', http://tckresearcher.net/ RHU%20bib%20v2%20copy.pdf (accessed 5 September 2023).

Walker, Rosanne, 'Tyndale-Biscoe, Cecil Hugh (1929–)', *Encyclopedia of Australian Science*, www.eoas.info/biogs/P003520b.htm (accessed 15 March 2018).

Welch, Ian, 'Poona (Pune) and Indian Village Mission (PIVM)', Working Paper, August 2014, https://openresearch-repository.anu.edu.au/bitstream/1885/13041 /1/Welch%20Poona%202014.pdf (accessed 6 May 2022).

'Woodstock School', www.woodstockschool.in/wp-content/uploads/2016/03/ History-of-Woodstock-School.pdf (accessed 4 February 2019).

Index

EU authorised representative for GPSR:
Easy Access System Europe, Mustamäe tee 50,
10621 Tallinn, Estonia
gpsr.requests@easproject.com